AQUINAS
God and Action

AQUINAS

God and Action

David B. Burrell, CSC

University of Notre Dame Press
Notre Dame, Indiana 46556

American edition 1979
University of Notre Dame Press
Notre Dame, Indiana 46556

First published 1979 by
Routledge & Kegan Paul Ltd.
39 Store Street,
London WC1E 7DD England

Photoset, printed and bound in Great Britain by
Weatherby Woolnough, Wellingborough, Northants

Library of Congress Cataloging in Publication Data

Burrell, David B
Aquinas : God and Action.

Includes bibliographical references.
1. God—Proof—History of doctrines. 2. Thomas
Aquinas, Saint, 1225?-1274—Theology. I. Title.
BT100.T4B87   1978   231'.042   78-51519
ISBN 0-268-00588-5

To
Frederick J. Crosson
Teacher, Scholar, Dean

Contents

Preface

This presentation of Aquinas was inspired by a structural parallel. Philosophical discourse over the past half century in the West – notably the Anglo-American world – has been forcibly guided by a sharpened logical and linguistic awareness. So deliberate a channeling of collective efforts has resulted in an enhanced respect and an insistent demand for clarity. Such a climate favors a thinker with reasoning as crisp as Aquinas. Yet few studies of Aquinas have underscored his keen attention to logic and language.[1]

In fact, however, nothing strikes the initial reader of Aquinas so forcibly as his logical acumen. Even a cursory reflection on his situation in thirteenth-century Paris tells us why. Aquinas inherited a century's intensive preoccupation with logic and language in the form of 'speculative grammars.'[2] The monastic and later cathedral schools of the eleventh and twelfth centuries began their reflections with the words of Scripture. Since words only make sense in an ordered context, these thinkers knew that their capacity to deal with those sacred words depended on their grasp of the form of language. Grammar and logic became indispensable tools.

As a student of those masters of the 'schools,' Aquinas worked to master their skills, and with his wit turned them to yet more systematic use. Despite the glaring cultural disparities between thirteenth and twentieth centuries, then, a structural parallel emerges: attention to logic and language. That parallel has guided this study.

Part I focuses on Aquinas' treatment of divinity: the critical test for a philosophical idiom. It shows how rigorously grammatical is Aquinas' discussion of the issues arising when we attempt to discourse about God. By paying close attention to the way he actually proceeds, moreover, we are in a position to test his treatment against two common criticisms associated with C. G. Jung and with Charles Hartshorne, respectively. On a rigorously logical reading, these criticisms miss their target, but the effort to meet them helps to clarify Aquinas' mode of discourse. And that clarification offers some illumination in the domain proper to philosophy of religion.

Part II concentrates on *actus* as a quintessentially analogous term. Tracing its multiple uses through many regions of Aquinas' thought offers a useful exercise in medievals' use of language. Expressions like *actus* were deemed particularly useful in philosophy since they can be used properly in disparate domains. The trick, however, is to guide the use in each area carefully enough to avoid illicit implications. For analogous terms are at root equivocal and hence not to be trusted in argument; yet we cannot avoid employing them when we tread beyond regions charted by theory. The key to controlling them is to locate paradigm uses sufficiently persuasive to initiate conversation with an interlocutor. The discourse which follows will prove the wisdom of that paradigm choice.[3]

The section on *actus* in fact completes the grammatical treatment of divinity, since Aquinas can allow himself to make only one direct statement: God is pure act. The connection between that sense of 'act' and acts as we know them cannot be directly established, of course, although it can be affirmed in acknowledging creation. So Part II confirms the studied impression of knowledgeable guides to Aquinas like Josef Pieper, who have long insisted that creation was the key to Aquinas' philosophy as well as his theology. A concluding chapter notes many affinities, however, between Aquinas' use of *actus* and eastern philosophical disciplines which remain silent on the central question of creation. So Aquinas' treatment of *actus* illustrates how an analogous expression may be understood even when one chooses a different exemplary instance. To appreciate this feature of language and especially of this class of expressions is to open a way to cross-cultural understanding.

On a more procedural key, this work adopts a referencing scheme to Aquinas' works to minimize the need for notes. References to the *Summa Theologiae* are abbreviated into arabic numerals punctuated by periods: e.g., 1.13.1.4 refers to Part I, question 13, article 1, response to the fourth query (or objection). Similarly, 2-1.12.2 refers to the first part of Part II (*Prima Secundae*), question 12, article 2 (the body of the response). The *Summa Contra Gentiles* is abbreviated *CG* 2, 24 (3), meaning Part II, chapter 24, paragraph number 3. References to *de Potentia, de Veritate,* and *Quaestiones Disputatae de Malo* are abbreviated *de Pot., de Ver., OD de Malo,* respectively. Commentaries on works of Aristotle are abbreviated: *In* 8 *Phys* 4 (4), meaning book 8, *lectio* 4, paragraph 4. The Marietti editions have been standardly employed, except where they are superseded in individual instances (e.g., Decker's *de Trinitate*); while the Eyre and Spottiswoode/McGraw-Hill text and translations of the *Summa Theologiae* have been used unless otherwise noted.

I am most grateful for continuing comments by my colleagues at Notre

Dame, notably Stanley Hauerwas and Ralph McInerny; and for the critical encouragement of Robert King, Barry Miller and David Tracy. The section on *actus* is the richer for the research efforts of graduate students in a philosophical theology seminar at Notre Dame in the spring of 1975. The reader will want to thank Sister Elena Malits, C.S.C., whose efforts at clarifying my prose mimicked those of Hercules. And I am especially thankful for the patience and care with which Mrs Anne Fearing produced preliminary and final typescripts for editors and publishers, as well as for the work of Roger Burrell and of the faculty steno personnel on earlier drafts.

Notre Dame, Indiana, U.S.A.

PART I

Scientia Divina:
The Grammar of Divinity

1

Background: Philosophical Grammar

Undoubtedly the medievals respected reason. But their conviction that understanding could be yoked to the service of something higher tempered their zeal for reason and checked it short of rationalism. Rationalists, enshrining reason, inevitably propose a canonical form of argument. Arguments are accepted or rejected by this standard alone, whatever purposes they may legitimately serve. The medievals were more wary. Their very confidence in reason, in fact, suggested that reason could be used in different ways.

The medievals were no strangers, certainly, to the paradigms of formal logic. They assumed that no proposed argument could contravene these paradigms. This test alone, however, was not regarded as a sufficient one. For besides the universal principles of logic there remain the principles proper to the domain under consideration. Anyone attempting to steer his inquiry by the paradigms of logic alone might be admired for his dialectical skill, but would be ridiculed as well for his lofty inattention to the lie of the land. To the medievals, the logician who pretends to universal knowledge presents a caricature of philosophy. Beyond the formal considerations common to any inquiry lie the material ones germane to the subject at hand. To overlook these is to find oneself in situations akin to category-gaffs. A repertoire of logical ploys does not make a philosopher any more than a habit makes a monk. A valid argument used inappropriately hardly credits its author.

Perhaps a thirteenth-century thinker could afford to be so attentive to the uses of reason because he was able to take logical proficiency for granted. To qualify as a student meant to be skilled in dialectic, the universal principles of argumentation. Furthermore, this dialectical science did not arise full-blown, but had grown out of several centuries of grammatical exercises. Attention to words came naturally to a religion of the Word, and man's more normal desire to understand found in the Bible

3

a source of questions as well as inspiration. The quest for coherence led to discrimination: the scriptures used language in many different ways. The task of classifying these uses and registering the responses appropriate to them generated a skill which came to be known as 'philosophical grammar.'

It was not one skill, really, but a set of related skills. Philosophical grammar embodied what we would list under logic, grammar, and criticism. Not unlike the grab-bag known today as philosophical analysis, this specialized training provided the historical context for those skills which Aquinas exhibits in argument. And in a society which valued its traditions, it was expected that every student of philosophy would have apprenticed himself to the masters who preceded him.[1]

1.1   Examples

The medievals' way of doing grammar is philosophical, since it reflects the background conviction that the form of one's discourse reveals something of the structure of the world. A conviction that language and reality are structurally isomorphic underlies every attempt at philosophical analysis, of course, even if it takes an exceptionally reflective thinker like Peirce or Wittgenstein to call our attention to it.[2] But the conviction alone will never suffice. We must be able to distinguish depth from surface grammar, and that project demands more than formal proficiency in logic. It calls for a close and discriminating attention to the material context of language use.

As already noted, the monasteries and cathedral schools prepared the way for just such philosophical effort by their attention to the different senses latent in the sacred scriptures. Two centuries of painstaking analysis are embodied in the distinctions which Aquinas invokes and in the moves he makes to resolve a problem. We shall examine three such maneuvers now to illustrate the hermeneutic contentions of this chapter and to prepare for the substantive issues which follow. In the first example he distinguishes *concrete* from *abstract* terms, showing how our deliberate use of one kind rather than the other carries philosophical consequences. In the second Aquinas distinguishes two sense of 'to be' to forestall too precipitate an ontological argument. In the third he takes an apparently familiar distinction between the thing signified and the way we signify it, and puts that to work to show how we can make true yet inadequate statements about the divinity.

1.11   *Concrete and abstract terms*

Aquinas tries to give philosophical expression to the divine transcendence by asserting that God must be simple. As we shall see, this assertion does ìot function like a description, or even an analogical description. It is rather a shorthand way of establishing a set of grammatical priorities designed to locate the subject matter as precisely as possible. So the assertion that God is simple claims, among other things, that God exhausts divinity. Of course, such a statement invites difficulties for the logically sophisticated.

An immediate objection to the claim that God is simple is that nothing can be identical with its nature. The formal structure reflected in predication demands that predicate outreach subject. Socrates is human but not humanity; Socrates is wise but not wisdom. Plato struggled to display a distinction which Aristotle could then announce: between the 'is' of predication and the 'is' of identity. To appreciate that distinction is to hold the key to many a metaphysical dispute. If Aquinas insists that God is divinity, and by extension, not only good but goodness, what will become of these hard-earned gains?

Aquinas' response indicates that he is quite conscious of violating a rule, and a universally valid rule. In fact, he does so deliberately in order to show that what holds for the universe cannot hold for the 'source and goal of all things.' God's transcendence does not admit of description, but perhaps we can get an inkling of it by determining what cannot be said of God. This strategy presupposes some sense of that transcendence as well as a grammatical grasp of the shape of our discourse. Aquinas' response leans upon the latter:

> In talking about simple things we have to use as models the
> composite things from which our knowledge derives. Thus when
> God is being referred to as a subsistent thing, we use concrete nouns
> (since the subsistent things with which we are familiar are
> composite); but to express God's simpleness we use abstract nouns
> (1.3.4.1).

Aquinas is reminding us of what we already know, and then going a step further to encourage us to act on our knowledge: it is *we* who use language to do what we want it to do. A knowledge of its rules affords us certain flexibilities if we dare to take them. He treats the same issue more explicitly in question thirteen:

> Since we came to know God from creatures and since this is how we
> come to refer to him, the expressions we use to name him signify in
> a way appropriate to the material creatures we ordinarily know.
> Amongst such creatures the complete subsistent thing is always a
> concrete union of form and matter; for the form itself is not a
> subsistent thing, but that by which something subsists. Because of
> this the words we use to signify complete subsistent things are
> concrete nouns which are appropriate to composite subjects. When,

on the other hand, we want to speak of the form itself we use abstract nouns which do not signify something as subsistent, but as that by which something is: 'whiteness', for example, signifies the form as that by which something is white. Now God is both simple, like the form, and subsistent, like the concrete thing, and so we sometimes refer to him by abstract nouns to indicate his simplicity and sometimes by concrete nouns to indicate his subsistence and completeness; though neither way of speaking measures up to his way of being, for in this life we do not know him as he is in himself (1.13.1.2).

This statement amounts to a summary of Aquinas' position on divine predication, but it can also function as a preview. What is of interest to us now is the way he takes for granted a formal isomorphism between grammatical and metaphysical structure (or 'composition'), and yet does not allow that fact to hamstring his efforts to express God's transcendence. To understand a rule is to abide by it except when an exception arises. And out original understanding is tested precisely by our capacity to recognize exceptions. If we know what we are doing when we use an abstract term, then, we know that expressions appropriately said of God can take an abstract form: 'God is goodness'. But we will also want to say 'God is good'. In fact, we will have to use *both* forms, and in doing so will express something else that we know but cannot otherwise state. The need for two shows that neither form is adequate, since we know that 'we do not know him as he is in himself.'

Where less patient thinkers would invoke paradox, Aquinas is committed to using every resource available to state clearly what can be stated. The resource he will rely upon most is his philosophical grammar. He is not directly engaged in praising or thanking God, of course, but in the reflective theological activity of making explicit what a religious life implies. None the less, this activity can also be considered a quest for God since its object discriminates between appropriate and inappropriate attitudes we might assume toward it. The mode of inquiry, however, remains reflective and explicitly linguisitc. For Aquinas is concerned to *show* what we cannot use our language to *say*, yet there is no medium of exposition available other than language itself.

But our language can be a medium of display only in the measure that we become aware of certain features recurrent in our use of it, and then articulate the meaning of this recurrence. When we can expose such a depth-structure in our grammar, we are able to use our language to show what we cannot bring it to say. Then we are in possession of the proper tools; it remains to be seen whether we can put them to use. A metaphysician outclasses a dialectician, Aquinas avers, not in possessing an arcane method but simply by the power of his intelligence.[3] Here is the place reserved for *intuition*: not some privileged noetic access, but an adept use of skills commonly possessed.

This commentary simply brings into relief what Aquinas does with distinctions like concrete/abstract terms. He is reminding us of certain grammatical features of our discourse to make us aware of how we might use those features to show what something which transcended that discourse would be like. We cannot pretend to offer a description of a transcendent object without betraying its transcendence. But reflecting on the rules of discourse brings to light certain contours of discourse itself. And those very outlines can function in lieu of empirical knowledge to give us a way of characterizing what we could not otherwise describe. I shall consider in chapter 4 just what characterizing amounts to. For now it is enough to examine other distinctions Aquinas proposes, noting how he uses them to increase our awareness of what we are doing in speaking as we do.

1.12 *Two senses of 'to be'*

Another implication of God's lacking composite structure is that his nature and existence cannot be distinguished. What it is to be God is identical with being it, for to be God is simply to be. In fact, the upshot of Aquinas' insistence on the utter absence of ontological composition lies in asserting that to be God is to be. Yet the assertion represents a highly refined form of shorthand, easily susceptible of misunderstanding. In chapter 3 I shall offer a substantive interpretation of it. For the present I want to indicate how Aquinas avoids the obvious suggestion that a claim like this represents a covert ontological argument.

If to be God is to be, how can we entertain a coherent conception which does not entail that God must exist? The objector puts it the other way around, reminding Aquinas that he has insisted 'we can know clearly that there is a God, and yet cannot know clearly what he is. So the existence of God cannot be identified with what God is, with God's "whatness" or nature.' Aquinas responds by reminding us:

> The verb 'to be' is used in two ways: to signify the act of existing, and to signify the mental uniting of predicate to subject which constitutes a proposition. Now we cannot clearly know the being of God in the first sense any more than we can clearly know his essence. But in the second sense, we can, for when we say that God is we form a proposition about God which we clearly know to be true. And this, as we have seen, we know from his effects (1.3.4.2).

This statement only apparently depends upon accepting the validity of Aquinas' ways of showing that God exists. Here he is rather distinguishing between two enterprises: one which results in affirming that to be God is

7

to be, and another which concludes that God exists. Although verbally similar, their grammar is quite different. 'To be' functions in the first as a predicate nominative, and in that role can 'signify [God's] act of existing.' Odd as it may seem, however, this assertion does not succeed in telling us whether God exists. For its form is not that of an existential assertion, but of a definition giving the nature of the thing in question.

If we accept grammatical form as the decisive clue to meaning, we will not confuse this assertion with an existential one. In fact, as we shall see, it is not a proposition at all since it links two unknowns. Rather it is one of those crucial tautologies defining the logical space of God-talk.[4] Nor is the affirmation of God's existence as absolute as it looks. The verb 'is' in 'God is' does not refer to God's existing; verbs never *refer* for Aquinas, but state the manner in which something is what it is.[5]

In this instance, Aquinas classifies 'is' among copulative uses, and reminds us of the manner in which the conclusion was drawn. It is as though in saying 'God is' one is uttering an elliptical form of the more complete conclusion: 'God is the cause of these existing effects' and hence can be said to exist inasmuch as they do. When the arguments are adequately attested, we can 'clearly know ... [such] a proposition about God to be true' because we are in fact speaking not of God in himself but of God in so far as he is the proper cause of certain effects.

This conceptual slippage enables Aquinas to hold that 'we can know clearly that there is a God, and yet cannot know clearly what he is.' It also suggests that the proofs play an ancillary role at best in the theological task he sets himself: to elucidate the parameters of responsible discourse about God.[6] But for the present, we can see how a foray into philosophical grammar clears up some crucial ambiguities in Aquinas' exposition and clarifies his enterprise for us.

1.13 Res significata *and* modus significandi

In his explicitly reflective remarks on religious discourse, Aquinas announces the general outline of his treatment and then offers the distinction which is supposed to carry it:

> How we refer to a thing depends on how we understand it. We have seen already (1.12.12) that in this life we do not see the essence of God, we only know him from creatures; we think of him as their source, and then as surpassing them all and as lacking anything that is merely creaturely. It is the knowledge we have of creatures that enables us to use words to refer to God, and so these words do not express the divine essence as it is in itself (1.13.1).

> God is known from the perfections that flow from him and are to be found in creatures yet which exist in him in a transcendent way. We

understand such perfections, however, as we find them in creatures, and as we understand them so we use words to speak of them. We have to consider two things, therefore, in the words we use to attribute perfections to God, firstly the perfections themselves that are signified – goodness, life and the like – and secondly the way in which they are signified (1.13.3).

The twelfth-century grammarians first began to distinguish the thing signified (*res significata*) from the manner in which it was signified (*modus significandi*) to handle permutations in the form of an expression. The simplest type are paronyms: 'good' and 'goodness'. The forms are different and their difference delineates distinct grammatical roles; one is not substitutable for the other. Nor would it do to write off the difference in forms as 'merely verbal.' One might come to understand certain verbal differences as unimportant (e.g., 'you run,' 'he runs'), but discounting them prior to such an understanding would mean disdaining the only available clues. A medieval characteristically demanded proof that a verbal difference was 'merely verbal.'

Considering for a moment the concrete and abstract manners of signifying ('good' and 'goodness'), how can we speak of the 'thing' they severally signify? Of course we are forced to use one expression or the other to do so, and thus find ourselves referring to the *good* or to *goodness*. The distinction between *res* and *modus*, then, cannot be considered an operational one: the only 'things' we can ever locate will thereby be *mannered*. What the distinction does is call attention to the fact that we can consider something from many different angles. Understanding this keeps us from confounding ourselves – but in no way promises access to the thing independent of any such angle: 'how we refer to a thing depends on how we understand it.'

Training these remarks on the subject at hand, Aquinas seems to press the distinction beyond its limits. When he says that 'we have to consider two things in the words we use to attribute perfections to God,' he appears to be prying 'the perfections themselves that are signified' apart from 'the way in which they are signified.' Yet he keeps reminding us that 'we understand such perfections as we find them in creatures.' So how can we consider the 'perfections themselves' apart from 'the way they are signified?' The answer, of course, is that we cannot.

What we can do, however, is to note that there are diverse ways of signifying, and let this diversity *show* us something about the thing signified. In the class of attributes mentioned – perfections – notorious diversities have been remarked since Socrates' discovery about wisdom: a wise man is one who realizes he is not wise. Expressions of this sort (e.g., 'goodness,' 'life') do not then simply mask differences in degree but cover discontinuities so radical as to approach contradiction.

The distinction between *res* and *modus* was originally introduced to release fixations which could follow from close attention to the forms of expression. Taught to remark the difference marked by '-ness,' a student might think that the abstract form requires another logical neighbourhood entirely, when in fact a more subtle shift is called for. But the situation regarding perfections is exactly opposite: terms like *wise*, *good* and *living* are used without changing their form in contexts so widely divergent that they defy comparison. We speak of a virus being alive, and apply the same term to a symphony performance.

How are such expressions related? That we cannot say. If we were able to say it we could not hope to use these terms of a God who transcends all our contexts. Aquinas does not recall an accepted distinction to resolve in short order the problem arising from religious discourse. Rather he invokes that distinction simply to remind us that we 'have to consider two things' whenever we employ a perfection-expression: the immediate context in which it applies, and the intention or scope latent within the term (which empowers the expression to do the job it does in that context). We discover this latent power not directly but indirectly, by attending to the other ways in which we press the same expression into service.

1.2 *Concluding observations: linguistic tools and their use*

The distinction between *res* and *modus*, then, does not yield any privileged access to the *res*. Nor have I given Aquinas' full-blown justification for our using expressions like *wise, good* or *living* properly of God when we cannot hope to know what they mean in that context. I have merely tried to show how he takes a well-established intellectual maneuver and puts it to work in regions quite remote from its original application. What remains constant, however, is the close attention all medievals paid to language, not only reminding us of what we can say but of the ways we can use it as well to show what cannot be said. Aquinas can draw upon a century or more of attention to uses when he invokes a distinction between the thing signified and the manner of signifying it. And we can test how well he has assimilated that preparatory work by the way he puts the distinction to work. A less attentive thinker might have tried to use it to license transcendent predication *tout court*. Aquinas simply employs the distinction to sensitize us to a special set of terms: perfections. Thus he alerts us to notice the things we ask these expressions to do and the ways we put them to use.

Many substantive issues have arisen in the course of displaying Aquinas' tools. The reason should be obvious: by displaying the way a thinker uses the tools he has at hand, we can catch a glimpse of his characteristic critical judgments. A philosopher differs from a logician, Aquinas contends, precisely in his power to discriminate among contexts. A logical instrument appropriate in one type of inquiry may be awkward in another. Aquinas relies on many such instruments. The medievals called them *distinctions*. We shall see how Aquinas displays his philosophic acumen by his choice of tools and the ways he employs the ones he chooses.

2

The Unknown

I have noted that Aquinas' theological inquiry into God does not pretend to supplant the awareness of God proper to a religious life. It is certainly construed on the model of any other intellectual inquiry: towards ascertaining the nature of the subject in question. Yet the discussion invariably centers on the propriety of certain forms of speech regarding the divinity. Anyone intent on contrasting a first-level inquiry (into natures) with a second-level inquiry (into linguistic proprieties) cannot help but find Aquinas' procedure confusing. But it will be helpful to recall that from the time of Plato and Aristotle, any philosophical investigation into the nature of something inevitably turned on ascertaining its logical neighborhood (recall Plato's *Sophist* or Aristotle's *Physics*). Inquiring into the nature of anything invariably leads one to linguistic reflections.[1] The distinctions embodied in ordinary language comprise the evidence available to us, and the way of interpreting and assessing those distinctions represents what is specific to one philosophy rather than another. Theology as Aquinas practiced it regarded its task as normative, but never in competition with the understanding appropriate to a religious life. Aquinas could walk this tightrope because his method was clearly a reflective, or as we could say, a meta-linguistic one.[2]

The issue of God, of course, raises special difficulties. It is one thing to amass reasons why someone might be constrained to acknowledge his existence. Such activity is neither religious nor properly theological for it does not pretend to deal with God in himself. Rather it is a means of leading to a point whence a person will have to entertain the subject seriously. Translated into linguistic terms, this initial intellectual exercise employed by Aquinas is designed to make plausible the formula: 'the beginning and end of all things and of reasoning creatures especially' (1.2.Intro). The ways he adduces to show that God exists offer diverse ways of showing that this formula has an application. In each way, our

12

attention is focused on something about things (that can be said of *all* things) which implies a beginning or an end. If something about a thing which in fact exists demands a cause, then *a fortiori* that cause must also exist.

I have said that considerations like these are not religious and are at best pre-theological. They are not religious since religious activity presupposes the reality of God. They are not yet theological since the God arrived at by each way is beginning or end after the manner conceived, whereas God himself is unqualifiedly first. That is why Aquinas can use the bare formula – 'beginning and end of all things' – as sufficiently expressive of the nature of God to guide his theological inquiry, yet also admit that 'we cannot know what God is, but only what he is not' (1.3.Intro).

Whatever is the beginning and end of everything else is not itself one of those things, so the formula distinguishes God from the universe. That is the logic of the matter. The inquiry 'must therefore consider the ways in which God does not exist, rather than the ways in which he does.' This maneuver defines Aquinas' strategy in questions which offer his reflective discussion of how one may and may not speak of God:

> Let us inquire then, first, about God's simpleness, thus ruling out compositeness. And then, because in the material world simpleness implies imperfection and incompleteness, let us ask, secondly, about God's perfection, thirdly, about his limitlessness, fourthly, about his unchangeableness, fifthly, about his oneness (1.3.Intro).

All this, remember, is by way of considering not what God is but what he is not. If this be a 'doctrine of God,' it is a dreadfully austere one. Taken as a doctrine of God, it spawns the notorious God of 'classical theism,' not unrelated to Blake's Nobodaddy.[3] But a perceptive reader would think twice before identifying a deliberate consideration of what God is not with a teaching presuming to say what God is. We could expect a doctrine of God to state what God is like, yet Aquinas is clear enough in warning us not to expect that of him. Nevertheless, commentators and critics alike have assumed that he is offering just that – a doctrine of God – in questions 3 through 11.

What people have failed to do is to take seriously Aquinas' disclaimer about our being able to know what God is. That explicit statement has been treated as though it were a bit of pious double-talk. And understandably enough, for he does go on to say much that apparently is about God. But only apparently so. By attending closely to what Aquinas does, we can see that he is scrupulously faithful to that original limitation. What God is like is treated in the most indirect fashion possible, and the only one available to an inquiry by one of his creatures. Aquinas shows under one rubric after another how it is that our discourse fails to represent God. It fails not merely by falling short but by lacking the structural isomorphism requisite to any statement which purports to refer to its object. Besides being unable to say the right things about God, we can never even put our statements correctly.

The end result of such an inquiry does succeed in delivering its object uniquely, it is true, but not in the manner anticipated by those expecting a doctrine of God. The inquiry into this particular nature cannot hope to circumscribe its object. One can only mark that object by noting precisely how different purported descriptions fail. In this way Aquinas fulfils his promise: to show what God is nôt. He also lays the groundwork for a 'doctrine of God,' even if these questions cannot be construed as providing such a doctrine. For they can supply the logical tools indispensable to anyone who wants to construct a conceptual image of what cannot be depicted.

2.1 *Structure of the inquiry*

How does one proceed to show what something is not? Can we initiate an investigation into the nature of something and avoid coming out with a doctrine? The first query can be met by a sensitive exposition of Aquinas' procedure. The second requires a more penetrating interpretation of his goals for philosophical theology. It seems that he regarded philosophy's role in these matters less after the model of a scientific demonstration than as a *manuductio*: literally, a taking-by-the-hand-and-leading-along. In our terms, Aquinas looked to philosophy for an appropriately intellectual therapy in the pursuit of religious questions, rather than expecting it to provide an explanatory framework. This somewhat novel contention is designed deliberately to help us to rediscover philosophy in its proper medieval dress. The following exposition of the way Aquinas proceeds will contribute to the plausibility of my contention as well as respond to the first question.

Aquinas outlines his strategy clearly:

> The ways in which God does not exist will become apparent if we rule out from him everything inappropriate, such as compositeness, change and the like (1.3.Intro).

The compositeness mentioned is the Aristotelian ontic composition of matter/form, or its ontological analogue of potency/act. Aquinas regards the latter feature to be constitutive of all things. Hence God will *not* possess it, since we know that the '[beginning and end of all things] has whatever must belong to the first cause of all things which is beyond all that is caused' (1.12.12). This much we can know without pretending to know anything about God, provided we are patient enough to let tautologies show us the way. Compositeness, of course, is not properly speaking a feature at all. It is not something we could discover all things to possess by examining each one individually. Rather it is what Wittgenstein called a 'formal feature': not patient of description yet displayed in the form of discourse itself.[4]

Whatever can be known (for Aristotle) is known through a set of formulae. The most perfect form of knowledge, science, is delivered in an ordered set of statements. The set begins with a definition of the nature in question, followed by propositions stating those features which follow from the initial statement of the nature.[5] Moreover, whatever is possessed as knowledge must be articulated. The form of that articulation reflects and displays the ontic composition in question: subject:predicate:: matter:form::potency:act. Although a formal feature cannot be used to identify an object or be part of its description, it is everywhere displayed – provided we are as sensitive to what our language shows as we are to what it *says*.[6]

If whatever we can say about something reflects the formal feature of compositeness, anything lacking it will lie quite beyond the range of our linguistic tools. The minimal structural isomorphism presupposed to successful reference will be wanting.[7] Aquinas means to be faithful to his warning: 'we cannot know what God is.' Note that whatever wants compositeness cannot be said to change, for it lacks the conceptual requirement provided by potentiality. This is a simple matter of logic, as anyone familiar with Aristotle's *Physics* can attest.[8] It has nothing whatsoever to do with a personal or cultural predilection for the enduring over the novel.

Since language is the only instrument the intellect possesses in its quest for understanding, our natural tendency is to regard something which cannot find expression through language as itself imperfect. What fails to meet normal requirements is normally considered deficient. So after inquiring 'first, about God's simpleness' and ruling out compositeness, Aquinas proposes four cognate topics 'because in the material world simpleness implies imperfection and incompleteness. [These topics are] God's perfection, his limitlessness, his unchangeableness, and his oneness' (1.3.Intro).

We shall have to guard against taking these as further characteristics of God which follow upon the defining feature of simpleness. That would be the normal pattern, of course. The result would be a scientific statement of the nature of God – a doctrine of God, if you will – providing a coherent account of divinity. But Aquinas warned us not to expect any such account; nor could we hope for one once we grasped what it means to lack compositeness. Actually Aquinas raises these further topics to offset any misunderstanding attendant upon ruling out compositeness in the case of God.

This is philosophy as therapy, not as theory, for Aquinas feels the misunderstanding will be endemic. The reason lies in our empirical bent

15

of mind, which he regards as more natural than a Platonic one. Aquinas holds that the object connatural to a human mind is a nature (= a *what*) located in a context of material objects.[9] Familiarizing ourselves with anything at all requires that we isolate it sufficiently from other things to consider it. Locating it in time and space is convenient, but failing that, we must have conceptual parameters which delimit the subject from everything else. Normally we manage this simply by saying something about it. That was Socrates' lesson; if it sticks, we have succeeded in identifying the object accurately.

Ruling out compositeness, however, removes the possibility of so identifying objects. That is why Aquinas says that 'in the natural world [= the world connatural to us, the world of ordinary language] simpleness implies imperfection and incompleteness.' Whatever lacks limits of any conceivable sort carries connotations of the boundless and the chaotic. Socrates had labored to release mankind from bondage to that fear by showing how we could train our minds to be discriminating. Reason's activity of delimiting offers the very touchstone of what is right and appropriate. So whatever professedly escapes that activity cannot but appear imperfect and even threatening.

Furthermore, by quite another line of reasoning, the only 'simple things' accessible to reason are those formal features themselves: matter and form, potency and act. But these do not present themselves as particulars that we encounter. We arrive at them only by a reductive analysis which finds them presupposed to the things we do encounter. Thus we cannot even call them 'things,' properly speaking. They are rather constituent principles of things, and for that reason radically incomplete.

So the connotations of *simpleness* are hardly positive. Aquinas needs to correct the spontaneous drift of our understanding in this regard by showing that simpleness in the case of God spells not imperfection but perfection, not incompleteness but undivided wholeness. Moreover, the limitlessness which follows upon simpleness does not have overtones of chaos in this instance, but of omnipresence. Similarly, the unchangeableness implied by simpleness here does not mark a divine indifference to change so much as it suggests a life not subject to the metric of time.

It has often been objected that the God so described would hardly inspire our worship. We should realize by now that this objection misses the mark, for in these questions Aquinas is not attempting to describe God at all. He is not proposing a synthesis of religious experience. He does not write to edify, nor does he appeal to religious life or practice as offering relevant evidence for his assertions. In fact, he permits himself only one such reference, and that is in question 13 where he is explicitly relating the import of questions 3 through 11 to our religious discourse.[10]

What then is Aquinas up to in these questions which treat of God's simpleness, perfection, limitlessness, unchangeableness and oneness? My contention is that he is engaged in the metalinguistic project of mapping out the grammar appropriate *in divinis*. He is proposing the logic proper to discourse about God. The terms employed here are not the ones a religious person would spontaneously apply to God: holy, compassionate, merciful, faithful. Nor are these predicates deducible from those associated with 'simpleness', as they would have to be if Aquinas were proposing a doctrine of God. They are no more deducible from *simpleness* than are Newton's laws from the principle of non-contradiction. Aristotle distinguishes the 'universal principles' of logic from the 'proper principles' germane to a specific inquiry.[11] A distinct act of understanding is required to formulate the principles proper to a specific inquiry; a physicist needs to know some logic, but logic does not make him a physicist.

In this instance, of course, the logic is developed expressly to handle discourse appropriate to a unique subject matter, God, so one could easily take the logical treatment for a more substantive doctrine. And this has certainly happened to Aquinas. He even encourages the confusion by using object-language constructions to do metalinguistic jobs. Yet he had clearly warned us that he was not undertaking to treat of God's nature. The 'features' which Aquinas regards it necessary to treat would not be found in an ordinary collection of God's attributes. We would not expect to find them in an invocation, for example, where God would more likely be addressed as bounteous, compassionate, just or searching.

Finally, the reasons he offers in support of these 'features' are never overtly religious ones. He is not concerned with what we might be able to say about God; he does not undertake to sift authentic from spurious experiences. Rather Aquinas is uniquely concerned with showing 'whatever must belong to the first cause of all things which is beyond all that is caused' (1.12.12). Such a task does not involve settling upon certain empirical generalizations and finding a theory to unify them. It is solely a matter of logical analysis, or as Aquinas understood it, of philosophical grammar. Carried on in these rarified regions and with this intensity, what he is doing rightly deserves the name *metaphysics* as well.

But whatever the name, the manner is invariably metalinguistic and the argument always indirect. The upshot of this exercise in transcendent logic is to announce concertedly the distinct ways in which any expression offered to characterize God – like 'wise and all-knowing' – will misrepresent its subject. In that indirect and reflexive fashion, something is conveyed to us of the nature of God. Grammar, after all, does give the nature of a thing, but never straightforwardly as people expect of a doctrine of God.[12]

2.2 *God's simpleness*

The title Aquinas gives to question 3, *de simplicitate Dei*, is already misleading. Anyone who passed lightly over the introduction might think that the author of the *Summa* was selecting one divine attribute among many for singular attention. Such a reader would spontaneously be on his guard against the particular biases working to construct this model for God. Why laud simplicity above, say, astuteness? A closer reading, however, shows these fears unfounded. Moreover, it is helpful to note that the little-used English term 'simpleness' provides a more felicitous rendering of Aquinas' use than does 'simplicity.'

He warned us in the introduction to this very question that the inquiry which followed would be a singular one. Simpleness does not name a characteristic of God, but a formal feature of God as 'beginning and end of all things.' It is a shorthand term for saying that God lacks composition of any kind. And that bit of metaphysical jargon is itself a shorthand way of remarking that no articulated form of expression can succeed in stating anything about God. God escapes our grasp because every bit of knowledge we possess is knowledge *about* something. Yet such a statement already violates the divine mode of being. It does so precisely because God's way of being is not a *mode* of being, but being itself. And we have no way of formulating that since all our expressions are articulated to fit modalities.

Perhaps a simple listing of the eight articles under question 3 will clarify what sort of analysis is being carried on here:

1 Is God a body? Is he, that is to say, composed of extended parts?
2 Is he composed of 'form' and 'matter'?
3 Is God to be identified with his own essence or nature, with that which makes him what he is?
4 Can one distinguish in God nature and existence?
5 Can one distinguish in him genus and difference?
6 Is he composed of substance and accidents?
7 Is there any way in which he is composite, or is he altogether simple?
8 Does he enter into compositeness with other things?

The translator has inverted the query which opens article 3; a more literal rendering would be: Is God composed of quiddity (essence or nature) and subject? The answer to this question and to all the others will be No. But notice what the questions come to: we are not asking whether God is composed of sugar and spice, but whether he is composed at all. The meaning of the term 'composed' shifts as the form of the question moves from an empirical to a logical one. In one article after another, Aquinas monitors each possible way to get hold of something: locating an object in space and time or saying anything about it. God escapes our grasp on every count. He concludes that God is 'altogether simple,' since the key to grasping anything lies in our capacity to articulate it.

A statement purporting to give the nature of a thing stands to be correct the more adequately our formula succeeds in articulating the structure of the object in question. God's lack of structure leaves us nothing to articulate. The final article heads off another way of mis-understanding God once we grasp that he is altogether simple. Overt pantheism would be a natural conclusion, since the closest analogue we have to something altogether simple is the *form* arrived at by reductive analysis. To say that God is simple might lead spontaneously to conceiving him as the form of the world. Aquinas finds that this conception betrays God's transcendence as much as thinking of him as the greatest thing around. So both misconceptions must be avoided in his effort to secure a logical space for the transcendence proper to the 'beginning and end of all things.'

His manner of arguing confirms Aquinas' intentions to ascertain not what God is like but what he is not like. To carry out his plan he called upon the resources available to him in philosophical grammar. So indirect an approach should help to warn those expecting a doctrine of God by underscoring that no features can be reported. At best we can try to ascertain what discourse is appropriate. The result of this strategy, we shall see, is even more indirect: to show even appropriate discourse must fail by misleading.

2.21 *God is not bodily*

Aquinas offers three arguments that God is not bodily. Logicians look askance at this practice: if one is conclusive, why the other two? If none succeeds, they certainly cannot hope to make it together? Yet so single-minded an approach misses the role of argument in carrying out a philosophical analysis. The aim is rather to reconnoiter than to capture, more to establish a beachhead than to win a battle. Arguments are marshaled in an effort to gain plausibility for an entire framework, not to prove or to refute individual points. When a framework is accepted, proof and refutation can proceed.

The first argument relies on a particular way of conceiving the begin-ning and end of all things: as the unchanging first cause of change. Were such a cause to function in a bodily way, then it could not be said to be unchanging. This seems to be a logical point, though Aquinas offers empirical evidence: 'experience can offer no example of a body causing change without itself being changed' (1.3.1). The argument comes to this: even were God to be bodily, it could not be in bodily fashion that he exercised the causality he does. Hence his bodiliness would be accidental

19

to his belief being the unchanging cause of change. But nothing is accidental to God. . . .

The next argument is more central: 'in the first existent thing everything must be actual; there can be no potentiality whatsoever (*necesse est id quod est primum ens esse in actu et nullo modo in potentia*).' The basis for such a statement could only be our inbuilt demand for intelligibility existentially interpreted: 'for what is able to exist is brought into existence only by what already exists.' As the first existent (*first* in the sense of the beginning yet also the end of all things) warranting the being of everything else, God needs no warrant. One shorthand for such a situation is to say that God is 'in act.' And since bodiliness brings extension which implies potentiality, 'God cannot be a body.'

The third and final argument is a Platonic one, as is often Aquinas' wont. We should not forget that Augustine had dominated the theological scene for eight centuries and that a syncretic form of Platonism quite hospitable to Christian revelation had been promoted on his authority. Aquinas could carry out his task of introducing Aristotle to Christendom more easily if he could show his conclusions compatible with the prevailing Platonic forms of thought. So he reminds us that 'a living body is not alive simply in virtue of being a body . . . , it is alive because of some other principle.'[13] Since this other principle, the soul, is more excellent, it more befits God to be like it than like a body.

Do these arguments prove that God is not bodily? Certainly not. For all we know, God might well have a body. But once again that is not the point of this inquiry. Aquinas deliberately eschewed any attempt to tell us what God is like. He did not feel himself or anyone else to be in a position to do that. He promised instead to underscore what God is not. That is, he undertook to map out the logic of divine matters, the upshot of which would be a series of restrictions on what we might appropriately say.

Perceptive critics have often remarked that such an undertaking is not so modest as it sounds; it presupposes some understanding of God, certainly. And of course they are right, for grammar does give the nature of things. But that is given indirectly and at an appropriate remove. If such critics had gone a step further to pinpoint the sort of understanding implied by Aquinas' undertaking, they would have seen how modest it actually is. For Aquinas says no more than must be said. He pretends to no acquaintance with his subject. All he knows is what his logic tells him should follow from being the beginning and end of all things. Bodiliness does not follow, so nothing licenses us to say that of God.

Correlatively, we are freed from having to pursue any queries which might presume God were bodily. And should someone come up with a report that he is, all we have to do is plead ignorance. We might try to help that person to recognize his own ignorance of the logic of the matter. But beyond that we could not go.

2.22 *God is not composed of matter and form*

The next article, asking whether God is composed of *form* and *matter*, is a more technical version of the first. Hence the central argument is identical: 'the very existence of matter is a being potential (*materia est id quod est in potentia*), whilst God contains no potentiality, but is sheer actuality' (1.3.2). Recalling the logical model for *actuality* as well as the standard analogy, matter:form::potency:act, Aquinas' argument comes to saying that nothing in God stands in need of warrant.

Of the supporting arguments, the first is explicitly Platonic, while the second is reminiscent of the *Phaedo* but Aristotelian in form. The first borrows the Platonic scheme: *ens per essentiam/ens per participationem*. On that scheme, the material component derives whatever it can claim to be by participation in the formal. Porphyry and others like him had long ago established this way of harmonizing Plato with Aristotle. God cannot in any way be said to be *by participation*, of course, or else he would not be the beginning and end of everything else. The next argument maps the syntax of *matter/form* onto that of *agency*: 'an agent acts in virtue of its form ...; a primary and immediate source of activity must therefore be primarily and immediately form. Now God is the primary source of all activity ...; God then is essentially form.' How else could we conceptualize the beginning and end of all things except as *form*?

2.23 *God is his own nature*

Article 3 states what one must state next, even though we have no idea what it would be like: that God is to be identified with his own essence or nature. The peculiar nature of Aquinas' program begins to assert itself as we come to appreciate the force of his initial description: 'to consider the ways in which God does not exist.' Individuality, as we normally encounter or experience it, stems most directly and immediately from matter. To be conscious of myself is to be embodied, and bodiliness forms the conceptual matrix as well for our dealings with individuals.[14] If it is not appropriate to think of God in terms which presuppose matter, however, then his individuality is in jeopardy. The only way out is to assert that 'such things are identical with their own natures.'

It is interesting to note how Aquinas makes this point in general terms, thereby indicating that he is laying down the universal (or logical) principles governing discourse about divine things rather than establishing a doctrine of God. (In this case he will want to apply the same scheme to the angels, but the modality would be no less one of logic were God the only conceivable application.) Such a logical advantage allows him to propose a principle of complementarity regarding our use of concrete or abstract expressions of God. This amounts to a slightly more appetible way of saying that we do not know how to say what we want to say about

God. Or more bluntly, that we do not know what we are talking about.

Aquinas' strategy does provide enough grammatical purchase, however, to head off a purely idealistic account of God. We need both concrete and abstract forms of expression. If 'God is justice' would do by itself, then so would 'justice is God', for abstract predicate terms call for the 'is' of identity. But if we are required to complement this way of expressing God's simpleness with the concrete form to express his subsistence, the 'God is just' construction reminds us that 'God' and 'justice' are not simply convertible. While a grammatical account cannot pretend to offer a proper account of the subject in question, it can discourage improper ones. This is another sense in which Aquinas' treatment could be said to consider what God is not.

2.24 *God is to-be*

Article 4 asks whether one can distinguish essence from existence in God. By denying even this much composition in God, Aquinas manages his most radical display of transcendence and comes up with the closest thing to an assertion about God that his professedly logical procedure will allow. Since this assertion and its implications will comprise the topic of chapter 3, I shall content myself with the barest outline of his arguments here.

Aquinas made his philosophical mark by a work published in his mid-twenties: *On Being and Essence*.[15] He used it to sort out the various senses of *ens* and of *essentia* from the Arab sources. Beyond clarifying their uses, however, he took this opportunity to argue a substantive philosophical issue, concluding that essence and existence had to be treated as really distinct from one another. In metalinguistic terms, this amounted to underscoring the difference between a proposition and an assertion; or in epistemological terms, to noting the gap between entertaining something and stating it to be the case. Although we can readily grasp the point when put this way, it can just as easily be overlooked because we have no structural notification whether a proposition is being entertained or asserted. A trained observer can usually distinguish subject from predicate; only a reflective participant can tell whether a proposition is in fact being asserted or not.

Hence this form of composition – that of essence and existence – eludes both saying and showing. It demands yet another frequency in one's awareness of language, beyond that attention to form or syntax which allows us to show what we cannot say. To grasp this difference we must be attuned to our use of language as a kind of performance, and be aware that we are doing something different with the same formula when we assert it than when we merely entertain it. How crucial a difference this is, and how central to inquiry of any sort, should be obvious. Hypotheses, models, and possible worlds are indispensable instruments to philosopher and scientist alike. Yet the activity of elaborating them must be completed by another activity of verifying them, if scientific inquiry is to proceed apace.

So when Aquinas denies even this much discrepancy in God, he is asserting that the very notion of many possible gods is incoherent. For once the pretenders have been eliminated there is only one God possible, and such a one cannot but be. As we shall see, that does not mean we will be in a position to assert this fact. Hence Aquinas' assertion does not issue in an ontological argument. But it will serve as a grammatical way of establishing uniqueness. And in the absence of the ordinary sort of individuality which bodiliness affords this will prove a welcome consequence.

The arguments, while necessarily indirect, are surprisingly spare. The first assumes the real distinction between what a thing is and the fact that it is, and notes that 'if the existence of a thing is to be other than its nature, that existence must either derive from the nature or have an external cause' (1.3.4). The first alternative is inadmissible because 'nothing with derived existence suffices to bring itself into being.' No reason is given for this assertion. Perhaps another rendering could make it as perspicuous to us as Aquinas felt it to be. We might make the identical point by noting that existence is not an attribute, and only attributes can be said to 'derive from the nature.' Such is the import of the real distinction between essence and existence. Thus the logical alternative of existence deriving from the nature is not a real alternative.

Nor can God's existence be externally caused, for he is said to be the beginning and end of all things: 'neither then can we say that God's existence is other than his nature.' The negative form of the conclusion is effective; without knowing what it is we are affirming, we must none the less affirm it.

The supporting arguments do just that. The second draws the analogy, essence:existence::potency:act, and uses it to argue that God's nature would be 'potential of existence' were it not 'itself existence.' And since 'God does not contain potentialities, so in him nature must not differ from existence.' The third argument is overtly Platonic, assuming that one can divide existing things into what exists *per essentiam* and what exists *per participationem*. Were God to partake existence, he could not be the beginning and end of all things. So God must exist by nature. Each of these arguments is rendered suspect by the way in which it deals with existence: as though it were a perfection accruing to something. The first argument suffices, however, to make Aquinas' point.

The point here is best conveyed by expressing it in a formula designed to display identity. When I want to assert that the presidency is identical with commander-in-chief, I can say 'to be president is to be commander-in-chief.' The repeated use of 'to be' is semantically redundant but syntactically significant; it announces an essential identity. In the case at hand, Aquinas is asserting: to be God is to be to-be, or (understanding the form being employed), God is to-be.

We have already noted in the first chapter how this differs from asserting that God exists. For 'to be' in this predicate usage 'signifies the act of existing,' and 'we cannot clearly know the being of God . . . any more than we can clearly know his essence' (1.3.4.2). What we can do is to link these two unknowns by inserting them in the scheme: 'to be . . . is to-be . . . .' And the upshot of Aquinas' argument is that we must do so. To assert that to be God is to be to-be, however, does not amount to a surreptitious proof that God exists. We shall have a chance to assay what it does come to in chapter 3.

2.25   *God is not in a genus, nor is he a substance*

Articles 5 and 6 complete the way in which God is not composed and hence may not be spoken about. Article 5 asks whether God can be articulated according to genus and species; and article 6 whether he can be thought of in substance/accident terms. The answer to both is, of course, negative. The central argument against locating God in a genus derives from the conclusion of article 4. If God's nature is to be, then the only genus to which God could belong would be that of being. And being, of course, is not a genus; Aristotle showed us that in *Metaphysics* III,3 (998b22). Aquinas seizes upon the import of this article to preclude our expecting theology to come forward with a doctrine of God in any straightforward sense:

> And this shows why one cannot assign either genus or difference to God, nor define him, nor demonstrate anything of him except by means of his effects; for definitions are composed of genus and difference, and demonstration depends upon definition (1.3.5).

In asking whether God can be thought of in substance/accident terms, Aquinas is inquiring whether it is proper to predicate something of God *tout court*. For in this utterly generic sense which includes properties, an accident is what belongs to a thing in that manner displayed by predication. We might expect him to deny this manner of being to God, and so remind us that the syntax of our language fails to reflect God's way of being. But his arguments are not so prespicuous as in the other articles. Aquinas seems to be presupposing a quality of attentiveness to the form of discourse that can only result from continued exercise in philosophical grammar.

The first argument counts on 'an accident being a mode in which the subject achieves actuality.' Given that God is in act, any such connotation of potentiality would be inappropriate. The reasoning turns on a subtle interpretation of the significance of the form employed to state that John is late, or walking home, or wise. Each of these statements remarks something about John, and so may be considered as announcing certain possibilities or virtualities present in John. In fact, only predicates which represent possibilities for John are properly said of him. So 'John is granulated' would make no sense, although in the case of persons, the field of metaphorical allusions seems to be nearly unlimited. What does not make sense in the case of God is that anything at all would be a virtuality for him.

When he reflects on actual religious discourse in question 13, Aquinas will distinguish among predicates and find those expressing perfections to be acceptable names of God. So it cannot be the intent of this present article to nullify all predication of God. Yet in the terms employed in the article, a modifying predicate expresses an accident, and the presence of accidents would imply virtuality in God. While it may be true to assert that God is wise, therefore, the manner in which we express that fact will fail to exhibit God's manner of being wise. In fact our mode of expression will give a false impression because we cannot say anything about God's wisdom without thereby showing it to be an accident of a subject. Thus even acceptable predicates will fall short of describing God. Furthermore, the failure will reflect not only a gap in our experience, but also an even more radical discrepancy in the form by which we can express and hence possess whatever experience we may claim.

The best we can do is to employ the principle of complementarity as a working rule: whenever I say that God is wise, I must be prepared to say as well that God is wisdom, and vice versa. Aquinas is reminding us that if the concrete form connotes a subsistent thing's being wise, it also expresses a note of possession which suggests achievement (and hence implies potentiality). So we must employ the complementary abstract form to show we know that God would not be wise in that way. His way of being wise would rather be to be wisdom itself: to be the norm rather than the normed.

The upshot of this restriction is to announce that all statements formed of subject and predicate – that is to say, all discourse – will falsify the reality which God is. Put in a slightly more rhetorical way, God is not an object. Ordinary objective discourse, which is presumed to display the mode of being of the subject in question, betrays rather than displays God's way of being. Aquinas makes this point summarily in a neglected aside: 'God is not even a prototype within the genus of substance, but the prototype of all being, transcending all genera' (1.3.6.2), for 'God does not belong to the genus of substance' (1.3.5.1).

Now *substance* cannot properly be said to be a genus, but it functions like one in delimiting that sort of thing of which something can be said to be the case. So properly speaking, nothing can be said of God. That is the consequence of his simpleness. Aquinas underscores this result in a more positive way in article 8 when he says that 'God is form itself, indeed existence itself; so he can in no way be composite' (1.3.8). This statement suggests the strategy he will employ to show that lacking compositeness does not represent a deficiency in God. But the over-all effect of question 3 should be to discourage anyone hoping to glean a doctrine of God from Aquinas. What we have is rather a gesture towards some unknown form of discourse, not objectifying, yet which will certainly elude our grasp.

2.3   Why simpleness is not a deficiency in God

After laying out the logic of divine things in questions 3 through 11, Aquinas provides an overview of the entire transaction in question 12: 'how God is known by his creatures.' This question seeks to relate his austerely grammatical treatment to the more pressing religious issue: man's desire to see God. In the several articles of the question, Aquinas contrasts the modest fruits of logic with these religious expectations and their fruition in the promise latent in revelation. In article 12, he offers this summary statement:

> The knowledge that is natural to us has its source in the sense and extends just so far as it can be led by sensible things. . . . [Inasmuch as] they are effects dependent from a cause [however], we can at least be led from them to know of God that he exists and that he has whatever must belong to the first cause of all things which is beyond all that is caused. Thus we know about his relation to creatures – that he is the cause of them all; about the difference between him and them – that nothing created is in him; and that his lack of such things is not a deficiency in him but due to his transcendence (1.12.12).

This statement, along with the outline of strategy introducing question 3, allows us to structure questions 4 to 11. Aquinas considers the other topics he does expressly 'because in the material world simpleness implies imperfection and incompleteness' (1.3.Intro). This motivates him to inquire into 'God's perfection, his limitlessness, his unchangeableness and his oneness.' He wants to show how each one of these formal features is a corollary of the central formal feature called simpleness. Yet some of these features also look like deficiencies. So Aquinas will have to show that each feature is not a defect but rather a way of articulating transcendence, and hence a perfection.

So the task is two-fold, especially regarding limitlessness and unchangeableness. In the case of perfection, he will have to show how we relate it to our ordinary use of pro-expressions. Oneness (or unity) seems to carry enough symbolic weight to stand without further elucidation. The result is the following scheme, where the entry in the right column suggests what each logical requirement might come to. Here we have an instance of Aquinas building some bridges from the more austere grammatical discipline of theology to its religious basis in experience.

Simpleness (3)	Perfection (4)
Goodness in general (5)	Goodness of God (6)
Limitlessness (7)	God's existence in things (8)
Unchangeableness (9)	God's eternity (10)
	Oneness (11)

Question 4 (God's perfection) elucidates article 4 of the preceding question by trying to convey what it means for something to be identified with its own to-be. From this angle, what scientific inquiry tends to bracket as incidental matters of fact assumes the utmost significance: 'the most perfect thing of all is to exist' (1.4.1.3). With sayings even darker than this one, Aquinas presses a metaphysical idiom into anticipating the intellectual attitude of existentialism. We will consider this particular strategy in chapter 3, however, and since questions 5 and 6 are more germane to our present development, let us focus on them for now.

2.13 God's goodness

Aquinas treats goodness under the rubric of perfection 'since things perfect are called "good" ' (1.4.Intro). It may seem trivial even to discuss God's being good; the terms have been practically synonymous since Plato. Yet the Judaeo-Christian tradition has been uneasy on this point from as far back as the book of Job. Once God's will and agency enter the picture, his goodness comes into question. What results for us is less praise than a problem: the problem of evil. How can we affirm his goodness in the face of our experience, given that he is master of the universe?

Following his over-all strategy, Aquinas will not attempt to take on this religious issue directly; he will rather work over the grammar of the situation to see whether the question should really arise. In this case, he will try to ascertain how we could possibly be using 'good' if we were to say that God is good (or goodness). So Aquinas will first examine how we use 'good' generally (question 5), and then work to relate that usage to the grammar of divine things (question 6). Since 'good' functions as a collective expression for any term of valuation or assessment, his resolution offers a form suitable to all of them.

Aquinas opens his general grammatical treatment of 'good' with the unlikely query 'whether being and being good really amount to the same thing (*utrum bonum et ens sint idem secundum rem*)?' Once we recover from the strangeness of the question, the answer seems obvious: of course not; you have to do something to be rated good. Aquinas notes this obvious reply and offers an explanation, but does not accept it. He notes that it is certainly more common and proper to speak of something's being good in the measure that it has fulfilled its potential than by the mere fact that it exists (1.5.1.1). Yet being something cannot be written off as a mere fact, simply because it does not represent an achievement. Furthermore, the potential that is fulfilled as well as the power to fulfill it stem from those resources latent in a thing's being what it is.

Aquinas' entire logical treatment is guided by these original convictions. The first announces his unwillingness to treat existence – the fact that something is the case – as a mere given. The pressure of intellectual inquiry is relentlessly essentialist, and Aquinas is skilled enough in philosophical grammar to appreciate this fact. But he will not be content to leave it at that, for we might well find our language expressing or showing what we cannot get it to say. There are presuppositions to discourse which quite instinctively guide the ways we use it. To bring them to awareness is to reveal something of the shape of discoursing itself. In this case, finding a way to characterize being will also show that valuation is not an extrinsic rating but represents an intrinsic realization. On the other hand, whoever takes for granted the fact that something exists will likewise be driven to extrinsic standards of evaluation.

Aquinas' argument apparently moves on a rarified conceptual plane. It begins with a summary of usage: 'good' means 'desirable.' What anything desires is its perfection. Yet 'the perfection of a thing depends on how far it has achieved actuality.' It is clear then that a thing is good inasmuch as it exists, ' . . . it is by existing that everything achieves actuality' (1.5.1). 'Actuality' functions as the middle term here, as in so many arguments regarding simpleness in God. The more actuality, the better the thing. Hence 'to be good without qualification is to achieve complete actuality.' But since 'to exist without qualification is to achieve an initial actuality,' one is entitled to say that a thing is good inasmuch as it exists (1.5.1.1). The term 'achieve' represents an attempt of the translator to turn a lapidary Latin construction into English; *actuality* need not denote the result of effort. One suspects a biblical origin for the notion as Aquinas uses it: 'and God saw that it was good.' Given that picture, existence can no longer be a mere given.

My suspicion is that Genesis provided the impetus for Aquinas to assert that 'being good does not really differ from existing,' so that whatever exists is thereby good. His training in philosophical grammar then helped him to explain why we can so easily overlook this fundamental fact about things: 'the word "good" expresses a notion of desirability not expressed by the word "existent".' In asking whether something is good, therefore, we are spontaneously diverted from its being to ask about its worth: how can I use it? where will it fit? what can it accomplish? how has he demonstrated his potential? Aquinas invites us to pause to acknowledge an existing thing's intrinsic worth. And since he is proposing the grammar of 'good' in general, he is also claiming that other ways of determining worth will be affected directly by how we handle the issue of intrinsic worth.

'Intrinsic worth' is not an expression Aquinas used, of course. Nor would he have thought that the issues latent in the notion of good could be resolved simply by invoking the term. The basic issue can be thus stated: are we entitled to treat the fact that something exists as a given or not? Put in these terms, we can draw fruitful parallels with recent discussions in epistemology about the myth of the given. Aristotle reminded us that a theoretical account must begin somewhere, and whatever we take as a beginning we must treat as a given. Yet what is inescapable for a scientific inquiry is reprehensible in philosophy; so Wilfrid Sellars will take to task those theories of knowledge which settle for a given, accusing them of relying on a myth at the precise point where analysis is called for.[16]

Conceptions of philosophy divide neatly at this point. Those for whom philosophy is a theoretical enterprise – albeit more general than others – can cite Aristotle's reminder and deny any culpability. But the upshot of Sellars' critique is that philosophy is more reflective than theoretical, and that it is more fruitfully pursued as ongoing criticism than as theory-building. Aquinas often appears to be constructing theoretical accounts in a deductive manner, but close attention shows him actually proceeding in a way which belies that approach. His explicit remarks about philosophy as handmaid of theology are vague enough to be satisfied by either way of doing philosophy. I have focused on what he did rather than what he said, on the general principle that a man's execution offers the best account of his intentions. This is not to attribute to Aquinas any reflective awareness of philosophy as a critical enterprise. I am simply concerned to show that he operated that way.

The issue is whether something's existence ought to be treated as given, that is, written off as mere fact. I have drawn attention to recent epistemological discussion to remind us of what is at stake here. The drift of intellectual inquiry is natively essentialist. That is, one simply presupposes the fact of existence, realizing that it defies expression; or else he tries to find a way of conceptualizing it. The metaphysical schemes reflecting these two strategies are called realism and idealism respectively.

Aquinas wants neither. His nose for philosophical grammar will not let him turn 'exists' into a predicate, nor will he be content simply to presuppose it. Rather he wants to be able to assume an attitude towards the fact of existence without pretending to be able to domesticate it within a conceptual framework. He needs to find a way of expressing the import of existence which does not amount to saying what it is. There is a strategy available from his exercise in philosophical grammar: pay attention to the form of discourse and see what that shows when used to say something. Then perhaps if we are unable to say what something is, our very efforts will show why.

If we are attentive enough to the form of discourse, then, we will be able to show how language expresses what we cannot get it to say. Again, Aquinas' recourse to this strategy was more instinctive than deliberate. He employed notions such as to-be (*esse*) and actuality – *esse enim est actualitas omnis rei* – which are even more abstruse than expressions like 'intrinsic worth.' Yet he used them not as components in a theory but to provoke reflection, as I shall show in chapter 3.

What about God's goodness? How does identifying being with good-ness, while acknowledging conceptual differences, help us to assert that God is good? And to do so without exacerbating the problem of evil endemic to a Judaeo-Christian picture of God?[17] The answer can be put in different ways, yet each sounds like a *tour de force*. On Aquinas' grammatical account, we can say that God is good without his having to do anything commendable. That is, we do not have to assess God's activity to conclude that he is good. In fact, when we say that God is good, we are not using 'good' as an assessment term at all. This statement does not envisage God's activities, but his being. The proposition Aquinas is arguing for is not the religious statement it appears to be; rather it is a logical reminder. But a reminder of what? Of a way in which we can use 'good' and the way in which we must use 'God.'

Aquinas expressly relies on Aristotle's account of good as what all things desire (*N. Ethics* 1,1 (1094a3)). This formula builds in a distinction between ultimate and instrumental goods, the latter desired for the sake of the former. As an account of practice, it turns on prudence; and many of us know Aristotle as proponent of the prudential rather than of the good. Yet while prudence expressly deliberates about means, ethics is concerned with analyzing the hold which a non-instrumental good might have upon us. Once we can ascertain that fact, the skills inherent in prudential judgment will have a context to guide their operation.

Aquinas notes elsewhere that fixing this context cannot itself be a prudential action under pain of regress.[18] We cannot deliberate about ultimate goals without turning them into means. And if deliberation is a key ingredient in choice, we cannot be said to choose our values. How then do we espouse those goods which determine which goods we shall choose? We either accept them or reject them. As Aquinas describes this activity, it is less something we determine than something in which we acquiesce. To consent to the inevitable remains a free act for Aquinas (following Aristotle); in fact it points to an interior refuge available to a man in the face of contingency and fate. Assenting to non-instrumental goods need not be so traumatic an action, but it springs from the same source. Such assent entails acknowledging (or refusing to acknowledge) and inbuilt orientation of one's own being. This is the orientation

described by Plato towards the one, the good, the true and the beautiful
– or towards whatever is true, good, and beautiful. It is expressed
archetypally in journeys and in ordeals, and in the mandala figure for
wholeness.[19]

This orientation is presupposed to any intellectual inquiry or any
activity which has a point. When he argues that God is good in the
context of an inquiry delineating what he is not, Aquinas is simply
reminding us that we cannot think of God without calling this orientation
to mind. And when we do, 'God' can be recognized as the name we give
to whatever is the origin and the goal of this inbuilt orientation. Of
course, he is the beginning and end of everything else as well; but this
orientation, brought to awareness, has a way of pre-figuring certain
'features' of God. Hence it can guide us in giving what account we can
of him.

Two citations will suffice to indicate that I have properly interpreted
Aquinas' intent. The first objection to the first article in question 6 (which
explicitly treats of the goodness of God) asks in effect how we can
associate goodness with God when he is beyond good or evil? Aquinas
responds that the good whereby we assess things ('created goodness') is
not at issue here, but rather its source (1.6.1.1). He uses the analytical tools
inherited from Aristotle to call attention to an underlying level where the
good sought after is what is desired by anything which desires its own
perfection. The source and goal of all things would represent such a level.

Hence we can say that God is 'good by nature' without his having to
do anything to be called good (1.6.3). For the good in question pertains
to the source and goal of all things, which is logically even if not
consciously desired in desiring whatever one desires. To assert that God
exists would be to affirm the reality of such an ordering. At this point
Aquinas is calling our attention to the ordering itself. That is why I persist
in calling his treatment a logical one.

2.32 *God's limitlessness and unchangeableness*

Among the formal features introduced to offset the negative connotations
of simpleness, two of them – limitlessness and unchangeableness – sound
deficient themselves. Aquinas complements his treatment of each of them
with a foray into those dimensions of our experience which might lend
plausibility to his logical contentions. This strategy shows how a logical
treatment can be guided by our key experiences, as well as shape the way
we comprehend them. I have suggested two columns to schematize the
complementarity between philosophical grammar and the language of
religious experience:

God's limitlessness (7)   God's existence in things (8)
God's unchangeableness (9)   The eternity of God (10)

2.321 *Limitlessness:* Whatever lacks limit lacks identity. We identify figures by their limits. Plato put reason to work to find the limits or joints of the world, lest man's psyche be left prey to the boundless and chaotic. Whatever is unlimited is thereby formless, arbitrary and without definite sense. Reflections like these cannot properly function as arguments, for their expression remains too vague. But they are no less compelling; such reflections evoke archetypal patterns endemic to any human undertaking, and constitutive of inquiry.[20]

None the less, Aquinas feels compelled to assert that God is limitless. The sense he gives to this expression, however, begins to allay our fears: 'the limitlessness of a form undetermined by matter' (1.7.1). His discussion does not move along mythic pathways, then, but along the tracks of philosophical grammar. The model is 'form itself'; that is, a predicate given substantive status. Take justice, for example. If, in fact, we were able to take justice rather than some example of it, justice itself would certainly be more perfect than any instantiation of it. Even a perfectly just individual could display only those traits which his time and circumstances elicited. We do not know how he would meet other tests. So Aquinas can truthfully say 'that the limitlessness of a form undetermined by matter is perfect in character' (1.7.1).

Justice is limited, certainly, regarding what it is and is not. It is unlimited in the scope of its possible realizations and in the number of instantiations. These limitations, in Aquinas' language, are those imposed by matter. When he asserts that God is unlimited he is thinking of limitations such as these. The notion of 'form itself,' however, or the role played by an abstract predicate nominative like 'justice,' offers no more than a model for Aquinas' inquiry into a grammar for 'God.' He has to find expression for something 'transcending all genera' (1.3.6.2) and hence not properly a predicate, for 'God is existence itself subsistent' (1.7.1).

God is to be regarded not simply as form itself nor even as the form of forms. He must be thought of as transcending even form as we understand it, although form will remain our model for grasping the logic of 'God'. Translated into terms more expressive of the philosophical grammar at work here, Aquinas is reminding us that abstract expressions have the merit of displaying God's simpleness. One of the corollaries of simpleness is, we recall, to lack all material constraints. Even more is at stake here, since God's nature cannot be distinguished from his existence. The abstract predicate nominative more properly used of God, therefore, is 'to be.' Because 'to be' is not a predicate like others, God must be thought of in terms transcending the ordinary predication relation; that is, in terms outreaching even those of form. But we have no such terms. We have reached the limits of grammar; we must use 'form itself' as our model for delineating the grammar of 'God.'

Aquinas elides this dialectical situation by announcing that 'to be itself is the most formal thing of all' (1.7.1). Perhaps our discussion will allow us to take that triumphant statement with the proper linguistic reserve. For it does not succeed in shedding any light on what one might mean when one asserts that to be God is to be. Aquinas can respond to the original suspicion, however, that lacking limits means lacking identity. He remarks that

> the very fact that God's existence itself subsists without being
> acquired by anything, and as such is limitless, distinguishes it from
> everything else (1.7.1.3).

He manages to clarify 'limitless' while showing that God's being limitless adequately serves to identify him. The argument is purely grammatical, using form or ordinary predication as a model:

> Just so, if whiteness subsisted of itself, the very fact that it was not
> the whiteness of something would distinguish it from all whiteness
> ingredient in things (1.7.1.3).

So God's limitlessness consists not merely in his being 'form itself' but in his being 'existence itself.' And existence is not just another form, or one predicate among many. Indeed, the fact that God is existence itself finds linguistic expression in the mandate to use a concrete expression to complement any abstract term we might use of him. For while concrete terms are more 'appropriate to composite subjects,' they also serve 'to indicate his subsistance and completeness' (1.13.1.2). Presumably that is what existence is all about.

This fact of God's existence will govern our conception of his relation to the world as well. For the model chosen – that of form itself – inclines towards pantheism. Hence Aquinas remarks, introducing question 8, that 'an unlimited thing ought it seems to exist everywhere in everything.' Question 8 will affirm that to be so, but not in the manner which the scheme of form-itself might lead us to think. Lest we allow that scheme to assume the status of straightforward expression, Aquinas offers a commentary reminding us that we are to use it as a model.

2.322 *God's existence in things:* Although the scheme of form-itself suggested that God should be present in all things, such a presence would make God the form of the world. Aquinas will not hesitate to use that notion as an image for the divine presence, as he used the scheme of form-itself as a model: 'just as the soul exists wholly everywhere in the body, so God exists wholly in each and every thing' (1.8.2.3). But the reasoning which tries to pinpoint the manner in which God is present stems directly from his unique mode of limitlessness. The limitlessness God enjoys is not just that of any predicate granted substantive status, but the limitlessness accruing to the *sui generis* predicate to-be: 'the very fact that God's existence itself subsists . . . distinguishes it from everything else' (1.7.1.3).

The manner in which God may be said to be in all things, then, follows from his being to-be. Since he subsists, he cannot be in things 'as part of their substance or as an accident.' It can only be 'as an agent is present to that in which its action is taking place.' But not just any agent or any action. For 'since his nature is to-be, he it must be who properly causes existence in creatures. . . . During the whole period of a thing's existence, therefore, God must be present to it, and present in a way in keeping with the way in which the thing possesses its existence' (1.8.1).

This argument turns on the fact that God's way of being is simply to be, and on the axiom that one's characteristic way of acting is congruent with his manner of being (*actio sequitur esse*). The effect proper to God (as agent) will not be any discernible feature of things, then, but the to-be of each thing. So God's mode of presence is a simple corollary of his unique limitlessness. We are still dealing with the logic of the situation, of course. And the argument is designed to go just that far and no farther. It licenses us to affirm what follows from the scheme used to display limitlessness and what religious sensibility demands: 'that God exists by presence in everything' (1.8.3). Yet the argument defies us to state how this presence might be understood – beyond recalling the grammatical restrictions we have already noted.

This challenge is hidden in Aquinas' apparently straightforward assertion: 'present in a way in keeping with the way in which the thing possesses its existence (*secundum modum quo esse habet*).' The awkwardness of the locution 'possesses its existence' should remind us that the fact that something exists cannot be counted among the qualities it possesses. The manner in which accidents may be attributed to something is displayed by the way we predicate them, and the manner in which anything is what it is can be exhibited by the role essential definition plays in a demonstration.[21] But the manner in which something exists is precisely what is nowhere displayed. The difference between a situation entertained and a real one is not shown in any of the statements articulating the situation. That difference emerges from the way we comport ourselves toward the situation.

A proposition asserted looks just like one that is being considered; my act of asserting it has no structural counterpart. Yet it is this act of asserting which provides the proper analogue for the fact that something exists. The shorthand for this semantic situation is a slogan: 'exists' is not a predicate. The slogan means that 'exists' does not function like those predicates which display what they are up to in saying what they say. And since philosophical grammar is based on such specialized attentiveness to the form of language, philosophers want to remind us how misleading

34

'exists' can be if we follow its surface grammar and treat it like other predicates.

When we use 'exists' to call attention to the reality of an object under consideration, we are not remarking a feature of that object, as predicates normally do. Rather we are using an expression within the language to call attention to an activity of the language which asserts that the situation under consideration is in fact the case. No doubt this activity asserts something about the thing itself. Philosophical grammar could not survive were language merely language. But we must be attentive to the grammar of 'about' when we remind someone that asserting a situation to be the case says something about it. And if we are attentive to it, we will realize that asserting is a *sui generis* activity, not to be compared with that talking-about which attributes, say, 'is walking' to the dog.

When we speak about a dog in that way, the form of the expression (taken as functioning within a framework) also manages to display the manner in which *walking* is related to *dogness*. And so with all predication. But not so with '. . . exists.' That is why we must be wary in our use of 'about' if we insist that asserting the dog exists asserts something about the dog itself. For the psuedo-predicate 'exists' does not succeed in displaying the manner in which *to be* is related to *dogness*. That is why philosophical grammarians insist on calling it a psuedo-predicate. And that also shows why Aquinas' statement conceals more than it reveals. For precisely what we do not (and apparently cannot) know is 'the way in which a thing possesses its existence.'

True to his intent in this question – to sketch out some points of contact between grammar and a religious way of life – Aquinas breaches the bounds of logical elucidation to say:

> Now existence is more intimately and profoundly interior to things than anything else, since everything else about a thing is potential when compared to existence. So God must exist in all things and intimately so (1.8.1).

As if to acknowledge that grammar is at a loss to display the way in which something exists, Aquinas has recourse to a poetic idiom to intimate what he cannot assert. The language is frankly evocative: *esse est illud quod est magis intimum cuilibet et quod profundius omnibus inest.* And the reason offered for such a statement is an adaptation of the triumphant formula of the previous question: 'to be itself is the most formal thing of all' (1.7.1).

Yet, as we noted then and clarified here, one cannot compare 'to be' quite so directly with other predicates as this superlative statement supposes. The best we can say is: were we able to do so, the most we could say about something is that it exists. Poetic language is meant to handle situations like this: to suggest what comparison would be like where a comparison cannot strictly speaking be made. Aquinas wants us to remark

35

the startling fact that whatever else may be said about a thing, it is quite irrelevant if we cannot assert that what we say in fact obtains. One way of linking that assertion to the entire set of propositions would be to say that they are all held in abeyance, as it were, awaiting assertion. Since it is normally by asserting something about something else that we make explicit what was hitherto implicit, we can say that asserting something to be the case is like making explicit the whole set of propositions which serves to delineate it.

In this metaphorical sense, then, 'to-be' is the predicate of predicates, 'the most formal thing of all.' And whatever else may be said about a thing could well be considered 'as potential compared to existence.' If this fact about a thing is considered as the proper effect of that which can be said without qualification to be, then God may properly be said to be in all things 'as an agent is present to that in which its action is taking place.' He may be said to be so necessarily, 'since nothing can exist except he cause it to do so' (1.8.4). Since, however, 'to-be' is not a predicate in our language and hence does not express a fact about a thing, we have no way of ascertaining what God's presence would amount to. We can affirm it to be the case, working with the psuedo-predicate 'exists' and the formal fact that something is the case. But we are no closer to knowing what God's presence would be like after question 8 than before. Even the articles which incline towards a religious manner of expression do not fulfill our desire for a doctrine of God. The mode remains grammatical.

2.323 *God's unchangeableness:* Nothing appears to remove Aquinas from our age so much as his insistence that God cannot change. Immutability has come to be synonymous with an entire theological attitude dubbed 'classical theism.'[22] The God which emerges is unresponsive and aloof, a useful tool for ecclesiastical tyranny and a convenient symbol for the super-ego, but hardly fit for Christian worship. Such a God has certainly been all too familiar to Western consciousness, and the image has doubtless been promoted and exploited by ecclesiastic and super-ego alike. Whether such a God-image stems from a theological account like that of Aquinas or from more persuasive political and psychological forces, however, remains a live question. For one thing, Aquinas does not propose unchangeableness as an attribute of God at this point. But even if we mistake the genre of his account, as people have for centuries, Aquinas clarifies his use of 'unchangeable' sufficiently to withdraw any support for an image of unresponsive aloofness.

We have already noticed, however, how misleading Aquinas' expression of these formal features can be. In fact, one of the primary aims of this commentary is to remind us that formal features are not to be confused with ordinary features. The difference lies in being attentive to philosophical grammar, and my contention has been that our experience with philosophical analysis in this century gives us a better grasp of Aquinas' working premises than even his most sympathetic commentators from the centuries intervening. Hence we were able to see that God's limitlessness represented nothing more than an elucidation of the grammatical fact that to be God is to be to-be. Aquinas felt compelled to spell it out in this way because of the negative connotations simpleness carried with it. Similarly, unchangeableness is presented merely as a corollary to logical (or ontological) simpleness. And like limitlessness, this particular formal feature carries negative tones of its own, as subsequent criticism has borne out. So Aquinas supplements his treatment of God's unchangeableness with a more evocative consideration of the eternity of God.

He offers a precise meaning for 'unchangeableness' as a parameter regulating any statement we might be inclined to make about God:

> In all creatures then there exists potentiality of change, either
> substantially as with perishable bodies, or in place as with the
> heavenly bodies, or in orderedness to a goal and application for
> power to different things as with the angels. And in addition there is
> a changeableness common to the whole universe of creatures, since
> whether they exist or not is subject to the creator's power. So,
> because God cannot change in any of these ways, he alone is
> altogether unchangeable (1.9.2).

A roomy medieval ontology offers Aquinas many different ways of using 'changeable,' and allows him to specify which uses he would find incompatible with the notion of God. Medieval usage also offers a precision which we might miss, and in responding to an objection from Augustine, Aquinas clarifies his own use:

> Augustine is here using a Platonic way of speaking ..., meaning by
> 'movement' any operation at all, even understanding, willing and
> loving; ... not however meaning, as we are doing at the moment,
> the movement and change of something potential (1.9.1.1).

So Aquinas explicitly removes intentional activity from the ambit of change, as Aristotle had taught him to do. Unchangeableness does not keep us from speaking of God in terms implying activity; it only interdicts those associated with striving and achieving.

And this is the sense of Aquinas' arguments. The first employs the notion of 'sheer actuality (*purum actum*)' so as to cancel out all potentiality. (I have already noted how little this notion of Aquinas manages to convey to us. Part II will elucidate its many senses.) The next argument reminds us that the logic of change-talk demands a persistent substratum and hence compositeness. In these Aristotelian terms, then, change-talk would be inappropriate in the case of something 'altogether simple' as God is. The third also relies on the grammar of change-talk:

Anything in change acquires something through its change, attaining something previously not attained. Now God, being limitless and embracing within itself the whole fullness of perfection of all existence, cannot acquire anything, nor can he move out towards something previously not attained. So one cannot in any way associate him with change (1.9.1).

The final argument builds on the sense of 'limitless' established in questions 7 and 8. The lyrical passage 'embracing within himself the whole fullness of perfection of all existence (*comprehendens in se omnem plenitudinem perfectionis totius esse*)' can be taken as a gloss on the logical fact that to be God is to be to-be. This should help us see that 'unchangeable' is not an empirical predicate, but rather announces a logical requirement to be met by any statement which purports to be about God. And since nearly any descriptive statement we might employ would carry overtones of a world in process, most of these would be inappropriate. If it should turn out that we had no other language available to us as religious persons to praise God or to speak of him, then this question would serve as a warning to guide our use of expressions, lest their overtones mislead us.

Being unchangeable, then, in the sense defined and in the metalinguistic manner Aquinas proposes, reminds us that God simply is what he is. Whatever is yet might not be, and whatever could be but is not, can be said to be in potency (1.9.2). There is no possibility of God's being other than he is, in either of these senses. Hence God must be said to be beyond the categories associated with plurality or change. Neither terms of motion nor of rest are appropriately ascribed to him. So 'unchangeable' does not mean 'inert'. In fact, God's activity 'preserves all things in existence ... by perpetually giving existence to them' (1.9.2). To say that God is unchangeable is to imply that this activity is effortless. To find analogues for it we will need recourse to intentional activities like understanding and living rather than to the activities we associate with work.

2.324   *Eternity of God:* If asserting God to be unchangeable does not entail his being inert, unresponsive, or aloof, what does it mean? Aquinas introduces question 9 by announcing: 'we must consider God's unchangeableness and consequent eternity.' 'Eternity' and 'eternal' are more characteristically religious expressions, so the consequential arrow inclines towards explicitly religious language and experience. If the upshot of God's unchangeableness was his being simply what he is, we should not expect a further elucidation in the direction of eternity to offer us any more information. At best we can hope for a set of reminders assembled to offset typical misunderstandings of unchangeableness, much as unchangeable was offered to correct the spontaneous apprehensions that simpleness expressed a defect in the divinity. The only difference will be

38

that these reminders promise to be more congenial to a religious sensibility.

Aquinas accents the negative note from the beginning. We can never have a proper conception of eternity: 'just as we can only come to know simple things by way of composite ones, so we can only come to know eternity by way of time' (1.10.1). Then he displays this contention by glossing Boethius' definition: eternity is the instantaneously whole and perfect possession of unending life (*interminabilis vitae tota simul et perfecta possessio*):

> So two things characterize eternity. First, anything existing in eternity is *unending*, that is, lacks both beginning and end (for both may be regarded as ends). Secondly, eternity itself exists as an *instantaneous whole* lacking successiveness (1.10.1).

The first characteristic harks back to unlimitedness and unchangeableness. What is beyond the constraints of material potency is beyond change and hence temporal categorization. The second reiterates simpleness in temporal terms and obliquely recalls Augustine's metaphor for eternity: the *nunc stans* of the elusive present moment.

Yet both of these observations simply affirm what is beyond change eludes the measure of change as well. Aquinas states (without argument) that 'eternity is properly the measure of existence as such (*ipsius esse*) just as time is properly the measure of change' (1.10.4.3). He tries to go on to elucidate this assertion: 'in so far then as any existence falls short of permanence in its existing and is subject to change, so will it fall short of eternity and be subject to time.' But so facile a Platonism hardly becomes Aquinas' guarded initial remarks. For 'permanence' or 'invariability' (cf. 1.10.1) are terms designed to span temporal process, not to transcend it. He notes how eternity differs from the 'now' of time, in which Augustine found the eternal suggested (1.10.4.2), but Aquinas nearly undermines his own treatment by using the careless metaphor of permanence.

There seems to be no way of clarifying the dark saying that eternity is the proper measure of existence as such, except to admit that we have no way of conceiving either. Then 'eternal' becomes a particularly poignant way of referring to whatever simply is what it is. Poignant because the ravages of time are more certain than future promise. So whatever simply is what it is will never no longer be what it once was, for it eludes temporal description.

Does the fact that something cannot be described in temporal terms mean that it is quite unrelated to process? If so, do we not have the stereotyped God of classical theism after all, once we mesh Aquinas' logical treatment with a more overtly religious expression? And if not, *how* might something eternal be related to things temporal? Aquinas gives a careful response to this question in a passage which demands close scrutiny.[23] In it he argues that 'since God is altogether outside the order of creatures, and since they are ordered to him but not he to them, it is clear that being related to God is a reality in creatures, but being related to creatures is not a reality in God' (1.13.7). It is also clear from the context that the relatedness in question is that of causal dependence. Similar to his treatment of unchangeableness, intentional relationships are left quite outside this consideration. So Aquinas is reminding us in effect that the beginning and end of all things is not itself dependent upon any (or all) of those things.

But there are certainly ways to relate to something other than dependency. In fact, the less dependency, the more spontaneous and free a relationship. Some will argue, however, that the grammar of 'relating' presupposes reciprocity; and while spontaneity may vary inversely with dependency, one cannot take it to the limit and still speak of a relationship. At this point some essential grammatical elements would be missing.[24] Aquinas is simply more radical in his outlook than such objectors are willing to be. We shall see (in chapter 6) whether his semantics can support a stance so radical as this asymmetric one. Here it is germane to note that something eternal can be related to something in process, provided that relationship is not one of causal dependence. What would it be like? We cannot know, of course, though Aquinas does offer a metaphor which suggests an analogy. The metaphor: 'his eternity comprehends all phases of time' (1.10.2.4); the analogy: 'as the soul contains the body' (1.8.1).

2.33   God is one

Aquinas' essay in mapping the grammar for discourse *in divinis* began by carefully establishing God's transcendence. The grammatical analogue was simpleness. And since this stipulation was so open to misunderstanding, he undertook to show these severe restrictions did not represent a deficiency in God. He aimed to mine the apparently empty grammatical notion of simpleness, by showing how it could function as a threshold to transcendence. His strategy lay in showing how certain other notions, equally grammatical in form but somewhat less austere in connotation, were in fact corollaries of simpleness. We have examined each of these notions but one, and seen how perfection required establishing a logical baseline for 'good', and how limitlessness and unchangeableness themselves required explicit commentary. In each distinct inquiry Aquinas aimed to express in yet another way what cannot be said (precisely because what is simple is not articulable), namely, that God is to be, that he simply is what he is.

The final notion is oneness. It completes the movement – from simpleness to oneness – as the initial rejection of articulation necessary to establish simpleness turns into an affirmation of undividedness: 'for to be one means no more than to exist undivided' (1.11.1). A conceptual sleight of hand? No doubt. But Aquinas, remember, did not promise us a doctrine of God: he proposed to 'consider the ways in which he does not exist' (1.3.Intro).

By tracing his execution, I have explicated Aquinas' intent as one showing the grammar of discourse *in divinis*. As an expressly metalinguistic inquiry, its movement is not measured by uncovering new information but by discovering conceptual corollaries. Its engine is analysis not synthesis, which is to say that Aquinas' inquiry seems to be going around in circles, somewhat as Socrates must have appeared to the milkmaid and to Meletus. But learning how to negotiate such circles can equip us with a useful set of skills. They may even prove to be precisely what we need to push on in the dark. From working with tautologies like these, we come to learn how to go on.

Oneness completes the circle, adding nothing, but reminding us that 'everything's existence is grounded in indivision. And this is why things guard their unity as they do their existence' (1.11.1). When we can assert things like that we can see why 'it is not ineffectual (*non est nugatio*) to say that what exists is one,' even though it may be tautologous to say so (1.11.1.3). To assert that something is one reminds us that to exist is to exist undivided. Philosophical reflection, after all, consists of reminders like these. Once made, they are superfluous and can be thrown away. But only after we have succeeded in formulating the tautologous statements and so appreciating their point.

Oneness or undividedness carries connotations of wholeness, and it is precisely these which Aquinas feared we would overlook because of the austere way he had to proceed in establishing God's transcendence by the logic of simpleness. These connotations are not a merely conceptual matter, any more than philosophical analysis is a merely linguistic procedure. These suggestions of wholeness, rather, reach to those preconceptual inclinations which Jung identified as archetypes. They demand our respect, much as Athena astutely offered the Furies a place of honor beneath the Acropolis. For such inclinations underlie any inquiry whatsoever, inasmuch as whatever is understood must be one. Little more can be said, however, especially in a deliberately grammatical essay. Aquinas does remind us in the final article that oneness is exhibited pre-eminently in God. For 'he exists supremely because he . . . is subsistent existence itself (*ipsium esse subsistens*),' and 'he is also supremely undivided because . . . he is altogether simple' (1.11.4). We have seen what simpleness implies. We have noted that it is best expressed by saying that God is existence itself: to be God is to be. It is time to examine that formula more carefully.

3

Showing a Way: *Esse*

The formal requirement of simpleness results in two assertions: (1) that nothing can properly be said of God except (2) that to be God is to be to-be. Once he had shown that nothing could be said about God, Aquinas proceeded on the strength of assertion (2): that in God essence and *esse* are identical. God is his own being (*suum esse*) (1.10.2); he is subsistent existence itself (*ipsum esse subsistens*) (1.11.4); to be God is simply to be (1.3.4). Whatever Aquinas does go on to say of God, after having shown how nothing properly can be said, is argued on the strength of this identification. Of course, these other things – perfection, limitlessness, unchangeableness and oneness – do not succeed in revealing anything more to us about God. They merely elucidate the sense of the original interdict: nothing can be said *about* God since he is altogether simple (3.7). Yet identifying essence with existence enabled Aquinas to go on; if not to assert at least to elucidate.

Whatever formula allows one to go on will assume the prominent role of definition. A useful scheme for essential predication is; 'to be *x* is to be *y*,' where the repeated 'to be' functions as a mere index of stating a property or offering a defining formula. This scheme permits us to state Aquinas' conclusion of 1.3.4, that God's essence is to exist, more precisely as: 'to be God is to be to-be'.[1] In this role, 'to-be' expresses the nature of God: that which we cannot know.[2] Aquinas is walking a tightrope here. While he must state that God's nature is to-be, that statement does not let us know what such a nature is like. The arguments in 1.3.4 maintain this 'infinite qualitative difference,' for they are uniformly indirect. There is really no choice but to assert that 'in him nature must not differ from existence. It is therefore God's very nature to exist (*essentia est suum esse*)' (1.3.4).

The grammar which enables Aquinas to shift the conclusion to a more positive voice does not effect any further illumination in the process.

Whereas a normal reaction to question 3 would have been to quit (whereof one cannot speak he should be silent), this formula does allow Aquinas to go on. However, it makes all the difference how we go on, and how we interpret what it is to go on. In a philosophical inquiry these amount to the same thing, of course, for a philosopher is called to be acutely conscious of the way he is proceeding. If that consciousness is not articulated, it will nevertheless be displayed in the questions he deems appropriate to pursue and in the arguments he offers in support of his position. In short, that consciousness will be exhibited in the direction a philosopher's inquiry takes.

I have indicated how Aquinas remained faithful to his original caveat by refusing to undertake a straightforward inquiry into the nature of God, settling instead for a circular elucidation. To show what he was doing, I have distinguished among levels of discourse and among kinds of statements. Some of these explicit distinctions were available to Aquinas, while others were not. The significant fact is that such linguistic in-struments help us to lay bare the joints of his actual treatment, showing why he used the arguments he did, and how his theological treatment remains a coherent one without betraying his original apophatic intent. I have expressed these results negatively and rhetorically by insisting that Aquinas neither intended nor delivered a doctrine of God. That amounts to reminding us once again that philosophical inquiry of this sort does not and need not issue in a theory. Its task is not to explain so much as to interpret: to remind us of where it is we stand by mapping the grammar of our situation.

Such philosophical inquiry moves by analysis and issues in elucidation. For those unable to escape the currently prevailing paradigm of scientific inquiry, it may seem idle to distinguish an elucidation from a theory. But there is no way to grasp the difference between these two modes of inquiry and to appreciate what an exercise in tautologies can accomplish, except by engaging in the sort of analysis Aquinas executes. To prod people into taking up this salutary form of exercise, one is prone to lapse into polemics. Hence the insistence that philosophy does not present theories and that Aquinas is not offering a doctrine of God.

What, then, of lyrical passages about *esse*, like 'existence is more intimately and profoundly interior to things than anything else' (1.8.1)? How is it that identifying God's essence with his existence allows Aquinas to go on – to elucidate, if you will? Where does this substantival use of 'to be' come from, and what gives him any right to use it at all? Furthermore, does not the charged expression 'existence itself (*ipsum esse*)' carry connotations which surreptitiously remove the treatment from the grammatical arena and convert it to a crypto-existential one? Is Aquinas more knowing than he pretends to be? Is not an implicit doctrine of God guiding the logical moves? What is all this about *esse*?

3.1 *Grammar of* esse

It was fashionable not so long ago to celebrate Aquinas as an authentic precursor of existentialism. He explicitly acknowledged a real distinction between essence and existence early in his philosophical life, and went on to exploit the existence-side of things in his theological writings. The attention he gave to *esse* not only affords Aquinas precursor status but also serves to distinguish him from Aristotle.[3] Aristotle was so wedded to discourse and to the paradigm of scientific inquiry that he could do no more than presuppose existence. He actively presupposed it, as even his logical treatises show, and so responded to certain issues left unresolved by Plato.[4] But Aristotle never had occasion to deal philosophically with existence itself. Aquinas did so, and in a manner whereby *esse* became a distinct ontological category.

For Aristotle, the potency and act of the *Metaphysics* correspond rather uniformly with the matter and form of the *Physics*. But for Aquinas the first set of categories becomes more programmatic or heuristic. The relationship of these sets is:

$$\frac{\text{matter}}{\text{form}} :: \frac{\text{potency}}{\text{act}} :: \frac{\text{form}}{\text{esse}}$$

One is tempted to say that the difference between the two views is that Aquinas added a new level to Aristotle's metaphysical analysis of the universe. Allowing for a certain crudity of expression, that is about what he did. Yet for Aquinas, the relations between one level and another remain that of act to potency. There are, furthermore, differences between the roles played by *form* as act and *esse* as act; these difficulties are apt to be overlooked by someone who simply speaks of adding a level. They will also be missed by anyone who fails to be attentive to discourse.

In fact, the most striking weakness in some philosophers who have celebrated Aquinas' existentialism lies in their inattention to language. They tended to treat the Aristotelian categories of matter/form and potency/act as metaphysical givens, overlooking the manner in which discourse embodies these fundamental distinctions. This oversight allowed them to treat Aquinas' discovery of *esse* as a philosophical breakthrough of a quite different order from Aristotle's delineation of the basic ontological categories. They were doubtless influenced by a similar claim on the part of contemporary existentialist thinkers, but closer attention to philosophical grammar could have compensated for that.

Although *esse* does differ from *form*, this difference is marked by the formal fact that '... exists' is not a predicate. Now a slightly different angle is required to note how a proposition asserted differs from the same proposition merely entertained. That was a difference which Aristotle

44

himself tended to overlook. Close attention to discourse, however, shows
how performance is as revealing as Aristotle found syntax to be. I am not
pretending to supply the genesis for Aquinas' grasp of *esse* as a distinct
ontological category. But employing a frankly linguistic matrix to
elucidate his practice pays dividends. I hope to show that basing the
distinction on discourse and its performance illuminates Aquinas' practice.
And a linguistic approach works more economically than the freighted
existentialist analyses. *Esse* remains mysterious on either count; it does not
find direct expression either in the words we choose or in the form they
assume to say something. By using discourse to guide us, however, we
should be able to display thus mysterious behavior without pretending to
explain it.

3.11 *Aquinas' uses*

In Aquinas' original arguments that God's nature must be to-be, there is
no hint of the import of the assertion. It appears to do no more than
renounce one more mode of compositeness in God. On the first opportunity to comment on the import of God's utter lack of compositeness (=
simpleness), however, Aquinas reminds us that 'the most perfect thing of
all is to exist (*ipsum esse est perfectissium omnium*), for everything else is
potential compared to existence.' The reason: 'nothing achieves actuality
except it exist.' Hence 'the act of existing (*ipsum esse*) is the ultimate
actuality of everything, and even of every form' (1.4.1.3).

We have already noted how Aquinas exploited Aristotle's basic
categories of potency/act as a scheme which can be reiterated. This
maneuver permits him distinct yet related uses for 'actuality.' Anything at
all which we consider must to that extent be actual, or else we could not
even consider it. Every thing – even imaginary things – must be a thing
of a certain kind, if only to be imagined. And that represents one sort of
actuality offered by form. But if the situation we are considering really
obtains, we have yet another kind with which to deal. Now we may be
likely to confront the situation. Aquinas handles this fact as well with the
scheme of actuality, using it now to express that the situation we have
been considering in fact obtains.

This fact makes all the difference in the world, yet descriptively the
situation remains the same. That something exists (or that a situation
obtains) demands expression, therefore, even though no feature of the
thing can express the fact. Aquinas reiterates the basic category of actuality,
which found its original expression in the predication relationship, to
handle this new situation. Although '. . . exists' is not a predicate (and
existence not a form), he proposes that we understand the role of *esse*
vis-à-vis what-a-thing-is, on the model offered by those predicates which do

express formal structure. This seems to be a genial way of calling our attention to something we cannot otherwise comprehend. It illuminates what is unknown by something we know, namely the predicative or formal relationship. By insisting that we have an analogy, however, Aquinas does not reduce an existential assertion to a predicative one. Yet every statement Aquinas makes about *esse* and the role it plays can be accounted for by this basic maneuver.

Anyone who has grappled with Aquinas' arguments for a real distinction between essence and existence (in *de Ente et Essentia*) has been schooled to demarcate *esse* from form. The effect is similar to assimilating G. E. Moore's essay, 'Existence is not a Predicate.'[5] It comes as a surprise, then, when Aquinas asserts (in the context of God's limitlessness) that 'the most formal thing of all is *esse* itself' (1.7.1). He offers no reasons in this place but refers us to what has already been said, especially to his treatment of perfection. *Esse* was there said to represent the ultimate in actuality since 'nothing achieves actuality except it exist' (1.4.1.3). The contrast drawn is precisely that between a hypothetical consideration and an assertion. Yet that very contrast accentuates the gap between form and *esse*, and so does Aquinas in treating God's perfection: '*esse* is the actuality of everything and even of every form' (1.4.1.3).

Here we have a case of feedback from the model to the thing modeled. The actuality existence offers to a hypothetical subject was explicitly modeled on that which form contributes to matter. It is this model which will allow us to speak of *esse* as the ultimate actuality of everything. Since the paradigm for actuality is predication (and form), one might be tempted to speak of *esse* and its role as the most *formal* role of all. This approach could be misleading because it suggests that '... exists' is a predicate like others, only superlatively so. That road leads to one or another form of idealism. But Aquinas' assertion is made in the context of God's limitlessness where the image of *form* dominates the discussion. Furthermore, a single assertion could not confuse what is otherwise so clearly demarcated.

What remains disconcerting in his treatment, however, is Aquinas' penchant for speaking about '*esse* itself.' I have suggested a test for language like this: peg it onto the performance of asserting a proposition otherwise merely entertained.[6] Besides discriminating sense from nonsense, applying this test has a cumulative effect. It brings the activity of asserting into clearer focus and forces us to inquire into its ingredients.[7] Applying the test clarifies Aquinas' decision to extend Aristotle's scheme of act/potency to discriminate assertion from predication (*esse* from form), and forces us to attend to the disanalogies as well. Let us see whether the test can also accommodate the lyrical statements we have come across.

The most challenging statement is the arresting claim that 'existence is more intimately and profoundly interior to things than anything else'

46

(1.8.1). Furthermore, the warrant Aquinas proposes for this claim sounds particularly suspect in the light of what I have just remarked: 'to be itself is the most formal thing of all' (1.7.1). Yet we have seen how both the claim and its warrant can be elucidated by the performance test: everything that we might say about an object could be considered held in abeyance, until we felt licensed to assert them. From this perspective, the fact that a situation obtains can be said to make explicit everything that might have been remarked about it.

But what of the bearing of such formulae? What sense have they? I have already noted how their specific application to God's presence retains the over-all attitude of unknowing, since we have no way at all of expressing how a thing possesses its existence (chapter 2.322). The final section of this chapter will examine more closely the related ways in which Aquinas appears to use *esse* to bridge the infinite qualitative difference between creator and creature. Here my concern embraces statements like these as prototypes of all those which speak of *esse* as though it were something, expressions like: 'God ... embraces within himself the whole fullness of perfection of all existence' (9.1); 'he preserves them in existence only by perpetually giving existence to them' (9.2); and 'eternity is properly the measure of existence as such' (10.4.3).

Do not statements of this form prove misleading simply because using the substantive form – especially the emphatic substantive: *ipsum esse* (existence itself) – leads us to think of *esse* as something we can characterize? Aquinas knows two ways to characterize, and they reflect two ontological modes: substance and principles of substance. We characterize substances simply by saying something about them. That is why substances are regarded as paradigmatic, as things *tout court*, for statements are what we normally state. We get some handle on the principles of substance (matter/form), however, in the measure that we school ourselves to notice what the structure of statements can show. But *esse* does not enjoy even this indirect characterization, since there is no structural difference between a proposition asserted and one merely entertained. To get any purchase on *esse* we must expand our awareness from linguistic structure to performance. Yet the substantival construction does not invite such a reflective attitude.

The results can be documented. The answer is yes; the statements about *esse* have definitely proved misleading. The temptation is classic: when the thing referred to cannot be characterized in the ordinary manner, it is regarded as mysterious. Instead of discovering dimensions within language which might show what could not be said, one so tempted assumes that such mysterious objects need an extraordinary language to articulate or a superior faculty to apprehend them. Possession of such a faculty then becomes the prerequisite for being a metaphysician. Call it superior insight or the intuition of being; the demand remains impregnable. Or impertinent. And when such a charge elicits a defense, the language employed tends to undermine whatever appeal the position may have held.[8]

Commenting on Aristotle's *Metaphysics*, Aquinas reflects that a metaphysician differs from a logician only by his power. Not by a separate faculty; a metaphysician is distinguished only by the astuteness with which he employs those faculties we all share and which logic can help to refine. The mode of metaphysics is not intuitive for Aquinas, but logical.[9] But his objective manner of expressing himself could prove misleading to those less versed in philosophical grammar. Whether he misled himself remains a question. Since he does not appear to have been so reflective about these matters as he was about others, we must scrutinize his performance to see.

3.12   *A systematic review*

We have seen how misleading the *ipsum esse* construction can be. Yet I have shown that each of Aquinas' uses – even the most outlandish – can be given an unobjectionable rendering. We must now ask whether such renderings allow these uses to be illuminating as well. If not, then Aquinas fooled himself playing with tautologies. If so, then we are a step closer to understanding what he was doing. For each of these renderings left intact Aquinas' apophatic intent.

One way of putting the question is to ask how '. . . exists' relates to *ipsum esse*? I have assumed a close relationship throughout, offering a reminder: that '. . . exists' is not a predicate is evidence that *esse* could not even be shown. Yet I have also taken for granted that stating Aquinas' summary formula as 'to be God is to be to-be,' is not to claim that God exists. Is there not some conflict here? The answer is abvious once we have clarified the different linguistic roles at work. Both assumptions can be justified by employing a distinction similar to Aquinas' *res* and *modus* (chapter 1.13).

The most fruitful way of explicating the claim that something exists begins by noticing that such a claim is not merely intra-linguistic. Whereas the question, 'What do you mean?' is ordinarily answered by an alternative synonymous expression, the existential 'Do you really mean it?' is best met by an action designed to effect a shift in orientation: an emphatic 'Yes' or even a kick on the shins. The expression, x exists (or x is real), then, is a way of stating within our language that x-language obtains. And since our normal presumption in speaking of anything is that the language obtains, we seldom advert to this device.

I have made much of the distinction between entertaining a proposition and asserting it. Real though this distinction is, it seldom amounts to a gap. A deliberate effort is required to carry out a thoroughgoing hypothetical inquiry; consideration is normally carried on with an eye to

48

affirmation. So we can easily understand how Aristotle could conflate the two in practice. He simply presupposed the existence of the subject in consideration, for in practice they tend to coincide. Any talk which does not obtain is considered idle talk.

The explicit claim that something exists, therefore, is a deliberate reminder that those expressions which serve to define and to describe the object do obtain. There are innumerable ways of making this claim, but they all come to showing that the object in question already figures into one's performance, linguistic or otherwise. An ostensive proof, for example, would indicate that I could not gaze or move in a certain direction without engaging the object. Aquinas' five ways intend to show that I cannot use language of a certain sort without implying a language suitably equivalent to discourse about God. So engaging in the one language implicitly engages me in the other; all the proof does is to remind me of the fact. That is what I mean by a language obtaining.

While 'God exists' makes such a claim about the God described, 'to be God is to be to-be' does not. We have already seen how Aquinas distinguished these two roles of 'to be,' intimating that 'God exists' is actually shorthand for certain statements. 'God exists' stands in for those elaborating the language which is said to obtain, such as 'God is the uncaused cause of motion' (chapter 1.12). In the formula 'to be God is to be to-be,' however, Aquinas says that the final 'to-be' is used 'to signify the act of existing' (1.3.4.2). This means that when the infinitive form 'to be' is used in a substantive role, it is not employed merely to indicate that the language in question obtains. Used substantively, the infinitive intends rather to refer to what-it-is for a language to obtain. Not that the expression 'to-be' has any magical power of its own; that is what the role makes it do.

Whether the formula refers successfully may be difficult to ascertain. There is certainly no single test available to find that out. It seems to depend on what we are able to make the formula do. In this case, when we utter 'to be God is to be to-be' we are saying that God *is* what it is for God-language to obtain. That is certainly different from claiming that a certain God-language obtains. Furthermore, since we are not in posses- sion of a God-language, but at best of some very general remarks about its syntax, we could have no clear idea what it would be like for such language to obtain. Hence Aquinas can affirm this identity without veering from his original profession of ignorance, for 'we cannot know the being of God (*esse Dei*) in [this] sense any more than we can know his essence' (1.3.4.2).

Without proving that '... exists' and *esse* are related, I have managed to go along with the grammatical presumption that they are different forms of the same expression. Aquinas follows the same path when he notes: 'the verb "to be" is used in two ways.' Furthermore, that presumption has not inhibited showing how these two roles carry quite disparate implications. So the grammatical presumption can stand without offering easy licence to an ontological proof.

But what is it for a language to obtain? Let us speak of x-language as though it comprised all those statements we might need to understand what x is, as well as to describe it adequately in different situations. Then the fact that x-language obtains would be a fact about the language itself, and not one of those facts we can use the language to state about x. That would make it something like a formal fact about x, like the fact that any account of x whatsoever will amount to a set of statements predicating different things of x. Hence we can say that x is composed of matter and form. This is a fact germane to any account of x, and hence a formal fact about x.

The fact that an entire language obtains is surely like that, so we can see why Aquinas found it plausible to reiterate Aristotle's scheme of potency/act to relate *esse* to form as form relates to matter. But in another sense, the fact that a language obtains is not formal at all. That is, it is not found imbedded in the grammatical structure of every proposition, as matter and form are. So it cannot be called a formal, in the sense of a structural, feature of discourse or of its object. The fact that a language obtains is reflected only in performance: in asserting a proposition hitherto entertained. It would seem more appropriate to call this a performative or existential fact about x. There is no call for any more than one such, however, so the fact that x-language obtains would be the performative or existential fact about x.

But here we find ourselves pressing 'fact' into an utterly new role without having any idea what it means. A normal fact is plausibly a fact because it can draw our attention to structural features – at least in the sense of 'depth structure.' But this new sort of existential fact can neither be expressed *in* the language nor *by* the language. What could license us to invent a new expression designed to call attention to x-language's obtaining as a fact about x, if we have no way of displaying what sort of fact it is?

On the other hand, however, it seems utterly ridiculous to claim there is nothing factual about x's existing. For the ordinary connotations of 'fact' and 'factual' seem more germane to something's existing than to any list of its attributes. So there you are! This impasse is what Aquinas' use of *esse* brings us to, and what repeated use continues to bring us up against. That is one accepted role of philosophical analysis: to display the limits of language not by pretending to have comprehended them, but rather by bringing one up against those limits hard enough to feel them.[10]

This is a Socratic strategy: coming to know more precisely what it is I do not know. As a strategy it seems particularly appropriate to philosophical theology. Yet the restless desire to know which animates the entire inquiry remains frustrated. Hence such a strategy is even more difficult to maintain than it is to execute. That might explain why so many commentators have allowed themselves to be misled by Aquinas' substantive use of 'to be,' often crediting him (and themselves) with an insight into the very act of existing which he nowhere claims nor confesses.

3.2   *How we are (not) able to use* esse

It is critical that we be clear about a responsible use of *esse*, for Aquinas' logical treatment hangs literally everything upon it. In the context of God's existence in things he argues: 'since it is God's nature to exist (*ipsum esse per suam substantiam*), it follows that created existence is his proper effect, just as fire itself sets other things on fire' (1.8.1). Now as the beginning and end of all things, God is the first cause of all and hence incommensurate with any single thing he causes.[11] Furthermore, since his normal way of acting is through secondary causes, Aquinas adopts the analogy of a God as a good administrator. So it is startling to hear anything referred to as 'his proper effect.'

Even more, such an expression is threatening to Aquinas' original intent, since the proper effect of a cause bears traces of its activity. Thus if created existence is God's proper effect, then it must bear his likeness. And Aquinas affirms as much. In the context of God's perfection, he asks whether creatures can be said to resemble God? After rejecting any thought of a specific or even a generic likeness, he does admit a sort of likeness. Creatures find themselves reflecting the creator 'by an analogical similarity like that holding between all things because they have existence in common. And this is how things receiving existence from God resemble him; for precisely as things possessing existence they resemble the primary and universal source of all existence' (1.4.3). So if we could know what it was for anything to exist, we would have a proximate lead to what God was like. Then we would be in possession of one of his proper traces, like Friday's footprints.

This statement can only be taken as a joke. A useful joke, no doubt, perhaps even a deliberate joke like a Zen koan, but a joke none the less. For while we may assert that something exists, we cannot know what it is to exist. We have no way of expressing the kind of fact that existence is, even though there be nothing more factual than existing. Using the language the translator adopts in question 4, we have no way at all of expressing the manner in which a thing possesses its existence (*modum quo esse habet*). When Aquinas used this expression in question 8, I remarked how strange a locution it is, since what is only possible cannot be said to possess its actuality (chapter 2.322). *Esse* can neither be something we have nor something we do; it simply calls attention to the fact that we exist.

And if we are not dealing with a feature, then how can we speak of resemblance at all?

We cannot, of course. That is the first response. God in no way resembles creatures, nor can we speak of creatures resembling God in any way determinate enough to find out what he is like. We cannot know what God is. But the fact remains that God is the source of all things, and hence on Aquinas' scheme he must be primarily the source of what puts the finishing touches of actuality on anything at all, its *esse*. This is a highly analytic way of speaking, of course. For the first cause causes things to be, not just the to-be of things; much as Hume really saw billiard balls moving rather than the motion of billiard balls. So even though 'nothing is commensurate with God, ... he is called the measure of all things, inasmuch as the nearer things come to God, the more fully they exist' (1.3.5.2). This final observation doubtless had experiential overtones for Aquinas, whose own religious form of life would provide contexts for 'nearer' and 'more fully existing.' As a theological statement, however, it appears tautological at best and misleading at worst, presuming as it does a scale of proximity to God.

Is there a second response to our query whether Aquinas has any right to speak of resemblance between creatures and creator? I think so, provided it is not proposed as an alternative response but remains a second one, only proffered after the first response has been given. For there is no resemblance to speak of, really. Yet if we attend closely to what Aquinas says, using the resources of philosophical grammar to interpret it, we may find some sense for 'resemblance' here. Things are said to 'resemble the primary and universal source of all existence ... precisely as possessing existence' (1.4.3). His own expression is somewhat less misleading: 'in so far as they are beings (*inquantam sunt entia*) they resemble him (*assimilantur ei*).' The translation is otherwise felicitous, however, for the medieval Latin *entia* certainly accentuates *esse* – something which its literal equivalent, 'beings,' would not do for us.

But how is it that things *are*? The question stands in contrast with one like, say, are things birds? For things are birds by being sparrows or robins, large or small, slow or swift, migrating or not, lifetime or seasonal mates, and so on. But the ways in which things can be said simply to exist would have to apply to all things, or to things simply as things. There is a classical listing of the manners of being – the ways in which a thing may (and must) be said to be what it is – known as Aristotle's categories. Substance, together with quantity, quality, relation and the other accidental modalities exhaust the manners in which something can be said to be. And nothing can be said to be except it be so mannered. (God, remember, is not said to be but to be to-be.) There are no 'bare particulars' in Aquinas' universe any more than in Aristotle's.[12]

The categories of Aristotle, then, represent the ways which things are things, or can be said to be. Following this lead, Aquinas would be saying that these manners of being are ways of resembling the source, while the source (which simply exists without manner) in no way resembles any single manner. God, remember, cannot even be said to 'belong to the genus of substance' (1.3.5.1). But what can these manners of being tell us about the unmannered source of being anything at all? The answer lies in accepting philosophy more as a therapeutic discipline than as offering a doctrine.

Could it be that the discipline to discriminate manners of being in the forms of our discourse will prepare the inquirer himself to recognize traces of God? These manners of being will not be found within our discourse; no descriptive feature of our world can pretend to be a trace of the creator. But some may be found in the ways we relate discourse to the world. To be sure, we cannot express this relation; hence it were better called a relating than a relation. Yet we can become more aware of doing than relating, or better, of living it. Curiously enough, logic and grammar can assist in this coming-to-awareness, as we have seen in trying to locate *esse*.

This awareness has come to be called (since Kant) a critical or trans-cendental attitude: it consists in becoming aware of how things as we know them bear traces of the manner in which we know them. While initially unsettling, such a critical awareness can move through many stages. All of these represent ways of relating oneself to oneself and the world.[13] The awareness itself can finally be exploited to acknowledge an unknown which bears no traces at all of our manners of knowing. We would then realize that we cannot conceive this unknown, yet we could state that realization by affirming the unknown to be altogether simple.

It would be a long roundabout way, but we could honestly say that it was through our understanding of how things are that we were able to make such an affirmation. Certainly no simple observation nor even any scientific theory could have issued in an assertion so studied yet so uninformative as this one. We need the highly reflective resources of logic to do it. For nothing less universal than logic can tell us how it is that things are (things). And no resemblance more definite than this could be countenanced between things and God.

Is this too sophisticated an interpretation of Aquinas' twin assertions that 'created *esse* is God's proper effect' and that 'things which come from God resemble him precisely inasmuch as they are things?' Doubtless it is, if one takes it to portray Aquinas working in so highly reflective a manner as this commentary. Yet great thinkers like Aquinas do make genial moves, operating better than they know how to say. I would welcome a less sinuous reading. None the less this one preserves his original intent while offering some sense for Aquinas' statements about *esse*. However oblique it may be, this interpretation at least fares better than postulating an intuition of what we know to be inexpressible.

Aquinas manages to employ the identity 'to be God is to be to-be' to help him to go on to make the grammatical points he does about 'God'. And he does so without presuming that we know how to use this substantival form of 'to be'. That is, none of the statements he makes using 'to-be' are empirical or informative. Taken together, however, these statements themselves display an ordered use of 'to-be'. Above all, the exercise I have undertaken to grasp how Aquinas is using this unusual expression has urged clarification of our own relation to the language we use, taken as a whole. I have relied on devices of philosophical grammar, many of which were available to Aquinas, to clarify some formal features of our language-world. In elucidating *esse*, I pressed beyond linguistic structure to performance. The effort to understand these uninformative statements - especially those comprising *esse* - has led us to a more exacting awareness of language, its limits and the part it can play in displaying what transcends those limits. In this way my insistence on a rigorously grammatical reading preserves Aquinas' original intent intact and illuminatively: 'to consider the ways in which God does not exist.'

If we were to state, along with Aquinas, that 'God is subsistent existence itself (*ipsum esse subsistens*)' (1.11.4), what would we be saying? We would be saying all that we can about God. Yet we have no way of fitting that statement into the rest of our discourses, except to work through this chapter once more. For this chapter aimed to show us that we cannot know what we mean by *esse*. Yet we are speaking appropriately if we have negotiated this exercise, for 'we have understood God perfectly when we realize that his nature transcends anything which we can apprehend in our present state.'[14] Language transcribes our present state. But we are nevertheless possessed of the capacity - the awareness and the tools - to use language as a pointer beyond that state, by carefully ascertaining its limits.

4

Analogical Predication

Aquinas is perhaps best known for his theory of analogy. On closer inspection it turns out that he never had one. Rather he made do with a few vague remarks and that grammatical astuteness which I have suggested as a replacement for intuition. Others, of course, organized those remarks of his into a theory, and that is what Aquinas has become famous for.[1] The misunderstanding resulted in the usual way: the philosophical activity of the master became doctrine in the hands of his disciples. Constructing a theory turned analogy into a method and gave the discussion a particular turn: does it work? The nearly unanimous conclusion has been that it does not. And that conclusion vindicates Aquinas, since it should direct our attention to his practice rather than to the theory.

Aquinas' own comments made use of Aristotle's initial and rough division of expressions and their senses into univocal and equivocal (or synonymous and homonomous). There is a set of expressions, Aquinas notes, which can be used in a fashion neither univocal nor equivocal, but somewhere in between. These expressions he calls 'analogous,' and can claim support from Aristotle.[2] There are different ways of finding this median, and Aquinas cites two specifically: (1) by reference to one focal meaning (attribution), and (2) by an ordered relationship among different uses (proportionately).

Noting these two ways of doing it adds some precision, it is true, to Aquinas' initial remarks positioning analogical expressions somewhere between univocal and equivocal. But not a great deal. Nor did he need to be too precise, since vagueness can be an asset. Aquinas will exploit the distinction so that the context can decide which kind of analogy to employ. He will also let the context suggest how to trace the reference or display the relationship. We shall see how he employed 'analogy' analogously, just as he used different analogies in making points of different kinds.[3]

Theory-builders, on the other hand, demand greater precision than this. If analogy is to be a method, 'analogy' itself must be a univocal term. This demand led Aquinas' followers to concentrate on the second way of making analogies: proportionality. For 'reference to a focal meaning' left indeterminate how that reference was to be established, while the second form offered a handy mathematical image: a:b::c:d. A reference to mathematical ratio is actually built into the term *analogia*, of course, which means 'proportionality' in Greek. So the theory-builders were bewitched into neglecting the analogous way Aquinas used 'analogy' when they hastened to identify that term with its mathematical sense.

This effort to make 'analogy' more precise by fastening onto its mathematical sense inspired a theory that will not work. It also succeeded in passing on two other distracting consequences as well. Preoccupation with *proper* (i.e. mathematical) proportionality diverted attention from an irreducibly metaphorical dimension in analogous expressions. And fascination with mathematical ratios led straight to the (mathematical) conclusion that a responsible use of analogous expressions presupposes a univocal access to the object in question.

It is hard to say which consequence was more deleterious. The first gave the impression that one could engage in strict philosophical analysis without benefit of any literary acumen, that is, without any feeling at all for nuance or plurality of uses. Such an attitude proved congenial, of course to many a philosophical temperament. Only recently has the philosophical community begun to feel the effects of Wittgenstein's dogged efforts to reverse the accumulated inertial force of this trend.

The second effect assures that analogous discourse itself become superfluous, just as the first dispensed with metaphor. If a univocal access to the subject is available, why rely on analogous ones? For filler perhaps, or suitable decoration, like metaphors. Or perhaps analogies should be reserved for religious expression which needs the imagination, while philosophy labors for literal understanding. This summary statement of Hegel's position certainly owes its plausibility to the two attitudes sketched above. Yet this position is undermined by Hegel's actual practice.[4] His performance and that of Aquinas prove to be closer than one might suspect. 'Dialectical' offers a useful rendering of 'analogous,' as Aquinas himself employs analogous discourse.

My contention that Aquinas had no theory of analogy parallels, of course, my insistence that he did not provide us with a doctrine of God. In both cases, he neither intended nor produced a doctrine. Furthermore, it took an understanding of philosophy quite at odds with Aquinas' to turn his treatment into one. My argument will be more easily negotiated with respect to analogy, since his own treatment of it is nowhere so compact or coherent as is his inquiry into what God is not. Aquinas undertakes a sustained inquiry into the practice of 'naming God,' which will form the focus of my treatment. But anyone intent on constructing a theory of analogous discourse from his writings must be content with collecting *ad hoc* remarks from diverse contexts, and with harmonizing the conflicting approaches which they take. This difficulty is acknowledged by all who try to do so.

More significantly, however, the theories gleaned from Aquinas' remarks on analogy offer at best a superficial illumination of his practice. I want to show not only that he did not state a theory of analogy, but that Aquinas did not operate from one either. He did not employ a theory explicitly or implicitly. My strongest argument derives from Aquinas' own performance with analogous expressions, and from his explicitly reflective observations about how we might responsibly speak of God when we set out to name him. This skilled philosopher had an understanding of analogous discourse, of course, and of how one should employ it – a very astute understanding. But such understanding did not amount to a theory, for the same reasons that we cannot come up with a method for using analogous expressions without betraying their very genius and utility to us. I shall demonstrate that Aquinas neither intended nor employed a theory by showing how unaffected he was by either of the consequences attending a theoretic posture.

Careful to separate obviously metaphorical expressions from those more properly used of God, Aquinas was not afraid to acknowledge a metaphorical dimension in these latter terms as well. In fact, it is this very dimension that will provide the purchase we need to use such expressions of God. Nor does Aquinas exhibit any anxiety because our discoursings of God are everywhere analogical. His elucidation of this fact does not lead him to look for a univocal core of meaning which could legitimize our using analogical terms. We have already seen how Aquinas' appeal to the accepted distinction of *res significata* from *modus significandi* suggested such a maneuver (chapter 1.13). But when we follow the ways he actually used this distinction, we never find him trying to turn up a pure *res*.

Some students of Aquinas may have gathered from his use of *esse* that at least this expression offers univocal access to God. After all, the author of the *Summa* will insist that 'He who is' is the most appropriate name for God (1.13.11). Yet our detailed examination of his uses and the claims they make has shown otherwise. However proper the formula 'to be God is to be to-be' may be, it does not offer us univocal access to God. And the reason is clear: *esse* is not a univocal expression in spite of its substantive form. In fact, the grammar of the term diverges so startlingly from substantives generally that it can hardly be called an expression at all. So it would prove chimerical to look to *esse* to provide a univocal baseline on which to peg one's use of analogous expressions.[5]

Most significantly, Aquinas did not even look for such a base line. What does ground his use of analogous expressions is not another expression, but a performance, his own performance.[6] And in this performance, Aquinas displays a consistency more akin to fidelity than to logical completeness. Whether that suffices to legitimize his claims about using such expressions to name God remains a moot question, I suspect, until we try out that performance ourselves. My efforts in this chapter to trace Aquinas' own practices are intended to assist others in themselves' making those motions.

4.1 Naming God

Nothing strains the resources available to human language so completely as our attempts to speak of God. We have noted how Aquinas identifies these resources as a specifically analogous potential present in a certain class of predicates. In offering a philosophical assessment of our attempts to speak of God, then, Aquinas will be constrained to sharpen his grasp of analogical predication. Hence the central role of question 13: *de nominibus Dei*, normally rendered *On Naming God* but given by McCabe as *Theological Language*.

Article 12 summarizes his entire treatment by putting the crucial question: can affirmative propositions be correctly formed about God? Aquinas' response recapitulates the previous articles and alerts us to the skills they were meant to form in us:

> In every true affirmative statement, although the subject and predicate signify what is in fact in some way the same thing, they do so from different points of view ..., while the fact that they are put together affirmatively indicates that it is one thing that is being looked at (1.13.12).

Making a statement announces our intent to say something of God, while the inner diversity endemic to a subject/predicate affirmation already misrepresents the simpleness of God. Yet we are aware of this discrepancy, for 'we also know that to each [way of signifying God] corresponds a single simplicity.' Hence we need not be misled into taking anything divine compositely, even when we must understand it in an articulated fashion.

But what will keep us from mis-taking God when the very form of our assertions misrepresents him? How can we properly use a language which we know to be inadequate? Finally, what can assure us that even a proper use is a truthful one? We will be in a position to answer the first two questions the more precisely we can show how assertions fail to represent God's manner of being. And a precise awareness of inadequacy should also offer a way to approach the issue of adequacy, or truthfulness. The earlier articles of question 13 are designed to develop the skills necessary to deal with the specific inadequacy our language suffers *in divinis*.

4.11 *Diverse ways of speaking*

Before proceeding to assess what we are saying when we speak of God, it would help to distinguish among different ways of speaking, if only in a preliminary and schematic manner. This will enable us to clarify some differences between religious and theological uses of 'God'. These distinctions can also accommodate the observation that we really don't talk that much about God – and if theologians do, that very fact poses difficulties peculiar to their profession.

A ready classification of ways of speaking presents itself by analogy with scientific inquiry. Our language is doing three different jobs when we use it (1) to observe what is the case, (2) to generalize about such happenings, or (3) to frame an hypothesis to help us get hold of yet wider ramifications. Similarly when we try to articulate man's relation with God, I shall suggest that we use language in one of three ways:

(1) to address God: 'O just one, who ordains all things, hear our plea.'

(2) to convey to ourselves or others the convictions framing our accustomed address: 'God is just.'

(3) to raise reflective questions hoping to gain a clearer grasp of what those convictions entail: 'if God is just, why does evil prevail?'

Classifying religious language in this way allows us to distinguish neatly between paradigm religious (1) and theological (3) uses; it also explains why much contemporary discussion fails to make that distinction. For what we might call the credal use (2) forms a bridge from religious to theological use, much as in scientific inquiry empirical generalizations often adumbrate a theoretical account by the way they are framed. Furthermore, it is asserions of the 'God is just' type which interest philosophers precisely because they look like straightforward descriptions and are cast in the declarative mood.

My classification is crude in failing to display the multiple uses to which we put statements like 'God is just.' Alistair McKinnon has developed an effective typology indicating how their descriptive form belies their primary function: to 'serve as the basis for the believer's attempt to determine more precisely the specifiable sense in which God is [just].' Expressions like these offer a 'foundation for belief as an ongoing interpretative activity.'[7] James McClendon and James M. Smith have also taken care to show how a statement conveying a conviction does more than offer a general observation[8] These uses could not hope to be effective, of course, if the statement were not true. Nevertheless, closer analysis forces us to take stock of the way we ask whether statements like 'God is just' are true.

Specifically, attending to the multiple and subtle linguistic functions played by such statements should warn us not to demand that they yield straightforward descriptions. As one might expect, surface grammar turns out to be especially misleading here. In the early articles of question 13, Aquinas will urge upon us the skills we need to appreciate this fact. Since he does not explicitly advert to convictional uses, however, the simpler classification I have suggested will suffice to understand his treatment of religious or theological language. The statements he has in mind are credal in form, presupposing the many forms of direct address familiar in liturgical prayer.

The examples Aquinas offers are few, and they cluster about 'God is good,' 'God is wise' and 'the living God.' 'Creator' and 'Saviour' are terms of a different sort, accruing to God as a result of his activity. And while 'He who is' is taken to be the most appropriate name for God (1.13.11), it is expected that we will use the more congenial expressions: good, wise or living. Aquinas' practice, then, confirms my contention that the terms employed in question 3 should not be considered attributes, in the normal sense of object-language predicates. Apart from 'goodness,' which can play both roles because it expresses what it says, those terms (simple, limitless, unchangeable, one) do not primarily express perfections; hence they do not exemplify that family of expressions spontaneously used of God.

These terms are of course analogous, and thus display a semantic structure isomorphic to that of perfection-terms. But they are proposed in question 3 to clarify the logic of the matter: to announce the manner in which any term used of God can only misrepresent the divinity. Question 13 will show how perfection-terms must fail to represent as well, even though they alone can be appropriately used of God. The predicates this question is concerned with, however, are those more amenable to direct address: O wise God! O living God! O just God! Hence, the credal expressions which question 13 focuses upon are to be taken more in a religious than in a theological sense. And it is these expressions which Aquinas has in mind when he speaks of the attributes of God.

4.12 *Grammatical observations about religious uses*

Aquinas summarizes our situation when speaking to or of God: 'we shall suggest that such words [like "good" or "wise"] do say what God is . . . but fail to represent adequately what he is. The reason for this is that we speak of God as we know him, and since we know him from creatures we can only speak of him as they represent him' (1.13.2). We cannot speak of God at all, in other words, unless it be under the rubric of 'the first cause of all.' Yet such a cause leaves no proper traces since its *modus operandi* cannot conform to the ordinary patterns whereby effect resembles cause. This is a logical constraint following upon the grammatical observation that God is outside any genus, even the comprehensive pseudo-genus of substance (1.3.5.1). In the measure, then, that our language embodies a subject/predicate, genus/species grammar (or any analogue thereof), no description can succeed in identifying a trace of divinity.

The inadequacy is two-fold: structural (subject/predicate) as well as categorical (genus/species). None the less, Aquinas claims that certain expressions can be trusted to 'signify something that God really is,' in the face of the two-fold manner in which we know 'they signify it imperfectly.' His claim appears to turn on a special class of expressions: 'words like "good" and "wise".' Since this class is defined by the capacity of its members to function appropriately across quite diverse genera, these expressions have been singled out as analogous terms. Using them properly of God, however, involves more than just noticing their inherent structure.

Using analogous terms properly *in divinis* demands that we attend explicitly to the two-fold manner in which even they will fail to represent God. But we have no way of translating this attention into the form of a declarative statement like 'God is wise.' The declarative form, further-more, itself presumes a certain adequacy in representing what it asserts to be the case. This form will inescapably mislead us *in divinis*, no matter how qualified the particular expressions may be. So besides isolating a class of expressions, Aquinas must lay down certain conditions for using them properly.

These conditions yield a rule demanding that we realize such terms will fail to express what they purport each time we use them of God. To employ them properly we must factor into our actual use the specific understanding that they cannot properly represent God as he is. It would prove inconvenient to state that understanding each time. So we must display it in the way we handle the declarative statements we do use, since there is no way of altering their form. Whether we are using the proper expressions appropriately, then, will be shown in what we feel entitled to go on to say.

The rules of proper use become rules governing implications that can or cannot be drawn. Hence the operating unit of appropriate discourse *in divinis* must comprise more than a single sentence. Aquinas had adumbrated this semantic feature in his earlier observation that we use both abstract and concrete terms of God, since neither alone is adequate to the task (1.3.3.1). If we were to transpose his observation into a rule, it would refer to what we go on to say: *in divinis* we can say 'God is wise' properly only when we are prepared to say 'God is wisdom' as well, and vice versa.

There will be more to it, of course, than simply adhering to such a rule. But the point of formulating the rule is to show how the conditions Aquinas requires for using expressions which improperly signify extend beyond identifying a special class of terms. These conditions invite us to consider more than just the sentence for adjudicating normal form *in divinis*. Yet they are not as clear in Aquinas as I have suggested. A closer look at what he does to justify his claim that 'words like "good" and "wise" when used of God do signify something that God really is [even though] they signify it imperfectly' (1.13.2) will indicate the conditions I find operating in his treatment. Watching his performance should also help us to formulate them more sharply.

4.2 Aquinas' treatment

Aquinas employs a conventional distinction to show how this class of terms can be used *in divinis*. He distinguishes between what an expression signifies (*res significata*) and the manner in which the expression signifies it (*modus significandi*). The terms we can use to speak of God – 'goodness, life and the like' – are said to apply more appropriately to God than to creatures 'so far as the perfections signified are concerned' (1.13.3). 'But so far as the way of signifying these perfections ..., the words are used inappropriately, for they have a way of signifying that is appropriate to creatures.' The reason is clear: 'we understand such perfections ... as we find them in creatures, and as we understand them so we use words to speak of them' (1.13.3).

Aquinas finds it helpful to distinguish what an expression signifies from the way it signifies, yet in nearly the same breath he reminds us there is no way of employing these terms other than the ways connatural to us. How can the distinction be put to work in the face of such a blanket restriction? We cannot use it to isolate what an expression signifies from the various manners in which it signifies, for there is no other access to the thing signified except a mannered one. Put in this fashion, Aquinas' restriction assures us that he will continue to rely on the structure and use of language to guide his inquiry, even (and especially) *in divinis*.

The *res/modus* distinction serves as a prototype for the difference Frege recovered between *Bedeutung* and *Sinn*.[9] Neither distinction, however, operates as we might expect: providing a method of isolating *res* from *modus* or *Bedeutung* from *Sinn*. For that very reason the distinction itself has often gone unnoticed, only to be recovered in the face of resolutely ostensive theories of meaning.[10] Aquinas does not introduce the distinction as a handy way to liberate ordinary language for use beyond its ken, but rather as a means of telegraphing the semantic model he will employ.

His model suggests that expressions signify not by pointing, as we might first think, but by fulfilling certain roles. Closer attention to these roles affords the clues we have to what it is the terms signify. And analogous expressions merit special attention precisely because of their capacity to play many different roles gracefully. Or, if you will, they perform their task effectively in quite unrelated contexts. On the strength of this semantic fact, we come to suspect that such expressions might prove useful in speaking of those things whereof we cannot speak. At least these terms show more promise than standard categorial forms of speech. How we can use analogous expressions appropriately of God and what this use comes to, however, remains to be seen. The rest of this chapter deals with those questions.

4.21 *The words are used literally of God*

Certainly the most startling claim Aquinas makes for perfection-expressions is that 'the words are used literally of God, and in fact more appropriately than they are used of creatures – so far as the perfections signified are concerned' (1.13.3). On the basis of this claim he will insist that such expressions can be used to state true things about God, even when they fall short of informing us about him. So we must ask how any term can be said literally of God, and what it could mean for perfection-terms to be so employed?

Two precisions are in order. By rendering *proprie competunt Deo* as 'used literally of God,' McCabe has challenged our native penchant to identify literal use with univocal or categorial expressions. This tendency is natural enough, since we spontaneously contrast *literal* with *metaphorical*, and analogous expressions inevitably retain a touch of metaphor. Analogical expressions, however, will differ from neatly metaphorical ones precisely in their capacity to function quite literally in diverse contexts.[11] For example, I can use 'in control' to describe the governance of a strict or of a permissive parent, employing that analogous term properly in each case. And I can recognize this situation, notwithstanding the fact that each of us tends to use the word by reference to certain paradigm situations. (This last observation acknowledges how analogous expressions like 'control' retain a touch of metaphor.)

The second remark is less telling, and for our present purposes, rather academic. It might seem that analogous expressions and perfection terms were coextensive. I deliberately chose a more neutral word like 'control' to make my first point, however, to ward off identifying analogous with perfection-terms. Yet someone could argue that 'control' represents a kind of achievement or perfection, and hence enjoys an analogous structure. Perhaps it does; perhaps that conceptual connection comes to an identity. But I am not interested in pursuing that connection here, even though I feel Aquinas sensed there to be one, and found that fact significant. It suffices for this account that all perfection-terms in fact enjoy an analogous semantic structure, and must do so in order to carry out their assessment tasks. I do not know whether all analogous terms are also and only assessment terms. Nor is it necessary to settle that question here. When I speak as though they are coextensive, it is for the sake of brevity. Understand: analogous terms which express perfections. It is this subset with which we are concerned.

These are those expressions 'that simply mean certain perfections without any indication of how these perfections are possessed,' and such words 'can be used literally of God' (1.13.3.1). It is not that we know how to use them, nor does Aquinas show us. But he offers three examples: 'being,' 'good' and 'living'; and he contrasts these terms with words like 'rock,' which 'can be used of God only metaphorically.'

The difference between the two kinds of expression has already been indicated. Terms used appropriately of God simply mean certain perfections, with no indication of how these perfections are possessed by him. So stated, however, the difference eludes us. For Aquinas offers no way of separating meaning from use, much as he warns us that *res* and *modus* cannot always be equated. In fact, he reminds us that 'what we mean by a word is the concept we form of what the word signifies' (1.13.4). Thus, whenever we say that something is good or alive, or simply that it exists, we assert these to be true in the manner appropriate to the object in question. If that object be God, however, we must say that 'we understand him through concepts appropriate to the perfections creatures receive from him' (1.13.4), because 'from the point of view of our use of the word we apply it first to creatures because we know them first' (1.13.6).

When we assert that God is living, then, we cannot know what we mean, since we are unable to form a concept expressing God's manner of being alive. Yet we are licensed to make the statement once we have become aware that we can use 'living' to express many ways of being alive, without thereby exhausting the range of this term. If we couple that awareness with Aquinas' formula that God is the source and goal of all things, his observations become more compatible. He can continue to insist, regarding terms like 'living,' 'that from the point of view of what the word means it is used primarily of God and derivatively of creatures.' This is so precisely because 'what the word means – the perfection it signifies – flows from God to the creature' (1.13.6). We need not know how to use the term of God, therefore, to know that it could be so used by someone who did know how. Furthermore, that use would certainly offer the paradigm for all others. We learn how to use perfection expressions by reference to the more perfect instances, much as we fix the range of generic terms by appealing to the better specimens.

If God's primacy were not originating, we would not be licensed to use even these expressions of him, of course. (Remember that an additional assumption is not being proposed here, but I am merely recalling the consequences of the formula Aquinas adopts to introduce the consideration of God.) Yet even God's being origin of all does not suffice to warrant our calling him 'living God.' We must understand the semantic structure of terms like 'living,' as well. And we can only discover that by using these terms and then assessing what such use shows us. So the *meaning* of these terms even when said of God, is never unrelated to the ways we use them.

Perfection-expressions are peculiar in being able to mean beyond the manners in which we employ them. This semantic peculiarity, however, does not warrant thinking we know what *we* mean when we apply them to God. 'When we say he is good or wise,' the terms are used *absolutely*; that is, without their indicating how these perfections are possessed. Yet what we mean to say by so using them is that God 'possesses these perfections transcendently' (1.13.6). Possesses them, that is, not as manners but as correlates to being God – which is to say, not as a possession. So the proper use of appropriate expressions turns not on acquaintance with divinity, but rather on a keen appreciation of the peculiar ways we must fracture logic to constitute a domain of discourse about God.

4.22 *The words are used truthfully of God*

These things having been said, the truth question appears relatively uncomplicated. If one is not pretending to know what he means in saying that God is wise, but at best to show how these traditional forms of addresses are legitimate ones, most of the knotty issues do not even arise. How do you know what God is like? is no longer a leading question. But even if you don't pretend to know that, what suggests these perfection terms rather than others? Their semantic structure, where one use outstrips another, and each does the job called for in the context. What warrants using them with confidence that they are being used properly? The active realization that one does not intend to state that God is wise in a particular manner, but that wisdom correlates with being divine.

The cash value of that awareness comes when we appreciate (as Job did) that 'wise' cannot be used to measure God's activity. Rather it is divine activity which constitutes wisdom. Normally, of course, the multiple ways we use 'wise' offer leading analogies for recognizing God's activity to be wise. But any particular conception might well be overturned. None the less, we are licensed to call God wise and to be confident that we have spoken truly. Such confidence is justified, however, only to the degree we realize that any given conception of wisdom falls short of characterizing God, though some of them may yield leading analogies to help us think of God.[12] What we state will never quite be congruent with what we think, however. That is the upshot of the initial distinction between *res* and *modus*.

4.3 *Analogy*

Aquinas manages to leave the grammar of ordinary language intact by insisting that 'we cannot speak of God at all except in the language we use of creatures' (1.13.5). Certain expressions of that language, however, offer possibilities the rest do not. These are called by Aquinas 'perfection-words.'

In their regard he highlights our capacity to distinguish between what a term signifies and its manner of signifying. This is not a capacity much experienced except in quite trivial ways, and when we pass over grammatical variants, judging they do not affect an expression's meaning what it *says*. Otherwise, the manner in which a statement is composed offers the most consistent guide for ascertaining what we mean by it. So the distinction between *res* and *modus* remains relatively inoperative, except in the special case of perfection-words. And even here, everything depends on how we employ that distinction.

We cannot rely on it to turn up a *use* of 'wise,' for example, which would be manifestly appropriate to apply to God. For any use whatever represents a manner of signifying. What we can do, however, is to reflect that our capacity to recognize distinct sets of expressions also allows us to make grammatical observations regarding characteristic ways we use them: 'thus when we say that a man is wise, we signify his wisdom as something distinct from the other things about him – his essence, his powers or his existence' (1.13.5). When we call someone wise, we are attributing wisdom to him. Not so with God, however. Despite parity of form, 'when we use this word about God we do not intend to signify something distinct from his essence, power or existence.' This fact of philosophical grammar was established already in question 3. It assures us that in using 'wise,' 'what it signifies in God is not confirmed by the meaning of our word but goes beyond it' (1.13.5).

The meanings of our words, including perfection-words, are exhibited in the ways we employ them. Should any word signify something beyond those characteristic uses, that meaning too must be exhibited in use. So it is in the case of God. Not directly, however, since 'God is wise.' But reflectively, in the measure that we acknowledge the shared form to be misleading. And that particular realization derives from an analysis of the logic of the matter, not from a direct experience of divinity. The logic which demands we mark a difference between the source of all things and the things themselves, furthermore, licenses us to use the same expressions in both domains. The only stipulation is that such expressions belong to the privileged set of perfection-words. For these terms shift their sense to meet their context, yet are at home in every one to which they are germane.

It is the analogous semantic structure of perfection words which make them apt for use *in divinis*. But Aquinas' original heuristic definition of God as the source of all things is what gives the formal license to use them: 'whatever is said both of God and creatures is said in virtue of the order that creatures have to God as their source and cause in which all the perfections of things pre-exist transcendently' (1.13.5). We cannot, of course, know the manner in which qualities like wisdom are possessed by God. Such ignorance was assured once we understood that God's simpleness means he has no qualities, even though we are forced to speak as though he had. This same ignorance is reinforced by recalling that the 'order which creatures have to God' utterly escapes us. The only common measure would be existence-itself, and we have no way of articulating *esse* to serve as a metric (chapter 3.2).

Whatever explains that which requires explaining must account for it adequately. There is a simpler way of putting this demand: whatever causes something to be what it is must possess the wherewithal to do so. In the case we are considering, it is the perfections – and particularly the fact that anything exists at all – which requires explaining. They provide parameters for our discussion of 'the order which creatures have to God,' for the perfections offer a way of speaking about whatever might account for them.

Aquinas himself does not try to show how perfections might adequately be accounted for. By choosing existence and attributes cognate to it, moreover, he assured that no one could propose a proper account. For existence is precisely what escapes scientific explanation; to account for it would be to supply the 'order which creatures have to God.' And that is a logical, not a theological, statement. But because the logical neighborhood proper to divinity is indicated only by expressions inherently analogous in structure, we have no metric for it. There is simply no way of articulating the 'order which creatures have to God.' We can, however, affirm there is one. And we can know thereby that perfection-expressions may properly be used of God. None the less, we will be conscious that we cannot know these expressions in speaking about him.

The peculiar semantic structure of perfection-words protects this transcendent use from charges of nonsense. That is so precisely because it makes sense to use words like 'wise' beyond their accustomed ken. For these terms embody a structure of assessment (*res*) besides an inherited history of uses (*modus*). Whether we use perfection expressions properly when we use them of God depends on an acquired skill: knowing how to respect the grammatical difference which logic demands for discourse *in divinis*. Genuinely learning how to respect these difference, however, is more than just a matter for logic. That task requires the disciplines traditionally associated with religious living and practice. For attending to differences, we must call upon the metaphorical resources of analogous terms. And the formation of apt metaphors is a matter for sensitivity, not for science.

At this point rules other than grammatical ones are needed. Of these Aquinas has nothing to say. He exhibits his adherence to them, however, by his manner of pursuing the questions he raises, and especially by not raising certain others. Aquinas displays his religious discipline most clearly by the ease with which he is able to endure so unknown a God.

5

Truth in Matters Religious

Aquinas was deeply concerned, as we have seen, whether men could say anything truthful about God. He was satisfied that certain human expressions, like wise or just, could be used of God and succeed in naming him. These would never be adequate to describe him because their characteristic use as predicate adjectives fails to display the manner in which God is either wise or just. Realizing this fact, the best one might do would be to assert that God is also wisdom or justice. That maneuver reminds the speaker himself, as well as his interlocutor, that his statement about God is inherently inadequate.

Then we shall never be able to know whether the God described by those statements which employ appropriate expressions of him is the true God. In fact, all we can do is acknowledge that the statements which purport to describe God truly will fail to do so if the God they would describe is the true one. For the true God cannot be circumscribed by any set of statements. Every one of them will fail by its manner, even when it states what is appropriate. This impasse, however, does not leave us paralyzed. We can use the expertise learned from Aquinas to rule out certain candidates for God. Any god described by an inappropriate expression cannot be God, and is unworthy of our worship. Because the expressions we do deem appropriate reflect our sense of what is worth while, furthermore, to worship such a god could only undermine one's sense of oneself.

Since we cannot know what God is like, it makes no sense to ask whether or not one has a true notion of him. This is but another way of remarking that any notion we have of God is inadequate, and hence none could be said to be true. Nor is the situation altered were I to speak rather of a concept or a picture of God. By 'notion' I wish to communicate in the most neutral way possible what each of these terms expresses: whatever is conveyed by a set of statements sufficiently precise to determine the item in question. But we are not in a position to determine sufficiently this 'item,' God, even to ask whether our statements are in fact the case. In this instance our statements fail inherently to yield the intended object.

It would be doubly obtuse, then, to ask whether Aquinas' concept of God is a true one. For such a question presupposes that he was engaged in developing a concept of God. Absurdly it goes on to wonder if Aquinas were successful in an endeavor which he has shown to be self-defeating. His practice of philosophical theology, as we have seen, proved to be more critical than constructive. This thinker's aims were modest: to ascertain what logical structure true statements about God would have to have, and to determine a class of expressions which could be used of him with propriety. Both objectives fall short of providing a doctrine or concept of God, although each proves useful in sifting out pretenders.

Ironically enough, any doctrine which pretends to offer an adequate concept of God is *ipso facto* just that: a pretender. There can be no conflict between the God of Abraham and the God of the philosophers, however, if we stick to the contours of Aquinas' treatment. For the critical philosopher has no god of his own; he knows that whatever god his skills yield cannot be God. The upshot of this should be clear: the verification of religious discourse will not itself be a matter of philosophy. Philosophical skill can be put to work to rule out unlikely candidates for god, but philosophy cannot decide the matter for us by ascertaining whether our God is the true one.

This overstates the matter, of course, since philosophy has seldom offered to undertake a process of verification. At best, philosophers have sought to clarify what verifying certain claims would involve. Actual verification is normally left to the mode of inquiry in question, be it physics or paleontology or criminal law. Since no inquiry proved up to verifying religious statements, however, it seemed logical that philosophy itself would fill the breach. The task fell naturally enough to metaphysics, whose office it became to yield a notion of God. One aim of my critical study has been to show that Aquinas did not demand such results from philosophy. Following him, we can say that in religious matters, as in others, a philosopher can at best help to discriminate sense from nonsense. The skills of the philosopher do not place him in a position to determine whether what can properly be said is in fact the case.

How then does a person ascertain whether his beliefs are true? Philosophy should help in suggesting various ways appropriate to the statements in question. Can it do so in the case of religious beliefs? Does Aquinas' way of putting philosophical skills to work offer any assistance here?

5.1 Art of using analogical expressions

Perhaps the most startling observation Aquinas makes about those expressions which demand analogous employment regards their literal or proper use. Were they to be used properly, he says, they would be said primarily of God and secondarily of whatever else to which they apply (1.13.6). The obvious implication is that we are never in a position to employ these terms literally (as McCabe aptly translates *proprie*); we must use them analogously if we are to use them in a manner appropriate to the syntactical structures available for them (i.e., in statements). We can use such expressions univocally, of course, but to do so would shear them of their intrinsic powers.

Nevertheless Aquinas presumes that we can have some intimation of a literal use of 'wise' which is not univocal. If that were so, this use would be the proper use of the term and would adequately express the divinity. But since there is no way of stating any of these expressions literally, how might we have some idea of this sense of 'wise'? A plausible account lies imbedded in our awareness of the analogous uses which constitute the semantic structure of such expressions. The single recurring fact is that we can always find a more comprehensive use of the term. In fact, a recursive formula displays the analogous structure of these expressions, e.g., the wise man is one who realizes he is not wise. And the formula has an inbuilt rachet-effect. The more accomplished the wise man is, the wiser he becomes in realizing that his accomplishments do not constitute wisdom.

Reflection on this recurring fact can intimate a literal use which transcends our actual employment. If we understand the proper analogous structure of terms like 'wise', however, we will not be tempted to insist that a transcendent sense is presupposed by our multiple uses. So characteristically neo-Platonic a move would be too facile in the face of Aquinas' sophisticated semantics. Yet he will allow the suggestion of a sense for analogous expressions which our propositional syntax will not permit us to state.

To the extent that religious language admits of using analogous terms in an increasingly comprehensive manner in speaking of (or to) God, we can approach that literal use. It will, of course, ever outreach us. Doubtless we can only use these terms concretely in an effort to express and interpret our ongoing experience. Awareness of being able to employ them in a more comprehensive manner would then constitute a progressive verification of the way of life which these expressions body forth. In short, such awareness offers a gauge for authenticity. If, as Aquinas insists, perfection terms apply primarily to God and secondarily to other things (1.13.6), their literal truth will be intimated to us via our felicitous analogical use of them. And that will be an issue of how we live as well as of grammatical skill.

Aquinas does not speak in this fashion, of course. He himself is single-mindedly taken up with the sheer logic of the matter, and appears to regard verification as belonging to the ascetical and spiritual disciplines.

Discernment of spirits, after all, already enjoyed a venerable tradition from the earlier monastic communities. I am simply trying to show what Aquinas' distinctive treatment of analogous expressions implies for undertaking the task of verification.

5.2 *Respecting divine transcendence*

Aquinas' preoccupation with divine transcendence suggests another angle on verification which is a variant of the approach just outlined. His austerely logical treatment of 'what God is not' generates a corollary for discriminating among religions: that religion will prove more authentic whose doctrine and liturgy assiduously avoid any pretense of circumscribing God. (This criterion will be familiar to readers of Tillich as 'the Protestant principle.'[1]) The use of language in such a religion to speak of or to God will reflect his transcendence by a set of functional rules which forbid employing any expression univocally.

The upshot, of course, will be to allow an increasingly comprehensive use of analogous expressions. In practical terms, an authentic religion need not try to explain what must be left mysterious. Logic can and should warn us when we are in such neighborhoods. But our native desire for explanation often overshadows logical instincts unless we are helped to reverence the unknown by a religious tradition. Nevertheless, Augustine became disillusioned with the Manichees precisely because they proposed a scheme which promised to explain everything. A Christian thinker like Ambrose, on the other hand, did not make such vain offers. He was able to respect the limits of available knowledge, and to live with issues beyond the reach of scientific explanation. Augustine was fascinated by this capacity and wanted it for himself.

5.21 *In the face of many religions*

Not too long ago philosophers of science discovered (or rediscovered) a very useful principle. Pondering the logical difficulties involved in verifying or confirming a theory, they found their task lightened by the reminder that we seldom (if ever) work with one theory. Rather confirmation is normally a matter of deciding among competing theories. The effect of this insight was, oddly enough, to alleviate a conceptual blind. Awareness of the presence of competing theories helped to fill the *prima facie* gap between theory and observation. In fact, we are always dealing with both, since our observations find themselves guided by the current theory.

The issues lie otherwise with religion, as the history of mankind testifies. Religions do not compete well with one another. Doubtless that is because each offers an ultimate horizon. The ubiquity of analogous predicates, moreover, militates against the clarity needed to determine conceptual differences among the various traditions. A plurality of religious ways can only complicate the verification issue for a philosopher of religion. This fact raises questions for us which Aquinas never had to face.

Christianity represented for Aquinas the authentic way to worship God. He believed it to be *the* revealed religion. As an historical institution, it was fertile enough in generating offshoots, but these could be shown to be either expressly heretical or unfortunately schismatic. (The first represents a deliberate tampering with the doctrinal synthesis; the latter has more often been a product of political causes.) Christendom faced the concrete challenge of Islam, and that had inspired Aquinas' apologetic exercise, *On the Truth of the Catholic Faith*.[2] But Islam was not a viable religious alternative for him. Even though he greatly respected its commentators on Aristotle, Aquinas certainly never would have entertained a decision to convert.

I say this without any direct evidence, of course, yet without hesitation either. Not do I base the observation on a preconception of the medieval world as a closed universe of Christian discourse. It is rather that the Christian way had become a total way of life for Aquinas, and one does not interchange ways of life. They represent, after all, an interlocking network of agreements in judgments.[3] And when we confront the issue of religious alternatives in this fashion, we must ask whether anyone ever succeeds in regarding a comparable religious way as a genuine alternative for himself.

By a comparable religious way, I mean one which confronts another head-on, as Islam does Christianity. Transition from one Christian denomination to another may be personally traumatic, but seldom demands adopting an alternative religious way. The fact and the aftermath of Vatican II have made the differences within Christianity largely a matter of historical record. (That is a theological assessment, of course. Human sensibilities and political arrangements are indeed another matter.) But the relations between Christianity and a traditional way like that of the Navajos, for example, are quite diverse. Many sensitive issues are doubtless involved in such a judgment. Nevertheless, levels of discourse can be sufficiently discriminated in such cases, so that a careful inquirer can generally avoid head-on confrontation.

Noting these significant reservations, what would it mean for a person to confront a comparable religious way, giving it serious consideration as a genuine personal alternative? The records are scant; they tend to show such people recovering their own religious tradition so that it is intimately affected by the intellectual and spiritual confrontation. Mohandas Gandhi offers a significant example of that process.[4] There is a growing body of literature, however, which documents a contemporary secular individual being confronted by a religious tradition or a holy and powerful man.[5] Even though these cases do not constitute a confrontation between religions, the resulting transformations are so startling that they should illuminate how we verify a religious way.

Enough has been said to relate Aquinas' situation to ours – perhaps too much on this topic. Yet one item deserves mention before leaving the question of verification in matters religious. Really, people seldom preach (or practice) a given religion precisely as 'the true one.' Outside of that peculiar and relatively recent historical scene of Christianity fragmented into competitive groupings, alternative ways were infrequently adverted to. More typically believers simply lived, and preached if called to, the tradition which was theirs. But immensely increased information about various religions (as possible within the last century) seemingly alters that state of affairs. It would be a mistake, however, to regard the kind of knowledge most contemporary Christians have of other religions as representing a concrete alternative. Only a very different sort does that. And the personal cost escalates beyond calculation when someone decides to forego scientific objectivity and to taste that knowledge afforded the initiates of a particular way.

Demands for personal growth and sacrifice (those patterns of formation which a genuinely religious way affords) are so encompassing that they render comparative considerations irrelevant. Of course, this is the very feature of concrete religious epistemology which so offends our demand for reasonable objectivity. A religious way asks a lifetime of fidelity; one is never quite granted the chance for dispassionate assessment. As a Navaho hero-story puts it: 'We shall know where we are going when we get there.'[6] But most of us react indignantly to such demands! So much is asked and so much promised that a reasonable man must know where he is going before he ventures forth. To insist on that, however, turns a religious way into something other than it is: a manner of living with those questions which outreach our capacity to answer. Attempts to speak about verification must respect that fact. Granting a legitimate demand for objectivity the status of an incontrovertible criterion pretends that such unanswerable questions never arise.

5.3   Status of Aquinas' account

I have deliberately strayed from Aquinas' own account to focus directly on religious discourse, mapping the peculiarities involved in verifying it. Moreover, I tried to indicate how as a theologian Aquinas was relatively unconcerned about such things. The evidence confirms that he was vitally concerned about the truth of Christianity in the life-and-death manner of a religious man. But he did not feel that philosophy could gain an independent vantage point on religion. Beyond offering logical clarification idispensable for discerning certain issues, philosophy had little more to say. The religious endeavor itself provided disciplines designed to ferret out one's own idols and to purify a person's perception of the ways of God.

But what about the clarifications Aquinas suggests in questions 3 through 13? What is their status? Granted that 'God is good' (question 6) or 'God is one' (question 11) are not to be taken as descriptions, are they nonetheless accurate statements? Is there any way they could be wrong? If so, how? If not, what is it such expressions tell us?

We know how to begin answering these questions; we do not yet know where that leads. Aquinas' account intends to lay out the grammar of 'God.' And grammar reveals the nature of things.[7] But at the outset he affirmed that we do not and cannot know the nature of God. The fact is constitutive of the grammar of 'God,' for it announces divine transcendence. The rest of the inquiry proceeds to show w it is that we cannot know what God is like.

This paradoxical procedure has been highlighted by my insisting that the results of Aquinas' inquiry do not yield a doctrine of God. We have seen, rather, that precisely in the measure he specifies the determinate ways the subject cannot be pursued, Aquinas succeeds in showing what we can know about God. Hence the entire treatment in questions 3 through 11 becomes an exercise in grasping limits. His own practice exemplifies how the grammar of 'God' indicates where and when we can go no further. And that point beyond which we cannot go defines itself as a limit to understanding rather than the end of the road. Once we have monitored Aquinas' use of the logic and semantics available to him to accomplish this task, we can better appreciate the purpose of his clarifications.

Aquinas' master formula giving a nominal definition for God is, as we have noted, 'the beginning and end of all things, especially of rational creatures.' That formula offers only a heuristic rendering of the object of anyone's quest for the sense of it all. But even a heuristic description, of course, presumes that the quest has an object. What if it hasn't? Such a question is freighted with that anxiety specific to a religious way: how can we ever know? It would seem peremptory to answer with a definitive negative that there is no point to the quest. Who could claim such a vantage point? And how would he argue his case? The feeling that one's search has no meaning cannot, after all, pretend to be a claim without further evidence. Tempting though it may be, one must leap from a sense of absurdity to 'the absurd.'[8] A more modest assessment of the situation would conclude that one failed to comprehend.

On the other hand, how can we ascertain whether there is some sense to it all? Aquinas' logical clarifications offer substantial direction here. First of all, they warn us not to try determining what that sense might be. They do this by showing that the object of such a quest could not be an ordinary object. So anyone who wishes to know the point of it all will be disappointed. Stronger still, whoever comes up with a description is bound to be wrong. Yet the quest is not rendered pointless for all that.

Why not? Because incapacity to formulate a terminus for our quest cannot cancel out the original impulse to find out if there is one. And a sign of that is the logical acumen which allows us to go on even when we have outreached the limits of descriptive discourse. We possess an ability to show why we cannot proceed any further. By exercising these logical powers to elucidate the limits of our understanding, we gain some intimation of a region beyond those limits, even though we cannot envision it or tell about it. This highly intellectual awareness confirms the original impulse, giving that precedence over our continued failure to answer the question which propels it.

The logical exercises thus show us how to go on by illuminating the peculiar character of this quest. Just enough light is shed to keep us from abandoning a task which proves so strange. In effect, these exercises help us through the temptation to think that reality is unintelligible. They enable us to see that whatever would explain the quest for understanding could not be comprehended by us. The exercises simply remind us that the sense-of-it-all cannot be something familiar to us, like the sense gravitational theory can make of falling bodies. Of course logical reminders never suffice to sustain such an odd paradoxical quest. But they do give room for the original impulse to proceed. And, needless to say, we are free to think of the quest in other than logical modes. Along with the rest of mankind, the logician too can conceive it in mythic terms.

Once again, the strictly ancillary role of philosophy appears. Logic cannot initiate the search for the source and goal of all things. It can only underscore how peculiar an inquiry it is, and so temper impatience when we are driven to take offense. But something else empowers the inquiry. That can touch us in myth and through musement.[9] We can follow it with our heart as well as our mind. What Aquinas shows us, through the rational idiom of logic, is the presence of that mysterious power. His witness to us: that reason may be employed with utmost sophistication in the service of this original impulse of our heart. And we need not feel that reason must always be used to check it.

5.31 *Putting it to the test*

If that is what Aquinas' treatment tells us, one lingering question remains. How do we know it is accurate? Could so logical an account of the grammar of 'God' be wrong? There is no obvious reason to distrust it since we have not turned up any notable flaws in his elucidation of 'beginning and end of all things.' The burden of that inquiry for Aquinas was to show how a definite conception of the-beginning-and-end-of-all-things eludes us. But lacking a definite conception, one may find that he has been guided surreptitiously by certain preconceptions. To bring these to consciousness would expose them for the pretensions they are; none the less, they may well have misled an inquiry whose logical form remains impeccable.

So long as the form of an account remains grammatical and does not pretend to be descriptive, the results of such distortions do not immediately come to light. But in•time they would, for our sense of the grammar of any subject gives a particular bearing to the ways in which we discuss it. This feel for the grammar manifests itself in the questions we entertain as in the tracks we think fruitful. That is what Wittgenstein meant what he remarked how grammar gives the essence of a thing.

We have already noted how Aquinas does not trouble himself to decide between a pantheist or creationist conception of the divinity. He did find it necessary to head off a pantheist line of thought by a specific article (3.8), clearly appended to the question giving a baseline for the logic of transcendence. Beyond that, however, he has little explicit to say. Aquinas might be criticized for not dealing more directly with pantheistic conceptions. (After all, there is a complementary tradition within Christianity itself – usually favored by the mystics – which prefers pantheistic language for describing the indescribable 'relation between' God and creatures.) But his avoidance of the issue is perhaps more a strength than a failing. Aquinas' account does not try to make a logic settle what logic cannot decide. That is a philosophic restraint even severe critics can appreciate.

There are two places, though, where Aquinas often is faulted for the preconceptions hidden under his logic. Critics claim his hand was guided by a particular picture of God, and that this picture is indeed woven into an apparently logical treatment. They insist, furthermore, that because Aquinas so effectively obscured the pictorial form in his account, the picture has been able to skew subsequent theological inquiry in a way which otherwise would have been detected. For this reason more than any, these critics object to Aquinas' treatment. They tend to regard it, in fact, as positively reprehensible.

But such critics are not always clear about the logical character of his account; some of them imagine Aquinas to be offering a doctrine of God. Most of Aquinas' theological successors made that same mistake, of course, and so charges regarding the effects of a certain conception of God should be leveled at them. None the less, these objections need to be examined. They can be dealt with more effectively when restated in a grammatical idiom, as I shall do in the following chapters.

The two target spots at which critics aim are Aquinas' elucidation of God as good (1.6) and his caveats about thinking of God as related to creatures (1.13.7). The first objection concerns conceiving evil as *privatio boni*. The second is directed at the impression of an impassive divinity. Each criticism can test the worth of Aquinas' logical clarifications. Let us begin by examining the charge that the God of Aquinas is an aloof one, taking up the issue of his conception of evil in the final chapter of this section.

6

A Philosophical Objection:
Process Theology

A most articulate objector to Aquinas' account is Charles Hartshorne, who
stands at the center of a movement called 'process theology.' The title is
both accurate and helpful if we let 'process' refer us to Whitehead's search
for a categorical alternative to Aristotle's 'substance,' and take 'theology'
in the sense intended by 'first philosophy' or 'metaphysics.' Classical in its
comprehensiveness, this way of thinking is consciously modern in adopting
process for its basic category. It seeks to incorporate into an ontological
scheme the revolution inherent in scientific method. Hence Hartshorne
describes his contribution as 'neo-classical theism,' and would doubtless
prefer this description to the more journalistic 'process theology,' a title
given to the movement as a whole.[1]

6.1   *Alternative roles for philosophy*

Hartshorne also follows Whitehead in adopting a straightforward interpretation of that enterprise which Aristotle called 'first philosophy.' On
this reading, philosophical reflection is taken to be 'the most general
consideration of all.'[2] What Aristotle left vague, of course, demands
clarification as science has developed independent of philosophy.

But it does not appear very illuminating to describe Aristotle as doing
something 'more general' in the *Metaphysics* than in the *Parts of Animals*.
Hartshorne's characterization simply overlooks the different kinds of
inquiry Aristotle undertook. By contrast with the theoretical mode of his
scientific investigations, the inquiry in which he engaged in the *Metaphysics*
might well be called 'reflective.' Our warrant for applying such a term is
the close attention Aristotle pays in that work to the leads offered by the
structure of our discourse. (One way of discovering the reflective character
of an inquiry is to attend to the clues which grammar supplies for
displaying the very form of discourse.)

78

What Aristotle could leave vague indeed we are compelled to clarify, but everything turns on how we do it. If we think of the intellectual enterprise he called first philosophy (also termed metaphysics and even theology) as the most general description and explanation of what is, then God would fall within that inquiry, albeit as its pre-eminent object. On the other hand, if we regard that activity as a reflective (or 'critical') one attempting to grasp those formal features of discourse which taken together supply the contours of our world, then God may well lie beyond its grasp. (One would still have to account for the issue arising within our language and way of life, of course.) The differences, while subtle, are central. And they are displayed as much in the way a philosopher proceeds as by what he actually says.[3]

So it will simply not do to identify the former conception of philosophy with a 'classical' outlook and refuse to see instances of the latter until after Kant. The thesis of this book is that Aquinas deserves to be placed among the 'critical' philosophers if we scrutinize how he employs philosophical grammar to circumscribe discourse about God. Aquinas is certainly one of the paradigms of a 'classical' philosopher. But he is forced to a critical posture as his convictions regarding divinity clash with the presuppositions of a straightforward scientific inquiry into the nature of God. That Aquinas would even launch an inquiry makes him 'classical'; the peculiar twist he had to give it makes him 'critical.'

What really identifies the critical approach, at least as Aquinas represents it, is his attempt to locate the parameters of discourse concerning God so that these very parameters display what cannot be stated. But that entire enterprise will be misunderstood if one takes the 'formal features' indicated by the parameters as offering a description of the object. Such a mistake results in the 'classical theism' which Hartshorne criticizes so passionately, and which Schubert Ogden calls 'the major obstacle to real progress in dealing with the problem of God.'[4]

If my interpretation is substantially correct, however, the fault lies not so much with Aquinas as with those who neglect his warning signals and mistake his inquiry into what God is not for a treatment of the divine nature. More specifically, the crucial oversight consists in failing to appreciate the philosophic virtue of the 'linguistic turn.'[5] Allow me to clarify this oracular pronouncement by examining more closely some characteristic statements of Hartshorne, as well as commenting on the manner in which he proffers them.

6.2 On conceiving God

For Hartshorne, Aquinas is the exemplar of a pernicious doctrine of God that has held sway since Philo: 'the "monopolar view" that God is wholly infinite, in no sense finite; wholly absolute, in no sense relative; pure being, in no sense becoming; wholly active, actual and simple, in no sense passive, potential or complex. . . .'[6] It is characteristic of Hartshorne to overlook the *Sitz-im-Leben* of individual thinkers and to proceed in dialectical fashion, taking issue with statements at their face value. He does allow himself some general interpretative schemes: remarking how 'the monopolar prejudice is pervasive in Philo,' and noting that Maimonides faced the same task 'of reconciling Judaism with philosophical tenets derived from the Greeks.'[7] Hartshorne is alert to an author's assertions which might belie such tenets or prejudices, but far less sensitive to the specific interpretative keys each of the authors offers, either explicitly or in their manner of prosecuting their task.[8] The result, of course, is that individual thinkers become representatives of the 'monopolar view of classical theism.'

More specifically, Hartshorne never adverts to Aquinas' demurring that 'we cannot know what God is, but only what he is not.' He simply assumes Aquinas to be giving an account of divinity. And the features which Hartshorne adduces he finds philosophically incoherent or unworthy of the divine: 'so I hold that being wholly immutable is not the most exalted status, but either an absurdity or else the status of something essentially abstract'; 'do we worship God, or do we worship certain philosophical abstractions inherited from the Greeks, e.g., immutability, independence or absoluteness, infinity, simplicity, and the rest?'[9] It cannot be abstractions themselves that put Hartshorne off; he is, after all, a philosopher:

> The point is not – far from it – that these abstractions have no application to God. But to grant that applicability is one thing, and to suppose that divinity just is absoluteness, infinity, immutability, so that the contrary terms relative, finite, mutable, in no way apply – that is quite another. For me, God is indeed absolute, but not 'the absolute,' he is infinite but not 'the infinite,' necessary and yet not simply *ens necessarium*.[10]

But the point is rather to determine just how these 'abstractions' function, and hence what sort of application they have to God. If they are not meant to describe divinity, but to proscribe descriptive attempts, then it would be illegitimate to use expressions like 'the absolute' or 'the infinite' as alternate names for God. It would also be inappropriate to ask whether the contrary terms apply as well. For all we know, they might be applicable to God; however, such terms could not do the same job of proscribing that 'infinite' and 'immutable' can. (It is worth noting for the record that Aquinas nowhere uses 'absolute' of God, nor does he regard *ens necessarium* as a felicitous name. The name he favors is *ipsum esse*: 'to be itself.'[11])

Yet does not the difficulty reappear at the level of linguistic prescription? Why so circumscribe what can be said of God? Do these very rules really betray a monopolar prejudice? In being so definite about what God is not, has Aquinas only smuggled in a conception of what he is, one which coincides with the monopolar view of classical theism? In short, has not the linguistic turn brought us face to face with the same impenetrable wall?

6.3 *An operative distinction*

This objection can be met most effectively by recalling Hartshorne's own strategy of distinguishing divinity from God. He contrasts the abstract divine nature with God's concrete existence, and is quite willing to concede to 'classical theism' an adequate analysis of divinity. What Hartshorne objects to is rather the manner in which such an account of abstract nature pretends to describe God as well: 'he is infinite but not "the infinite".' This use of 'abstract' and 'concrete' harks back to White-head's metaphysical constructions (*eternal objects* and *actual entities*), but we can grasp Hartshorne's point without entering that particular thicket.

To begin, try aligning Hartshorne's distinction with Aquinas' discrimination of levels of discourse:

Hartshorne	*Aquinas*
abstract (divinity)	grammatical prescription
concrete (God)	direct statement

I have elucidated Aquinas' treatment in a programmatic idiom, showing how his manner of proceeding embodies a logician's better judgment. Hartshorne speaks in a more straightforward way of abstract and concrete 'aspects' in God. One suspects, however, that the two ways of distinguishing are isomorphic in several respects. At least a comparison suggests that we are now in a position to locate Hartshorne's dissatisfactions more accurately than he has been able to.

What if Aquinas' treatment in questions 3 through 11 was not intended as a series of direct statements about God's nature, but as a coherent set of grammatical prescriptions relevant to discourse concerning God? Would not the results epitomize what Hartshorne calls an abstract treatment of divinity? Nothing is learned directly about God by insisting that he must be good, limitless, unchangeable and one. Rather, Aquinas shows how these predicates are equivalent to the key predicate *simple*, which in turn serves as a systematic reminder that nothing can be said of God. Many have overlooked the explicitly grammatical cast of these questions, of course, and confused such predicates with divine attributes like loving, merciful, just, and faithful. The result fits neatly with that classical theism Hartshorne deplores.

If 'unchangeable,' for example, is taken as a descriptive term rather than a proscription, we can only regard it as characterizing a situation. And 'static' means 'zero motion.' Aquinas, however, derives unchangeableness from simpleness. As we have already noted, he makes that derivation precisely to remind us that God is beyond the very category of motion (with its contraries of movement and rest). To miss Aquinas' distinction here is tantamount to confusing concrete with abstract aspects in God, in Hartshorne's terms. Of course Hartshorne himself insists they be kept distinct, presumably for reasons similar to those motivating Aquinas: to allow human discourse to display the otherness or transcendence of divinity.

On my analysis, Aquinas adheres to this important distinction by using the predicates in question (simple, good, limitless, unchangeable, and one) prescriptively but never descriptively. And he must adopt some such strategy to observe his own warning that this particular inquiry is unlike any other. It will differ notably from a straightforward investigation into the nature of a thing, for this inquiry yields only what God is not rather than what he is. Aquinas' strategy, furthermore, seems preferable to Hartshorne's distinction regarding aspects in God, since levels of linguistic use allow for more precise differentiation than the much-abused couplet: abstract/concrete. Finally, if Aquinas remains faithful to his distinction between grammatical prescription and direct statement, he appears no more subject to monopolar prejudice or philosophical tenets derived from the Greeks than Hartshorne who insists on God's abstract divinity. In fact, one advantage to displaying the relevant similarities between the programs of these two thinkers could be to lay slogans like these to rest.

6.4 Relating levels of discourse

Distinctions differ from divisions, of course, by serving a specific purpose and leaving the subject intact. Otherwise Hartshorne leaves us with two gods, and Aquinas' grammatical achievements would be merely verbal ones. But to what end the distinctions these two employ? What bearing has God's abstract on his concrete self? Or precisely how do grammatical prescriptions guide direct statements? Put baldly: if grammar has nothing to do with the nature of the thing in question, of what use is it? And if grammar does yield the nature, how would such an inquiry differ from a straightforward demonstration of properties? Aquinas tells us what not to say of God, not what we should say. But that preliminary dodge will not suffice: this cryptic remark is more a warning than an elucidation. His practice, however, reveals something more at work.

Each of the prescriptive rubrics Aquinas gives is followed by an observation that is related but cannot be said logically to follow from it. The observation is of another sort. After remarking God's simpleness Aquinas affirms his perfection; after showing good to be equivalent to being he can speak of God's goodness. Having derived limitlessness from simpleness he speaks of God's existence in things, and after showing how unchangeableness follows from limitlessness Aquinas talks about the eternity of God. Unity carries two dimensions within itself: on the one hand, whatever is is one; on the other, oneness suggests wholeness.

I have already remarked how in each case the second terms are more properly religious ones, susceptible of direct statement: perfect, good, present, eternal, whole. But Aquinas apparently feels some affinity between the members of each pair, as the first term suggests the second, and the second casts light on the first by offering an opportunity for appeal to the religious dimension of our experience.[12] Now the grammatical prescriptions are strictly speaking vacuous, since nothing follows from them except coextensive prescriptions which add an intentional note but do not extend the range of implications.[13] Yet these prescriptions do suggest certain religious attitudes; they guide our thinking and our sensibilities. In such manner, grammar reveals the essence of things.

Thus far, Aquinas' account nearly matches Hartshorne's critique. All the former would need is further to remark our inveterate tendency to fill in the logical notions with cultural accretions. And historically, indeed we have done that. Aquinas' grammatical notions (simple, good, limitless, unchangeable, and one) have been taken to picture a self-sufficient, all-powerful ikon of divinity, set off in solitary splendor. I have been arguing all along that such a construct may be ours, but not Aquinas'. Moreover, there are counter-forces to such a conception in his account. These are the more properly religious predicates (perfect, good, present, eternal, and whole) which are suggested by the grammatical notions. The power of these predicates is that they articulate entire dimensions of religious experience. As inherently mythic notions, they possess a structure of their own. So the guidance offered by the grammatical notions tells only a part of the story. The religious predicates become vehicles for bringing other dimensions of our experience into play; and the effect of that is to enable us to challenge and correct any surreptitious content which may have accrued to the vacuous grammatical notions. The religious predicates, therefore, serve as idol-breakers.

Theology and religion are related dialectically, not consequentially. Philosophers are prone to overlook that fact. Although Hartshorne affirms such a relationship, he seems to disregard it in bemoaning the dire *consequences* of classical theism. Aquinas, however, acknowledges this dialectical character by the very way he works. Allow me to illustrate more concretely his operative understanding by examining closely his insistence that 'being related to God is a reality in creatures, but being related to creatures is not a reality in God' (13.7).

Someone persuaded by my interpretation of questions 3 through 11 might be generally willing to exempt Aquinas from Hartshorne's accusations. But the assertion that 'being related to creatures is not a reality in God' sounds preposterous! It has become the central stumbling block for appreciating Aquinas' treatment of God, the clinching evidence that he does in fact exemplify classical theism. And this particular statement has provided contemporary thinkers the strongest motivation for seeking an altogether new framework according to which God will be 'really related' to the world.[14]

6.5   *God and the world*

The context of Aquinas' handling of God's relationship to the world in question 13.7 is whether we can use words that imply temporal succession in speaking of God. His actual treatment, however, extends to any form of natural relatedness (attaching to divinity as such), though it prescinds from intentional relationships which a God might freely initiate. This strategy of Aquinas should be familiar by now: determine what must be stated grammatically, so that we can recognize what sort of things cannot be asserted of God. Such prescriptions offer a grammatical base for learning how to interpret the things that are in fact asserted.

Aquinas' motivation for this grammatical determination is explicit: 'since God is altogether outside the order of creatures, [i.e.] since they are ordered to him but not he to them, it is clear that [whatever we might say about God which implied his being ordered to creatures] we say it about him because of the real relation in creatures' (13.7). He lifts an example from Aristotle to illustrate the point, and this example has proved unfortunate: 'just as we can say that the pillar has changed from being on my left to being on my right, not through any alteration in the pillar but simply because I have turned around,' so it is that 'words implying temporal sequence and change' apply to God 'not because of any change in him but because of a change in creatures.' But certainly Aquinas, who finally licenses but one assertion about God (that he is to-be itself), does not intend any straightforward comparison of God with a pillar. Rather he must be using the example to make a precise point about how we may and may not employ working relations when trying to conceive God *vis-à-vis* the world.

The background here is philosophically complex: Augustine's preoccupation with *ordo*, an Aristotelian tendency to identify *real* with *natural*, and a long tradition of logical work on the theory of relations. (Both Augustine and Aquinas were particularly concerned with ordering relations, of course, as a way of dealing with intellectual difficulties arising out of a trinitarian revelation. And both drew on the considerable work which had been done in this regard by the Cappadocians.[15]) The upshot of all this is encapsulated in question 13.7: relations are ways of ordering things one to another, and these ways differ according to the reasons we adduce for so relating the things. These reasons are called 'respects'; hence the grammar of 'is related to' demands that we specify the respect: x is related to y in respect of z. This innocent reminder Aquinas gives will help remove a fateful ambiguity from his terminology and free us to attend to his practice.

Aquinas distinguishes 'real' relations from those 'that are set up as part of our thinking' (*relatio realis/rationis*) by the *respects* involved. Father and son are related by generation, larger and smaller by quantity. Wherever we can specify the respect to be either an inherent property or a natural process, the items are said to be really related to one another; this signifies that the relationship is grounded in the concrete nature of the things themselves. On the other hand, where the respect cannot be so specified, the relation is said to be merely one of reason. Aquinas offers two examples of *relatio rationis*: X is identical with X, and X is better than nothing. The first generates a paradox when we try to press it into canonical form 'X is related to X in respect of being the same thing.' The second example simply will not fit into the form. Lewis Carroll has displayed how that inability to fit leads directly to nonsense. Aquinas contents himself with remarking that we are consciously constructing in the attempts such examples illustrate. The same thing can terminate a relation of identity only because 'the mind takes one thing and thinks of it twice, thus treating it as though it had a relation to itself.' So in the other case, 'the mind treats *nothing* as though it were a term.' And similarly with classificatory schemes relating species to genus.

The difference between a *relatio realis* and a *relatio rationis* reduces to the reasons which can be offered for adducing a relationship: do they refer to natural processes or inherent properties, or are they intellectual fabrications? Such fabrications have a point, of course, in constructing theories which can lead us to discover more about natural process. Not even the highest degree of confirmation, however, warrants an assertion regarding the relations among the theoretical terms themselves. To neutralize the misleading effects of Aquinas' choice of terms, we might say that a real relation designates one where a reason can be discovered; on the other hand, a relation 'set up as part of our thinking' must be such precisely because no reason can be found.

Now we are in a position to assess the worth of Aquinas' using this distinction to treat divinity's relations with contingent things. In saying that 'being related to creatures is not a reality in God,' but 'that God is said to be related to a creature because the creature is related to him' (13.7.4), Aquinas is reiterating a point made earlier. There is no process or property inherent in divinity which demands or results in creatures. A later article clarifies this: '[God's] relation (*habitudo*) to creatures does not flow from his nature. He does not produce creatures out of the necessity of his nature, but rather by intellect and will (cf. 1.14.8, 1.19.4). *For this reason*

85

we cannot speak of a "real relation" to creatures in God' (1.28.1.3 – emphasis added).

If 'real' respects are limited to natural process or inherent properties, then a free creator could not be said to be 'really related' to his creation. From *that* perspective, God can be said to be creator or lord only 'in so far as creatures are related to him.' A structure inherent to creatures will display their createdness (elusively, their *to-be*), but nothing in the structure of divinity requires creation. None the less, 'God is *really* lord. It is the relationship of lordship *in* him that is supplied by our minds, not the fact of his being the lord' (1.13.7.4 – emphasis added). God's being creator is not a fabrication; what is our intellectual fabrication is only the fact that we ascribe creating to him as a property.

We can see now that Aquinas' point in denying God to be 'really related' to the world is limited: to assert the one thing we can know about divinity, its transcendence. And this assertion shows that transcendence can be displayed in the technical language of relations as well. Such is the grammar of divinity. Aquinas does not hesitate (in 1.28.1.3) to speak of God's relation (*habitudo*) to creatures; but he states the respect in which God is related: in producing creatures by intellect and will. Since this relation follows upon what God does rather that what he is, it is not a *real* one. Rather, the creator bears to creatures an *intentional* relation. Aquinas speaks of this relation when he specifically takes up creation, and his treatment is open to a great deal of development along more personalist lines.[16] At this point, however, we remain focused on the grammar of divinity. Itself inscrutable, this grammar can certainly offer no clues at all to what God might freely do.

The most that can be said of God, as we have already seen, is that to be God is to-be. We can go on to show how certain grammatical prescriptions are equivalent to that assertion. Such an elucidation issues in a clearer grasp of God's transcendence, or a better sense of what he is not. So we cannot say, for example, that God is creator if the consequence of that statement would be to ascribe a property to God beyond that of simply *to-be*. That God is creator is true enough, but we know it only as a fact, not as a 'reasoned fact.' No reason can be adduced from our examination of what must (not) be said about divinity. It is only from the fact of creatures (and specifically their created to-be) that we can reason to God as creator; we have no inherent reasons in support of such a statement. If we wish to speculate about it, we can only think of creation as a free activity, and even that will prove misleading.[17] Short of such speculation, we can only keep to what can be said (grammatically) about what should be said or not. And at best we will remind ourselves that ascribing creator to God as though it were a property or natural process can only be a manner of speaking.

The point of Aquinas' treatment of relations between God and the world would better be expressed, then, by denying that God is naturally related to the world. With such terminology we could accurately parse the equivocal observation that God is not *really* related to it. Such a grammatical treatment remains open to God's *freely* relating to the world. And if so, we are led to think of him as related to the world much more intimately than by virtue of natural process. Thus by denying that God is by nature creator, Aquinas is actually setting the stage for a more effective affirmation. The relatedness that comes with knowledge and love is of another sort entirely, and the function of these denials is to display that clearly.[18]

6.6 *Grammar and religious affirmation*

Dealing with one more issue raised by the 'process theology' movement will help us appreciate its rhetorical appeal, and shed more light on the manner in which grammar guides what we objectively state. It is unclear whether some 'process' thinkers fail to grasp Aristotle's distinction between activities which are changes and those which are not, or whether they simply reject it. At any rate, these theologians contend that if knowing and loving the world cannot change or improve God, then he cannot really (i.e. personally) be related to it. In short, if God does not need us, he cannot *really* love us. The essential independence which follows from our grammatical account may leave room for freedom, but it certainly removes any possibility of mutuality. And what is love without mutuality?[19]

The epistemological basis for such a critique has been articulated by Schubert Ogden in reliance upon Hartshorne. Ogden insists with Whitehead that God 'is not to be treated as an exception to metaphysical principles, but rather to be understood as exemplifying them.'[20] He calls this method one of 'strict analogy,' and means thereby to deny that the metaphysical principles in question are themselves cast in analogous terms. The upshot of this position is to deny to expressions like *just* or *loving* that very capacity for transcending any particular exemplification which originally licensed them for use *in divinis*.[21] By insisting, for example, that certain features commonly associated with loving (as we find it) must always characterize it, that prescriptivity which gives such terms a greater-than-descriptive force and makes them appropriate religious predicates is threatened.

Let us examine 'loving' in particular. Does the absence of need which follows from asserting that to be God is to be undermine the mutuality we associate with a genuine loving relationship? By asking the question in this fashion, I am acknowledging that certain characteristics may well be essential to loving, while others are not. The criterion I shall employ is a linguistic equivalent of Aquinas' demand that such characteristics themselves be 'perfections'; I ask that their semantic structure be analogous as well.[22] Moreover, I am deliberately submitting to the guidance offered by Aquinas' grammatical prescription of a relation of dependency of God upon the world. Finally, I remain acutely aware how primitive our understanding is of psychological notions like *need* and *mutuality,* to say nothing of *loving* itself. We are but minimally conscious of the basic grammar of these terms as they might function to clarify *our* experience, to say nothing of God's activity.[23]

Can we conceive of someone loving another when he stood to gain *nothing* from it? Or is love built inescapably on need? We tend to be such needy individuals that the question fairly answers itself. Furthermore, often we come to recognize how needy we are only after being compelled by experience to come down from a posture of independence. So our perception of need is as acute as our judgment on what passes for independence. Conceivability in these matters, however, cannot be confined to what we can imagine. We need to take a more fruitful tack. I would suggest one which relativizes the issues in question. Is it our experience that we love more authentically the less we relate to others *as* fulfilling our needs, and the more we come to enjoy them for what they are in themselves?

I suspect that asking the question this way solicits a positive answer, and initiates a line of reflection countering one's response to the earlier question of whether the absence of need undermines mutuality. Undoubtedly, coming to love another for himself alone in fact *does* fulfill our needs, but in the process we have learned to comport ourselves in a less self-serving manner. Would a love that was totally altruistic, then, be the most authentic? Or would it be incoherent? Could the absence of any need at all on the part of one party make him infinitely solicitous, or would it turn the whole thing into a sham?

I submit that we simply are not in a position to answer such a question, as the vagueness of the language itself should testify. First of all we are unclear how the grammatical parameters translate into an absence of need in God. Then we are unable to get sufficient hold on the grammar of 'need' itself: we cannot chart its various senses carefully enough to see how they function at different levels of inner freedom. All we can ascertain is that it *seems* to be possible to become less preoccupied with fulfilling one's own needs, and as a result to experience a greater freedom to give and to share lovingly. And we can argue that *seeming* is *being* in this situation, given certain sustained strategies to offset self-deception.[24] Beyond programmatic observations like these, though, we do not know how to proceed.

Traditional Christian theology never attempted to respond to such issues merely with a philosophical theology, but turned to revelation for specific direction in resolving these baffling human questions. The process theology movement faults classical theism with a God too remote from the Gospels.

But the God they propose, while inspired by the Gospels, would not need to have been the agent of such a revelation. Appearing more Christian in spirit, this God of process theology could also dispense with his self-revelation in Jesus. Aquinas, on the other hand, needs the specific revelation of the scriptures to fulfill those aspirations which the austere prescriptions of grammar can only disappoint. Yet those same prescriptions do have a guiding role to play in removing *ersatz* notions of divinity. And if, when properly understood, Aquinas' strategies cannot be convicted of untoward psychological or metaphysical consequences, they remain a powerful and viable way of conceiving the inconceivable. These strategies show what cannot properly be said of God.

A Psychological Objection: Jung and *Privatio Boni*

Aquinas' treatment of goodness in general (question 5) and of God's goodness (question 6) considers evil to be a lacuna: 'if we take evil itself, it cannot be anything, but is rather a lack of some particular good.'[1] The technical term for 'lack' is transliterated 'privation,' hence the rubric: evil is a privation of good. Jung traces this doctrine to the earliest Church fathers. He attacks it, indeed, with a vehemence parallel to that which Hartshorne and others direct at the tenets of 'classical theism.' In fact, the similarities of the two critiques are striking, although Jung's perspective is more explicitly psychological than overtly philosophical. Nonetheless, his objections presuppose and in part propose an alternative grammar for the matter, as Jung's predilection for gnostics and alchemists suggests.

The confusions run parallel as well. Perhaps these are more tolerable in Jung since his philosophical penchant never received the rigorous training of a professional. But confusions there definitely are regarding the *privatio boni* of Aquinas. My strategy in handling them will be like that for Hartshorne's objections: notice where Aquinas explicitly displays the grammar of the situation; then draw out the consequences of that grammatical effort for a more substantive discussion of the issues involved. With Jung, these issues have both psychological and ethical implications.

Of course, Jung is not the only one to have mistaken the essentially grammatical character of Aquinas' definition of evil. Were it not for egregious misuse by theologians, Jung probably never would have fastened upon it. The immediate targets of his polemic, however, are not culture-theologians. It is those who found in the tradition a theological way of celebrating the prevailing ethos of progress. And this construction provided the context for Jung's rejecting the notion of evil as a lack.

So Jung's preoccupation with *privatio boni* does not represent a simple confusion of levels of discourse. He is astute enough to acknowledge that it 'may be a metaphysical truth; I presume to no judgment on this matter.'[2] The issue is rather the effect such a metaphysical (or grammatical) statement can have in lulling us to disregard evil as an operative force. And this particular heedlessness goes hand-in-glove with unsullied convictions about precisely what is good. The connection between moral righteousness and naïveté in the face of evil needs to be clarified; but for now that affinity can stand as a reason for Jung's resentment at the *privatio* teaching. Needless to say, manifold cultural and historical factors influence Jung's remarks. The presence one allows to the devil, for example, noticeably affects the import of thinking of evil to be a lack. If a force like the devil is in the foreground of people's awareness, the grammatical status of a definition of evil as *privatio boni* would be evident. On the other hand, if that force recedes from consciousness, we might be tempted to think that grammar offered a description of our actual situation.

Dealing with Jung's objections, then, offers a two-fold opportunity: to test the resources of the main strategy guiding this analysis of Aquinas, and to illustrate how carefully an interpretation involving different cultural settings must work to lay bare the layers of accumulated meaning. The first task would be quite straightforward if we simply remarked the distinction of levels which Aquinas observed and Jung overlooked. Closer attention to the precise role of *privatio*, for example, could show that many of Jung's objections were in fact unfounded. Yet the intent of these objections presses beyond the accomplishments of simple clarification. It touches our attitude toward whatever we find unwelcome or unmanageable. That attitude eludes grammatical formulation, of course, but mightily affects the way we use such formulae. So meeting objections like Jung's will force us to a more careful demarcation of Aquinas' statements. That work will help us appreciate just how *grammatical* a goodness it is which Aquinas attributes to God.

7.1 *Positions outlined*

Despite Jung's protestations that his assertions are not philosophical but psychological (i.e., never outreaching the evidence available to him from therapeutic encounters), some of them are overtly metaphysical. For example, there is his statement that 'evil is the necessary opposite of good, without which there would be no good either' (9.1, 323). This amounts to a grammatical legislation that we treat good/evil as contraries, where understanding one includes understanding the other. The pair thus provides parameters for the genus which one must negotiate to grasp either one of the terms. Aquinas' assertion that evil is a privation, on the other hand, is designed to head off any suspicion that the grammar of good and evil is that of contraries. Citing Simplicius' commentary on Aristotle's *Categories*, he notes that when two items are contrasted as *habitus* (or inclination) and *privatio* (or lacuna), they do not fulfill the defining characteristics for contraries. For contraries must both share a genus and hence 'are something according to nature.'[3] Examples of contraries would be hot/cold or large/small, whereas good/evil function more like sight/blindness. Blindness is opposed to sight, certainly, but is so precisely because it denotes the absence of all power to see in something which ought to have that capacity. Good and poor eyesight, however, qualify as contraries; one is defined in terms of the other, and both by a common measure. We would not get very far defining sight as the absence of blindness, to be sure. But we can define blindness no other way. It is just this asymmetry which Aquinas' grammatical remarks are meant to corroborate.

Aquinas' motivation is primarily a systematic one, although one can catch resonances of common experience. The roots lie in Plato's contention that whatever we decide upon must present itself as good. No one can deliberately choose something he perceives to be evil, unless it be for a good end.[4] The point is at once logical and psychological. To act is to act for an end. Only those ends that are 'worth my while,' however, can elicit the activity required to achieve them. Hence an activity must be perceived as good (= 'worth my while') for me to decide to undertake it. This fact of analysis locates the logical and psychological priority of good over evil, suggesting that good be characterized as a capacity and an inclination (*habitus*) and evil as a deficiency in one such inclination.

Besides the analytical point, we have the moral maxim: *bonum ex omni parte, malum ex quocumque defectu*. It refers to our experience that a constructive enterprise demands co-ordinated planning and harmonious activity, while destruction requires little effort at all – a match or a monkey wrench will do. (The flick of an oiling switch can turn a massive and intricate hydroelectric generating plant into a twisted mass of metal.) Granted we are never in a position to use *good* or *evil* at the level of generality on which we have been considering them; still it seems clear that what these terms express are not contraries but something more like a capacity and its privation.

Jung, however, speaks from another sector of human experience. Initial success led him to adopt a therapeutic strategy which proved to be of powerful assistance. The way to wholeness for an individual invariably lies in accepting what he regards as evil – his dark side. Such a procedure left Jung impressed with the relativity of our assessments of good and evil: 'life is always bringing us up against ... the uncertainty of all moral evaluation, the bewildering interplay of good and evil, the remorseless concatenation of guilt, suffering and redemption' (9.1, 217). Good and evil often appear as contraries, then, and in fact, the goal of therapy (or of development itself), 'individuation, or becoming whole, is neither a *summum bonum* nor a *summum desideratum*, but the painful experience of the union of opposites' (9.1, 382).

So Jung finds that our perceptions of what is good and what is evil are normally related as contraries are related. We come to know one through the other, and vice versa, as in sobriety and drunkenness, fidelity and infidelity, justice and injustice. The context of his findings is psychological in two senses: commonplace and analytic. He is speaking of our level of appreciation of such things, and he is also speaking of the power which they carry and release. Jung is speaking of consideration and of the unconscious. But it is in the latter especially that the unexpected reconciliation of apparently irreconcilable opposites play such a key role:

> I must emphasize ... that the grand plan on which the unconscious
> life of the psyche is constructed is so inaccessible to our
> understanding that we can never know what evil may not be
> necessary in order to produce good by enantiodromia [reconciliation
> of opposites], and what good may very possibly lead to evil (9.1, 215).

Of course, one could observe that Jung is addressing a different issue from that with which Aquinas is concerned, and argue that the very listing of polarities (justice/injustice, fidelity/infidelity) presupposes the grammatical point about one term being the privation of the other. And it might also be noted that Jung himself attaches a primacy to one *good* which does not itself require to be reconciled with an opposite: the quality of consciousness in which opposites find their reconciliation, individuation. However fertile the unconscious, Jung gives decisive priority to consciousness – provided it respects the context provided by its opposite and does not pretend to autonomy.

Thus the scheme of contraries or opposites cannot tell the whole story of our use of *good* and *evil*, even for Jung. Moreover, he can appreciate how formal a fact is the 'tendency, existing right from the start, to give priority to "good." ... So if Christian metaphysics clings to the *privatio boni*, it is giving expression to the tendency always to increase the good and diminish the bad. The *privatio boni* may therefore be a metaphysical truth' (9.2, 54). Were Jung to substitute 'consciousness' for 'the good' in his own statement, he could see precisely how *privatio boni* expresses a metaphysical (or grammatical) truth.[5] Yet the fact remains that the grammar of capacity *v.* privation offers only the barest hint of the power which evil schemes can muster. Nor does that grammar readily display the contrary ways in which good/evil present themselves in our development.

A closer look at *privation*, however, can offer more illumination than Jung suspects. For Aquinas defines evil as a privation of some particular good, and the term 'privation' itself means 'lacking something which ought to be present.' (There is nothing wrong with a man without wings, but one who has lost his legs is maimed.) Perhaps we can best grasp Aquinas' intent if we think of our expectation of straightforwardness in human dealings. This common trust, which forms the basis for all social intercourse, makes deceit and misrepresentation the evils which they are. If we remember, moreover, the pervasive natural inclination to a good of order which supplies the background for Aquinas' treatment, *privation* turns out to be more than a mere lacuna. *Privation* can be seen as that which generates frustration, resentment, and a host of cognate agitations. Furthermore, the specific *animus* which disorder can elicit appears sharpened by something missing when it ought to be there.

In short, however, remote capacity/privation may seem to lie from our experience of evil, that scheme serves to illuminate evil better than speaking of simple contrariety. Jung goes on to complete the paragraph just cited: 'I must only insist that in our field of experience white and black, light and dark, good and bad, are equivalent opposites which always predicate one another' (9.2, 54). As evidence for this alternative proposal he cites Origen: ' "To turn aside from good is nothing other than to be perfected in evil." This shows clearly that an increase in the one means a diminution of the other, so that good and evil represent equivalent halves of an opposition' (9.2, 45, n.). Yet simple contrariety is not the only way to account for the opposition that holds between good and evil, as we have noted. Capacity/privation has the same effect, without demanding the parity which contrariety presupposes. And we have seen how postulating a parity runs counter to our common experience.

7.2 *Mediating the positions*

Clarifying the conceptual confusions involved will help us to appreciate the force of Jung's criticisms as well as the astuteness of Aquinas' grammatical observations. Let me focus on three confusions: one hermeneutical, another logical, and a third metaphysical. The first touches Jung's polemic and the way in which established religion and a liberal ideology wedded to progress found it congenial to think of evil as a mere lacuna. The second difficulty concerns his predilection for the abstract terms *good/evil*, and for opposition as an engine of forward motion, after the manner of Hegel. The third examines Jung's supposition that evil must have a cause, and in clarification suggests that Aquinas' alternative – that an evil action has *no* cause – captures the perversity of evil forces even more poignantly than Jung's common-sense proposition. In examining all three conceptual confusions, we shall see how one's convictions regarding the presence or absence of influential evil forces affects the entire tone of the argument. The aim of Jung's polemic might well be to persuade us to restore the powers of evil their proper place.

7.21 *Conventional wisdom* v. *therapeutic insight*

Jung's practice as a therapist led him to become conversant with unwelcome dimensions in himself and in others, and forced him to deal with responses customarily deemed wrong. He came to realize that the 'individuation process is invariably started off by the patient's becoming conscious of the shadow, a personality component usually with a negative sign' (11, 197). And since individuation represents the highest goal to which a man might aspire, he can generalize to say that good can only come about through 'accepting the dark principle' (9.1, 337). We might propose another shorthand for the shape of the individuation process: the way to wholeness lies through the opposites, sorting out the *prima facie* goods and evils to discover the way that is one's destiny (or true good).

It is this experience of the struggle to release what is truly good from the grip of ambivalent forces of good and evil that makes Jung furious when faced with *malum = privatio boni*. No wrestling, it seems, no ambivalence expressed in that formula! The negative cast of *privatio* offers a comfortable suggestion that evil is not really real. And just a short step more brings me to the welcome 'conclusion' that there is no evil in me to contend with, since it is but nothing after all. In this instance a misleading formula, mistakenly applied, would help the ego attain a position it always craved: moral righteousness.

The movement here is not logical; we are seduced by suggestion and ambiguity. If evil is a mere negation, then it is nothing to be reckoned with and my impulses must be good, as I always figured they were. This attitude may be reinforced collectively by church or society; it is especially enhanced when the conventional wisdom of both coalesce. So Jung can justly deplore that, 'as a result [of such psychological naïveté], Christians rely on the doctrine of the *privatio boni* and always think they know what is good and what is evil, thus substituting the moral code for the truly ethical decision, which is a *free* one' (10, 358). This is a long way from Aquinas' careful grammatical statement of the matter (although Jung uses *free* as Aquinas would *good*); we are being shown how confusion can spawn abuse.

Jung is careful to avoid a simple relativism. It is impossible to assess what is good and evil, and moral codes help one in doing so. But 'the paradox is just that for this particular stage of development [what is evil] may be good. . . . Perhaps he *has* to experience the power of evil and suffer accordingly, because only in that way can he give up his Pharisaic attitude to other people' (10, 459-60). A philosopher can readily remark how Jung clearly subordinates *prima facie* good and evil, which he considers as simple contraries ('the opposites'), to something like Aquinas' *habitus* or capacity. In this case, 'good' is subordinated to 'giving up his Pharisaic attitude'; in general, to individuation or wholeness. But the force of Jung's discovery and the vehemence of his objection to *privatio boni* lie in the connotations of the formula: a suggestion that evil is something that can be *overlooked*, since it really isn't anything.[6] Such a suggestion releases us from the painful duty of *facing* what is unwelcome. It licenses, furthermore, that common form of psychic overlooking: *repression*.

Here too religious maxims reinforce this process of deliberate failure to bring to consciousness, by treating evil as a 'thing of ill omen, that which is tabooed and feared. . . . We should, so we are told, eschew evil and, if possible, neither touch nor mention it' (10, 297). And repression, made more plausible by a sophistical rendering of *privatio boni*, abets the all-too-welcome ploy of projecting 'the unrecognized evil into the "other".' The result is to 'strengthen the opponent's position in the most effective way,' and 'what is even worse, our lack of insight deprives us of the *capacity to deal with evil*' (10, 297). Here is an astute description of the liberal ethos, convinced of its rectitude, and confident that rational planning can fill whatever lacuna of ignorance remains.

In such a frame of mind there is 'no imagination for evil,' since we know what is good and have the power to achieve it. And besides, evil is nothing. It is in the face of this legacy from Christendom and its secularized offshoot, the liberal ideology of progress, that Jung must insist:

> If one can no longer avoid the realization that evil, without man's
> ever having chosen it, is lodged in human nature itself, then it
> bestrides the psychological stage as the equal and opposite partner of
> good. This realization leads straight to a psychological dualism (10,
> 297).

The dualism which Jung espouses presents itself as a fruitful therapeutic hypothesis: that each of us has two sides, this side and the other. Each side takes on ambivalently the face of good or evil, and both must be reconciled if the self is ever to emerge. That alternation of struggle and concession which spells the individuation process, however, represents an unequivocal good, even if it may not always be expedient to initiate it.

The dualism of which Jung speaks, then, is really limited to the *prima facie* good and evil represented by a moral code on the one hand and the shadow on the other. The threatening aspect of the shadow – especially of the far-reaching archetypal realities of the psyche – announces not evil, but mystery. These realities are rightly to be feared (as power always is), though they must be faced. This is the realm of nature, not of evil. In commenting on this process, Jung states:

> I do not feel qualified to go into the ethics of what 'venerable
> Mother nature' has to do in order to unfold her precious flower. . . .
> It will be objected that my respect for Nature is a very unethical
> attitude. . . . People who think like this evidently know all about
> good and evil, and why and for what one has to decide.
> Unfortunately I do not know all this so precisely, but I hope for my

patients and for myself that everything, light and darkness, decision and agonizing doubt, may turn to 'good' – and by 'good' I mean a development such as is here described, an unfolding which does no damage to either of them but conserves the possibilities of life (9.1, 337, n.141).

This passage sums up Jung's point about good/evil as *prima facie* contraries, and confirms my insistence that he needs an unequivocal use of *good* as well. The fact that 'the psychological self, [as] a transcendent concept, expressing the totality of conscious and unconscious contents, ... can only be described in antinomial terms' (9.2, 62) is Jung's central anthropological discovery. Rather than contradict the basic grammar of good/evil as capacity/privation, this insight actually shows how unexpectedly ambivalent our conscious judgements are. The seemingly disastrous consequences of the *privatio boni* formula, furthermore, turn out not to be consequences at all. Even if we call them *effects*, we are speaking more of those psychic forces attached to ego and intent on preserving it, than of the formula itself. It is, after all, easy enough to account for misunderstanding such a formula, especially its grammatical form. But something more is needed to explain the gross and sophistical ways it has been misappropriated. And such forces are the very ones which Jung calls to our attention.

7.22 *Good/evil, or good actions and evil actions*

One of the barriers to reading Jung is certainly his predilection for abstract discussion. Although he insists: 'as a therapist I cannot, in any given case, deal with the problem of good and evil philosophically but can only approach it empirically,' he certainly does not shrink from reflecting upon that experience in an idiom as abstract as German philosophy ever developed. He recommends his therapeutic discovery that 'the self is a *complexio oppositorum*' to us 'precisely because there can be no reality without polarity' (9.2, 267). Jung characterizes the most painful and intimate moments of self-discovery as a grappling with opposites, usually of cosmic stature. He even suggests that 'if we look closely we shall see that good and evil are, as I said, *principles*' (10, 458).

This is the language of a man for whom philosophical – even grammatical or metaphysical – language brings clarification. (Most people, however closely they looked, would never turn up a *principle*.) But such language creates its own mystification. Jung's preoccupation with his therapeutic experience offered a powerful corrective, it is true; nonetheless, we have already seen how misplaced his polemic could be. My contention is that an inherited Hegelian predilection for contradiction as the source of development fixed in Jung a penchant for *opposites* and *polarities*. To find these was to display the dynamism inherent in the psyche. Hence the tension of opposites would provide for Jung an appropriately developmental model for the self.[7]

The presumption is Hegel's. It organizes his logic and his philosophical method. To lay out the basic antithetical structure inherent in any process shows what makes it a process. Of course, structure or form is *ex professo* abstract, and so must the language be to match it. Jung was drawn to this Hegelian idiom, I suspect, by more than familiarity. Adopting the language of structure would help an empirical age to locate those forces Jung encountered in therapeutic exchange, which the common-sense division of the world into real (substances) and imaginary (thoughts) could not accommodate. But the idiom mystifies precisely because it collapses the distinction between grammar and description, and so tends to reify the structure it means to convey.

I can illustrate this effect by offering an observation of Aquinas' and then examining Jung's contention that good and evil are principles. Aquinas opens his discussion of evil with a grammatical distinction: just as the term *white* can stand for something white (as in 'whites') or for the property of being white, so it is with *evil*. One can perpetrate evil, and that certainly is to do something. Evil actions, inclinations and intentions are real enough. Considered in itself, however, evil should not be understood as a simple contrary of good but rather as a particular deficiency. And a deficiency is not something so much as it is a lack of something.[8] Jung is usually thinking of evil actions, inclinations or intentions, even of the force behind them, when he insists on the reality of evil within and without us.

In fact, Jung insists that 'the reality of good and evil consists in things and situations that happen to you' (10, 462). That corresponds to Aquinas' distinction between evil things and evil taken abstractly (or grammatically). Of such things and situations, however, Jung goes on to say that they 'are too big for you ... something stronger than oneself, invincible, is at work and one is up against it' (10, 463). Here he is clearly speaking of good and evil as *principles*. This is a description of forces which affect us and show themselves to be real, even if they are not distinct entities. If not substances, such forces are indeed substantial.

Following the pathways endemic to the individuation process in the various places where Jung traces them, however, we find that the psychic forces themselves cannot be denominated simply good or evil. Everything depends on the attitude which we consciously assume in their regard; and we cannot know which attitude will be appropriate until the time comes to assume it. It was precisely this ambivalent feature of the individuation process, moreover, which originally encouraged Jung to regard good and evil as opposites (or simple contraries). So we must conclude that he was misled in insisting that good and evil should be regarded as principles. When we examine the situation more closely, it is evident they cannot be that.

The category of principle as 'a supra-ordinate thing, mightier than I am' (10, 458), is a useful one for conveying the status of psychic powers. But good and evil just do not happen to be among these. A predilection for the language of form and structure to convey what empiricism systematically overlooks, however, could lead one to miss its propensity to reify and hence to mystify. That is why I have called this particular confusion of Jung's a logical one.

7.23 How else can evil be explained?

In calling the third area of conflict between Jung and Aquinas a conceptual confusion, I have unfairly begged an important question. For in this case Jung allies himself with a long-standing tradition, one which should antecedently qualify as an alternative way of organizing the data. If it embodies a confusion, that should be argued, not assumed. So it shall be.

The position Jung is led to adopt is an expressly gnostic one. Here he appeals to something more than the way in which good and evil manifest themselves contrariwise; he takes up the demand that evil has a cause. Hence I have called this argument a metaphysical one.

Jung's basic argument occurs in criticizing an exemplary patristic account of Basil, who 'asserts on the one hand that evil has no substance of its own but arises from a "mutilation of the soul." ... [But if] he is convinced that evil really exists, then the relative reality of evil is grounded on a real "mutilation" of the soul which must have an equally real cause' (9.2, 48). Or 'if the devil fell away from God of his own free will, this proves ... that the devil already had a "mutilated" soul for which we must hold a real cause responsible' (ibid.). In another place Jung bolsters this straightforward appeal for sufficient reason with a more properly archetypal demand: 'the conception of God as the *summum bonum* ... inevitably requires the existence of an *infimum malum*. No logical reasons are needed for this, only the natural and unconscious striving for balance and symmetry' (11, 313).

The gnostic contention for two eternal and opposite principles – one good and the other evil – appears more and more plausible. It answers directly to Jung's experience with therapy, satisfies the casual principle, and provides an appropriately symmetrical cosmic pattern. The doctrine of *privatio boni*, on the other hand, seems 'a regular *tour de force* of sophistry' (11, 313), – an intellectualist failure of nerve in the face of a God who 'fills us with evil as well as with good' (11, 461). Conceived as a philosophical corollary to monotheism, this doctrine must deny 'the independent existence of evil ... even in the face of the eternity of the devil as asserted by dogma' (9.2, 48). (One is reminded of a process theology epithet: 'monopolar prejudice.')

Alternative metaphysical positions are difficult to adjudicate. But Jung reminds us of a way in which they can be – perhaps the only way. He concedes that 'in the metaphysical realm, . . . good may be a substance and evil a *m′ e on* [*non-being*]' *(11, 306).*[9] Nor is this an empty concession, for Jung admits it to be 'possible that here, as in the case of other metaphysical statements, especially dogmas, there are archetypal factors in the background' (11. 306). The presence of these ideally would 'be accessible to empirical research.' The fact is, however, that Jung's own experience 'permits of no definite conclusion as to the archetypal background of the *privatio boni* . . . : I know of no factual experience which approximates to such an assertion' (ibid.)

This may sound like a backwards manner of validating metaphysical statements. Jung is certainly employing *factual* and *empirical* in an unaccustomed way. Nonetheless, the procedure is reminiscent of C. S. Peirce's contention that metaphysical assertions reflect basic logical strategies, which can themselves be justified only 'aesthetically.'[10] And the entire burden of Jung's reflections on his therapeutic experience is to enrich and extend the range of the factual amd empirical. Aquinas' own elaboration of the asymmetry of good and evil, furthermore, can be read as appealing to just such archetypal aspects of experience.

This is not surprising if we keep in mind that Aquinas took his cue from the *Confessions,* where Augustine had been so disconcerted in reflecting on having wantonly destroyed some pears. Recall his account: Augustine was looking back on a boyhood adventure of stealing pears from a neighbor's tree and pelting them against his wall.[11] Suddenly he is appalled at the senselessness of what he and his friends had done. There was absolutely *no reason* for it at all! This realization forces Augustine into a detailed analysis of motives and influences; bad company notwithstanding, nothing can explain so wasteful and useless an episode. Could it perhaps offer a naked paradigm for sin? Growing up develops in all of us resources for justification. But in those pricileged moments of self-knowledge when our justifications appear as precisely that, do we not perceive the utter senselessness of our destructive deeds? Augustine clearly grasped that point. And so would Aquinas.

Stripped of those specious 'reasons' which are designed precisely to provide us with cover stories and convey the appearance of *good,* what makes an evil action evil is that it makes no sense. It simply answers to no reason. In action-theoretic terms, such an action has no cause.[12] Aquinas understood that. In fact, he so organized his grammatical analysis that the necessary conclusion that evil has no cause would answer quite neatly to our experience.

So runs the substance of Aquinas' account of sin. God is the cause, ultimately, of whatever we do, even of the action whereby we transgress the order of things. But he cannot be made responsible for that action's being a transgression. The reasoning is straightforward, even if the conclusion sounds contrived.

The fact of creation bolsters our pervasive experience of contingency to suggest for Aquinas a general theorem of dependence: whatever we do we do as secondary causes, and all such actions by definition must be referred to the primary cause (*QD de Malo* 3.2). An instrument is different from a secondary cause in that the latter can function as an agent in its own right. In their subordinated role, however, Aquinas does conceive secondary causes instrumentally. The rule he lays down has even been called the 'theorem of universal instrumentality.'[13] But since everything both acts and is caused to act according to its nature, universal instrumentality does not entail determinism. Rather, the effect of these two theorems is to accentuate the transcendence of the first cause who disposes natural things to act according to natural laws, and intentional beings to act freely.

Any act, then, must be referred ultimately to the first cause. In the case of an evil act, however, we are forced to distinguish between the act itself and its malicious aspect. The malice (or sin) consists formally 'in the created will's turning away from its ultimate end. And it is impossible that God would make anyone's will turn away from its ultimate end, since he himself is the end' (*QD de Malo* 3.1.). Interestingly enough, Aquinas does not appeal to God's goodness as a *motive*. Rather he attends to the logic of the matter and focuses on the universal tendency among agents (including causes) to attract others to themselves: 'Whence it seems fitting that God would turn all things to himself and as a result turn nothing away from himself. As the highest good, he could not be the cause of a free agent's turning away from its primary good' (ibid.).

Aquinas does not presume to set a rule for God's free activity: we can neither know what he is nor how he might act. All that can be done is to lay out the logic of the situation. As Aquinas does that, it is not God's goodness (in a moral sense) which constitutes the reason why he cannot be the cause of sin. Rather, it is impossible that God cause sin because to do so would be to turn creatures away from himself. And that would be not evil, but unnatural! (Many will perhaps find this a strange argument; Jung would not.)

The evil dimension of a sinful action must then emanate from a secondary cause no longer acting instrumentally, but on its own. According to Aquinas' theorem, however, a secondary cause can act only in a subordinate capacity. But there is a subset of creatures endowed with freedom, and the real difference freedom makes does not lie in a simple capacity to choose. What defines the created agent as *free* is precisely the power to accept or to reject what it itself is: its ontological status, if you will. To accept the status of a secondary cause is to act accordingly; to reject it is to (pretend to) act in some other fashion.

Augustine's consternation at the senselessness of an action which became for him a symbol of sinfulness finds logical expression in Aquinas. Whatever we *do* maliciously is truly a mediated effect of God as transcendent first cause. But the malice of such a deed can be traced no further than ourselves: to a desire, based on pretense, to be what we are not. Pretense exposed looks silly; rationally, it is indefensible. And since the causes appropriate to actions are reasons, we must say that an evil action, in so far as it is evil, *has no cause*. Its evil aspect may even be considered to consist in the fact that it is senseless or without cause. In which case, the 'archetypal background of the [doctrine of] *privatio boni'* would be pressed more forcefully upon us.

7.24 *The limiting case: refusal*

The issue shows up clearly in the angels, in whom none of the 'excusing causes' are operative. Their evil actions consequently display the formal feature of sin: a created will turning away from its ultimate end. The angels display this feature in an especially lucid manner, since their purely intellectual mode of apprehension brings whatever is ultimate into immediate focus. The clarity of the angels regarding their own situation, furthermore, would prevent them from pretending to be what they were not. The angels' sin, therefore, could not consist in a rejection of their ontological status. The self-defeating character of so obstinate a posture would be evident to them. In the case of the angels, sin had to consist in turning down a gift, either outright, or by preferring to achieve what God offered gratuitously.[14]

What of the refusal – is it an action or not? Here Jung's demand for a 'real cause' joins forces with the widespread dissatisfaction among nineteenth-century romantics. These, remember, had faulted the classical view of sin and evil precisely for being too pale and logical. Can something so adamant as a refusal be grounded in a mere overlooking? If evil 'exists, so to speak, only as a by-product of psychological oversight, [then] it is a factor that can be got rid of by a change of attitude. We can act differently if we want to ... [yet] it took the intervention of God himself to deliver humanity from the curse of evil .... One must be positively blind not to see the colossal role that evil plays in the world' (9.2, 62). How can the origins as well as the encircling power of evil be explained if we insist on grounding it in a *failure* to see or to act? Yet if we do acknowledge that refusing is an action, what happens to Aquinas' general theorems?

Oddly enough, Jung himself accepts the substance of Aquinas' schematic solution. The action gains its force from being an action; the malice involved trades on this original power to wreak its destructive effect. Not that Jung would have distinguished so carefully, but for him the evil dimension is always related to *unconsciousness*. Yet not to *the* unconscious (as to a cause), nor to any lack of consciousness whatever. The evil dimension, rather, can be traced to a specific failure to be conscious: namely, to that degree which the action and its potential consequences demanded. As an action, an evil deed is consciously perpetrated; as evil, it lacks the degree of consciousness whence such an action should emanate.[15] This can be confirmed by reflecting on the way we accuse ourselves once we have seen what we did without seeing.

For a more 'empirical' and less Jungian response to this dilemma, we need only attend to the manner in which refusal or obstinacy manifests itself. Active and aggressive as it may be, there is something about such a posture which encourages us to call it a non-action. If we follow up this feeling, we will see just how value-laden is our working notion of *action*. Without explicitly attending to the Aristotelian analysis that every action is for an end, we nonetheless assume that actions carry purposes. Instinctively we believe they are out to accomplish something, and that actions generally represent ways of 'getting on' with things. (If understanding is 'knowing how to go one,' acting is a way of 'getting on with it.'[16]) Refusing to do something represents a surd in this procedure. Such an action – if an action at all – is one of a peculiar sort which denies what we associate with activity.

Does not Aquinas' grammatical analysis lead us to that precise point: 'evil, in itself, represents the privation of some particular good' (*QD de Malo*, 1.1)? Activity is what moves us along; refusal blocks that motion. (Of course, in certain circumstances the proper thing to do might well be to refuse acting. But then usually we feel constrained to explain that the course of activity would lead to untoward consequences.) Whatever evil is perpetrated, moreover, invariably is accomplished in a context which contains much good – and the action itself may indeed be a courageous one. It is often that very context which increases an action's potential for destruction: evil is the privation of a particular good. Nor is it inappropriate to read 'privation' as 'inverse', provided we do not regard the latter term as an equivalent contrary.

The senselessness of a destructive deed amounts to the fact that it cannot be explained. Jung's innocent assumption that evil too must have a cause fails to appreciate the specific power and malice of evil: its senselessness. While this feature is clouded in most human situations by countless excuses, refusal displays it more clearly. In the constructed world of angelic intellects, the sheer obstinacy of the refusal stands out most starkly of all.

7.25 *Reflection on method*

I have spent much time grappling with Jung because he presents a

103

common and forceful objection. More intimate access to what Aquinas was doing has been provided by unravelling Jung's confusions. That task, furthermore, has shown us how misleading it can be to mistake grammatical assertions for something else. Paradoxical as they sometimes sound, grammatical statements turn out to be indispensable instruments of conceptual clarity. Even the paradoxical ring itself might serve to warn a cautious reader that something out of the ordinary is going on with grammatical assertions. And an effort to 'straighten it all out' may well sacrifice the gains embodied in ordinary life and language – these same gains made explicit by exercises in philosophical grammar.

Interestingly enough, attention to grammatical achievements can often clarify what their critic is seeking as well. Jung concludes a major analysis of the principal archetype of the self, *Aion,* by remarking how 'we are unable to give a definition of good and evil that could be considered universally valid' (9.2, 267). True, for what he rightly wants from a definition is a rule stating how to label situations as they arise. The upshot of Jung's practice leads him to marvel at the ambiguities which arise when we assess situations to be good or evil. But what if '*malum = privatio boni*' were not a definition in the operative sense Jung assumes? Rather if the formula is an elucidation of the structure inherent in those terms he freely uses (as well as in the realities they express), then something else is going on.[17] And that is a kind of therapy in its own right: a philosophical exercise aimed at making us more conscious of what is happening when we use ordinary language to describe or evaluate our situation. To become thus conscious one must shift to a reflective level of discourse; and the need to find a formula for *good* or *evil* is another way of acknowledging that 'we are unable to give a definition [of them] that could be considered universally valid.'

In an extemporaneous address entitled 'Good and Evil in Analytical Psychology,' Jung delineates how it is that 'people behave when they are faced with a situation that has to be evaluated ethically . . . : suddenly they see both sides' (10, 462). He goes on to observe: 'once one has experienced a few times what it is like to stand judgingly between the opposites, one begins to understand what is meant by the self' (10, 463). Now 'the opposites' represent conventional good and evil; on the other hand, 'what is meant by the self is not only in me but in all beings, like the Atman, like Tao. It is psychic totality' (ibid.). Again speaking of 'the opposites,' Jung concludes: 'I can master their polarity only by freeing myself from them by contemplating both, and so reaching a middle position. Only there am I no longer at the mercy of the opposites' (10, 464).

It is clear from this statement that the good which Jung presupposes (and whose grammar Aquinas elucidates) is not one of the poles of conventional morality. This *good,* rather, is the 'middle position between' those poles; it represents that very self to which Jung aspires. Indeed, what is so insidious about conventional morality is that it can only deceive us by presenting its rules as our good and transgressions thereof as evil, since the very grammar of these terms outstrips any general rule.

Perhaps I have said enough to show why 'privatio boni [is] a metaphysical truth' (9.2, 54). The formula is precisely that – a grammatical elucidation. Clarifying what Aquinas was doing in using the formula illuminates our experience to confirm Jung's suspicion. He suspected, indeed, but could not verify 'the archetypal background of the privatio boni' (11, 306). Regarding Jung's preference for the gnostic perspective, it should suffice to reproduce a paragraph in which he states his allegiance:

> Paradox is a characteristic of Gnostic writings. It does more justice to the *unknowable* than clarity can do, for uniformity of meaning robs the mystery of its darkness and sets it up as something that is *known*. That is a usurpation, and it leads the human intellect into hybris by pretending that it, the intellect, has got hold of the transcendent mystery by a cognitive act and has 'grasped' it. The paradox therefore reflects a higher level of intellect and, by not forcibly representing the unknowable as known, gives a more faithful picture of the real state of affairs (11, 275).

We can appreciate the irony in this paean when we recall how paradoxical Jung himself found the *privatio boni* formula in the face of a gnostic symmetry between good and evil.

7.3 *Reinstating the devil*

At the outset I suggested that several of the consequences Jung attributed to *privatio boni* might better be traced to a gradual erosion of the sense that lively evil forces affect our world. This has happened, of course, since the Enlightenment. Perhaps his polemic was aimed at reinstating in us a vivid awareness of the devil and a wariness at his guises. Jung's goal would not be undermined by our showing how his generalizations regarding good/evil as contraries are misguided. For the devil need not be a divine *alter ego* to offer effective opposition to God's plans. The formula which represents a practical corollary to *privatio boni* assures that: *bonum in omni parte, malum ex quocumque defectu*. A carping critic can effectively block a proposal with but a fraction of the effort it takes to construct and present it.

It simply is not true, as Jung claims, that 'the position of the devil in Christian dogma is so very unsatisfactory' (9.2, 124), or that the doctrine of *privatio boni* reduces him to a 'shadow-existence' (11, 169).[18] Christian doctrine in fact presents the evil spirit for what Jung perceives it to be: 'a factor of quite incalculable potency' (ibid.). And Aquinas' theoretical construal of the doctrine reinforce that judgment. What is indeed true is that the devil has all but disappeared as a factor in Christian consciousness – at least until quite recently. Yet the reasons for this outstrip any mistakes theology might have made. They are lodged in the near-complete hegemony of a crudely empiricist *Weltanschaung*. On this view only material objects are real or objective, while everything else is taken to be subjective and imaginary. The position is incoherent, for it also acknowledges that our (subjective) perceptions organize the (objective) world. Thus insubstantial mind dictates what shall be substantial. Collective opinions, however, need not be coherent.

Of course, it must also be recognized how popular images for the devil conspired to banish it from our imagination and reduce the devil to ridicule. Here above all Jung's critique offers positive guidance in presenting a more sophisticated set of images, ones that can capture our imagination and illuminate our experience. This is a vastly different project, I might add, from one which intends to shift the devil's status from real to symbolic. Jung's program can be described in terms directly contrary: he is concerned to show how real is the symbolic.[19] More straightforwardly, forces are as real as substances, especially when they really affect the course of our lives. Jung's idiom for the evil spirit sacrifices individuality to offer us insight into how such forces can influence our behavior. What in fact affects us must be real, however we picture it.

Aquinas most concretely treats of devils when he asks whether they can cause men to sin (*QD de Malo* 3.3), and if so, how (ibid., 3.4)? He also asks more particularly whether evil spirits know the 'thoughts of our hearts' (ibid., 16.8), and how they are able to influence our powers of imagination (16.11) and our minds (16.12). As pure intelligences, evil spirits exercise immense sway over our imaginations; they could also affect our minds directly. The devils do not meddle directly with our minds, however, because a human intellect strengthened by their powers would more easily see through the particular species of deception being planned (3.4). But it suffices for the evil spirits to hold sway over our imaginative powers, since these are the key to concept-formation and mediately to judgment (16.12). Agitation or distortion of the powers of imagination can throw a person mightily off course, as prolonged confinement or excessive fatigue proves so well.

The only way a devil can cause us to sin, however, is by interior or exterior suasion (3.4, 16.11). Evil spirits cannot touch the well-spring of activity itself: either the act of willing (3.3) or that personal judgment by which each of us directs the course of his thoughts and of his life – what Augustine called 'thoughts of the heart' (16.8). As intellectual beings superior to us, the devils can know our characteristic thoughts; what they cannot discern is how we will *use* them. Nor can they know our innermost feelings. These spirits are canny, nevertheless, in spotting the slightest expression of our hidden emotions (16.8). But they absolutely cannot touch the act of willing which naturally inclines to happiness. That act can only be moved from within, by the judgment we make regarding some particular good and its connection with true happiness (3.3). Devils can indeed propose enticing objects – thoughts or images. These never suffice to move the will, however, although such objects can powerfully sway it.

So much for Aquinas' highly intellectual way of construing the common belief regarding evil spirits. The presumption remains that these intelligences (the evil ones along with the good) are individual agents, although we have no earthly way of conceiving their individuality. As spirits they are immaterial, and therefore bereft of the ordinary parameters for identification and re-identification.[20] Aquinas asserts their individuality semantically by insisting that each angel exhausts its species. But how *that* spells individuality, we simply cannot conceptualize. So it seems one is granted much latitude with this particular characteristic in attempting other ways of construing evil spirits. Perhaps even an idiom which carries no hint of individuality would do, so long as some measure of agency is retained.

Jung models his interpretation of devils not on angelic intellectual substances, but on powers of the unconscious. He adopts the Greek *daimon* to speak of such powers. These Jung finds represented mythically by gods and demi-gods. The figures who people the world of myth express in appropriately symbolic terms the forces of the unconscious. The hero's ordeal takes place through encountering these symbolic figures. Each human being learns to respect them by coming to recognize their effect on his life. Such forces are no less real for eluding the direct light of consciousness.

Jung does not consider these powers of the unconscious to be evil in themselves. None the less, they often present themselves in a threatening guise or in an antagonistic pose. What has the aspect of evil, moreover, often turns out to be our precise good. The threatening mien bespeaks the mysterious nature of the unconscious. And the danger associated with the unconscious comes from our ignorance and unfamiliarity more than from malice on the part of the forces themselves. In fact, as part of nature these powers are not really susceptible of ethical evaluation. That can only come with consciousness.[21]

The devils of Judaeo-Christian tradition cannot simply be identified with these psychic *daimones,* of course. But not because such powers are 'merely psychic' and so hardly to be reckoned with. Quite the contrary: psychic powers are never 'merely' so. They are neglected at serious risk to body and soul. The fact that these forces cannot present themselves to us as individuals do in no way makes them less real. Indeed, we run up against them in confronting other individuals, as we do in ourselves. And we can become aware of the powers of the unconscious through our dream and fantasy life. Theirs is a different mode of presence, to be sure, but no less real for being different.

What keeps us from identifying the devils of tradition with these powers is their moral ambivalence. The devil is confirmed in evil; psychic powers are part of nature and thus premoral. Despite appearances, they are neither good nor evil. Should such forces succeed in taking possession of us, the results are certainly destructive. But it is we – not they – who perpetrate the evil. Or more properly, it is we-possessed who act in a destructive manner. Even if the agency seems more daimonic than personal (and one can normally tell), the *daimones* are incapable of acting maliciously without hitching their powers to a human being's imagination, reason, and volition.[22]

For Jung, then, *daimones* become devils only when they are in league with an individual human consciousness. Unconscious powers cannot act autonomously except in relation to that which bestows autonomy: consciousness. A schizoid situation is defined as that form of possession in which certain psychic powers have 'captured' enough consciousness so that it splits off and acts semi-autonomously. In less dramatic and more normal situations, we simply find ourselves overreacting or systematically heedless of facts we knew were important. Sometimes in retrospect we can see how monstrous was a pattern of behavior that we had allowed ourselves to regard as quite acceptable.

Often it is difficult to assign responsibility for such oversights. Traditional moral philosophy regarded them generally as excusing causes, while recognizing that we might be faulted for failing to correct our self-deceptions. Consciousness is the only protection one has; and consciousness can be overwhelmed – though when that happens we speak of sickness rather than culpability. Moreover, consciousness alone can take praise or blame. So if *I* am not responsible, no one is! It may or may not be proper to blame me, but I can never blame a *daimon*. That would represent a logical evasion.

Jung's position has some obvious advantages from the Christian standpoint. If I conceive the devils as malicious beings able to manipulate my very imagination, I must rely on incessant prayer to God who can restrain them (without having promised to banish them entirely). Gradually I should then become more capable of discriminating spurious from authentic wishes, and so be more selective in my appeals for help. That would be the normal effect of baptismal grace as it developed within me, eliciting and responding to my prayer. None the less, 'the devil as a roaring lion goes about seeking whom he may devour.' The critical factor remains the devil's active malice, however. If we are really dealing with an individual, and with one so richly endowed, what hope of success do we have?

Without doubt the devil has steadily waned in Christian consciousness since medieval or even Reformation times. All the cultural factors which spell Enlightenment can be considered as causes. We could also speculate, however, whether an evil spirit such as Aquinas describes might not have induced a paranoid psychological situation? Believers would find themselves unable to sustain such anxiety, and so banished the devil from individual and collective awareness. Only popular images of the devil could endure – and these reflect a characteristically human way of bearing the unbearable: humor. Thus the very laughable quality of the commonplace images bespeaks a repression. Modern man had outsmarted the devil and acknowledged him at all only as the butt of jokes. But a little reflection on the odds will suggest who has the last laugh. And yet reflection alone does not accomplish that; it is faith which shows us what we are up against.

Here we have the classical Christian *Weltanschauung*. Faith lets us in on an inner scenario that otherwise we could only suspect: our wrestling is not with mere flesh and blood but with principalities and powers. To be cognizant of the devil and his blandishments is to learn to seek assistance from God. So the dynamics of a Christian life offer the only feasible way of correcting that penchant towards an illusory autonomy which seems to be born with each one of us.

Where the watchword is autonomy, as in the Enlightenment, dependence of this sort – even on a transcendent God – becomes repugnant. Not so with Jung, however. His quarrel really is more with rationalism than with classical doctrines, including *privatio boni*. In fact, we have seen how his polemic against that doctrine tended to fasten on the way it lent support to an illusion of rational control. Jung enhances the picture of the self as a battleground for opposing forces, by naming the principals and mapping out their characteristic maneuvers. But he does not think the conscious self capable of sustaining a victory. The odds are against it. Persons are poorly endowed for the struggle that is demanded of them: conscious, they must nonetheless gain consciousness.[23]

Furthermore, 'the progressive development and differentiation of consciousness leads to an ever more menacing awareness of the conflict and involves nothing less than a crucifixion of the [conscious] ego, its agonizing suspension between irreconcilable opposites' (9.2, 44). The appropriate symbol for progress here is the Christian one of the cross. Jung's experience with therapy will not permit him to describe individuation by the more comfortable natural metaphors of growth and development. He finds himself constrained to speak of the process in the explicitly religious idiom of life through death. While he can sketch the parameters of the struggle, those very terms prohibit his describing its resolution. This is 'always felt as a "grace".'[24]

Jung's language surrenders the devil as autonomous individual. What replaces that conception is a legion of impersonal forces. These can enhance our consciousness or impede it; they assist us powerfully or possess us destructively. It is up to us, yet we are not sufficient to the task. Jung provides us a profound respect for such powers, impersonal though they be, as ingredient in the self I am called to become. And he alerts us to the compelling need to discover a way through those forces that threaten to overwhelm me. I must find their helping side and learn to live with the powers of the unconscious. Better, I can become myself only by letting them reveal and nourish my true identity. That way I might call my destiny, or God's will for me.[25]

It is difficult to adjudicate between metaphysical scenarios, of course. And those are exactly what Jung and Aquinas present in proposing the parameters for a self's becoming oneself. Jung offers us a tactical way of reinstating a healthy respect for the powers of evil, and a needed corrective for an ethos dominated by rational control. It also suggests a way to construe self and world which demands that we find both language and strategies for dealing with impersonal forces as well as objects and persons. This might, I suspect, bring us closer to the medieval category of *spirit* than our current notion of person ever could. In that case, the individual angelic spirits (each of whom exhausts a species), might look to us more like impersonal forces than other persons.

Finally, Jung's notion that devils can perpetrate evil only when they succeed in capturing a human imagination, reason, and will, is intriguing. It locates the agent quite effectively, and offers at least a conceptual possibility for discriminating degrees of possession and responsibility. Above all, such a conception removes the threat of a wily and malicious agent intent upon doing me in. I have suggested already that so formidable a threat tends to be self-defeating, for we cannot long sustain it.

7.4 Concluding observations

I have focused on Jung's objections to *privatio boni* for the same reason I did on those of process theologicans to 'classical theism.' These objections seemed to offer the most trenchant possible critique of Aquinas' philosophical theology. And philosophical theology can be regarded as Aquinas' distinctive contribution to philosophy as well as the linchpin of his systematic theology. Neither Jung's nor process theology's objections could be called purely technical, for each purported to pinpoint a widespread feeling of discontent by tracing the difficulty to its roots in a classical doctrine. By meeting the objections we have been able to test Aquinas' skill in propounding the doctrines at issue.

More particularly, these objections offered a test of my own way of interpreting what Aquinas was doing. Since it is a fairly radical one, that interpretation gains plausibility if it helps Aquinas to withstand such patent criticisms. By showing how metaphysical assertions function as grammatical elucidations, the polemical thrust of both objections has been deflected. At the same time, their intent is preserved. That is a standard way of demonstrating the superiority of a conceptual strategy: show how it allows one to parry the primary objection while meeting the objector's legitimate demands. Readers can measure the success of that strategy for themselves.

PART II

Actus:
The Operative Analogous
Expression

8

Actus: an Inherently Analogous Expression

Philosophical discussion breeds disillusionment when so much is promised and so little accomplished. What better example of offering stones for bread than Aquinas' providing a grammatical treatise in response to humankind's search for divinity? I have tried to counter the disappointment by showing how – in their own lean way – the logical exercises can nourish our minds and spirits by pointing beyond themselves. Yet grammar remains a thin gruel, indeed.

Joel Feinberg puts it nicely by reminding us: 'here as elsewhere in philosophy, analytic techniques help to answer the penultimate questions, while the ultimate ones, being incapable of *answer*, must be come to terms with in some other way.'[1] If we can learn how to unravel the tangle of penultimate issues effectively, however, we find ourselves squarely facing the ultimate ones. And on reflection, we can ask no more of philosophy. At that point logical analysis can take us no further; we are on our own, or need assistance of another sort.

Thus far I have worked to let Aquinas bring us through a maze of questions with grammatical finesse. I also tried to show how to employ the skills acquired in that exercise to attain some clarity on two keenly contemporary questions. Aquinas' way of doing grammar *in divinis*, it appears, proves more successful than these contemporary contenders for illuminating the very issues on which they sought to fault him. Yet for all that, something is missing in our consideration of Aquinas' philosophical logic.

His answer to the ultimate questions, perhaps? Hardly, since we have no right to ask that and Aquinas had more sense than to try to give it. Some indication, then, of the insight animating his analysis? Is that what we've not yet discovered? I think so. Of course, such an insight will not be expressed in the formal features which grammar employs. It must be articulated in a different language – one which does not give answers, but

115

offers new realizations. Hegel spoke of notions. I prefer to call such expressions 'master metaphors,' noting how they guide our grammatical analysis. As metaphors, these terms are inherently analogous; we use them better the more we realize how using them reveals us to ourselves and shapes the self we will become. In short, inherently analogous expressions are inescapably performative in character. *Actus* is certainly one of these.

Actus stands out as the master metaphor guiding Aquinas' grammatical treatment of divinity. In one of his initiating arguments, Aquinas gives a new twist to the nominal definition of divinity from question 2: 'what is the first existent thing must be in act (*necesse est id quod est primum ens esse in actu*)' (1.3.1). Insistence on God's actuality is the only clue Aquinas will provide for our grasping what it is to be divine. *Actus* alone suggests the point of his painstaking grammatical elucidation.

We are not surprised, then, to find Aquinas reminding us that *actus* and *esse* are in the same logical neighborhood. *Esse* itself is the most perfect thing of all, to be compared to everything else as act (*ipsum esse est perfectissimum omnium, comparatur enim ad omnia ut actus*) (1.4.1.3). And God, we recall, is '*esse* itself subsisting (*ipsum esse subsistens*)' (1.11.4).

In Part I I have shown how statements like that come to nothing. That is quite simply the logic of the matter, and to try to attenuate it would undermine Aquinas' masterful strategy of pressing logic to show forth the transcendence of God. *Actus*, however, does introduce something more than logic into the discussion. By showing how *actus* functions, Part II of my study will work like the second column in Aquinas' grammatical treatment, suggesting how what we cannot say may none the less be taken (see chapter 2.3).

Once we recognize how *actus* functions as the master metaphor guiding Aquinas' logical analysis, showing how it works is all that remains to be done. To do that, however, we must trace its use throughout the writings of Aquinas in domains wide of philosophical theology. If the notion is truly central, such a survey should introduce us to much more of Aquinas in the process. It will certainly show *actus* as sufficiently analogous to embody the insight animating his grammar of 'God'. And the exercise itself may even persuade us of the plausibility of that austere analysis. That was, after all, what the notions discussed in column two were meant to do.

8.1 *Characteristic uses of* actus

It is the distinctively human activities of knowing and loving which offer Aquinas a paradigm for understanding action more generally. The bulk of the *Summa* is devoted to human acts; its master plan would show how humankind, created by God, proceeds to find the way back to its source. Even where the topic at hand is divine activity, Aquinas conceives it intentionally and models it on the intellectual activity of knowing and loving with which we are intimately acquainted.

Aquinas' treatment of causality follows the analysis of Aristotle, whose controlling metaphor for nature was art. The Greeks accepted art as an imitation of nature. Aristotle neatly inverted the dictum: 'art imitates nature,' to explain the processes of nature by the more familiar procedures of articulation and fabrication. For that reason, Aristotle's analyses of causality remain linguistic in character, and fall short of the kind of theory we have come to expect. The same must be said for Aquinas, yet these grammatical observations can show how to overcome the spontaneous demands of imagination to find some *influx* from cause to effect.

Whatever is 'in act,' as Aquinas puts it, need do nothing further to become a cause. Its capacity for acting is inherent, although that power will not ordinarily be evident until some object which it can affect comes within range. At that point, the inherent activity shows itself, and the thing in question becomes an agent. Notice, however, that the agent itself does not change in becoming an agent. It is the object acted upon which is changed: first, by being brought under the agent's sway; and second, in the manner that the object is thereby affected.[2]

Aquinas' point regarding causality may be summarized by this formula: the act of the thing changed is that of the agent (*actus motus est moventis*). Closer scrutiny of his treatment will show how it meets the demand for a clear-cut description of those situations gathered under the rubric of cause-effect. His concerns did not require a more specific theoretic consideration. As a bit of philosophical grammar, however, Aquinas' handling of the matter exorcises many questions which bedevil our common-sense expectations concerning cause-effect relations.

Finally, just as Aquinas does not hesitate to characterize divinity as *actus purus* (1.3.2) in the midst of an argument that God cannot be characterized, so will he employ *actus* to articulate divine activities. It is traditional to distinguish God's action *ad extra* in creating and sustaining the universe from his own inner life elaborated in the trinitarian processions. The salvific activity of God will not fit neatly into either bracket, yet Aquinas handles all three modalities of divine activity under the rubric of *actus*.

It should be clear by now that the distinct contexts in which *actus* functions exhaust the ways of parceling out what is. So in effect *actus* is coextensive with *ens* (being) for Aquinas, as his argument in 1.3.1 indicates: in the first existent thing everything must be actual (*necesse est id quod est primum ens esse in actu*). By insisting that 'whatever is is in act,' he offers one of those illustrative tautologies. Aquinas is reminding us that individual existing things afford our paradigm instances of *being*. Potentialities, moreover, are discerned only by reference to such full-fledged instances – even when they can only be imagined.

8.2 *The paradigm use*

One can readily observe how the intentional activities of knowing and loving, proper to human beings, provide Aquinas the paradigm for so extended a use of *actus*. This perspective would also be consonant with the humanism proper to his times. If we take the epic of a period to express its characteristic spirit, Dante's *Divina Commedia* displays the significance with which medievals freighted human actions. Incapable of being reduced to their causal components, human actions give testimony that men and women are created in the likeness of God, and so are truly capable of originating chains of consequences.[3]

Bernard J. F. Lonergan has shown how Aquinas locates the originative nature of human actions in an immanent act of understanding.[4] If we grasp how Aquinas characterizes the act of understanding at the heart of the originative (and hence responsible) nature of human actions, we will be in possession of his account of *actus*. The only accounting we can give for analogous terms is to show why the accepted paradigm use is plausibly paradigmatic. Furthermore, when a term is so pervasive as *actus*, we cannot elucidate that paradigm use in terms more basic than *actus* itself. Thus at some point the account must be sufficiently perspicuous so that the very elucidation of a typical act of understanding will be the paradigm form of activity. An account can only perform this office, of course, when it becomes itself a performance. We shall see that this is precisely Lonergan's own strategy as well.[5]

8.3 *Order of treatment*

The following chapters will begin by canvassing Aquinas' uses of *actus*: for the range of intentional performance (9), for natural process (10), for divine activity both creating and immanent (11). Chapter 12 will show how Aquinas' rendition of the act of understanding offers a perspicuous accounting for the panoply of uses of *actus* which we have observed. This same chapter will rely upon Lonergan's analysis to shed light on the actual practice of Aquinas, comparing that practice so illuminated with the work of some contemporary philosophers of action.

In a more reflective and final chapter (13), I shall try to relate Aquinas' uses and the account offered to those paradoxes of action that bedeviled Wittgenstein and which suggest the fascination of Zen. I will indicate how proper attention to language can attenuate some of the paradoxical features, while others resist any further elucidation. In an indirect way, this irreducibly paradoxical character of action confirms Aquinas' choice of *actus* as a primary notion. The ways that these paradoxes emerge, furthermore, offer striking structural parallels to the therapeutic manner in which Aquinas employs *actus* to disabuse us of some common-sense expectations. It should not be surprising that a notion so basic would incite parallels in quite disparate traditions. On the contrary, the structural similarities serve to remind us just how fundamental a notion Aquinas is offering us in his elucidation of *actus*.

9

Intentional Activity and Performance: Paradigm for *Actus*

9.1 *Understanding as active receptivity*

The shared human fact of wanting to understand, together with the particular acts of understanding which answer that desire, provide Aquinas with the materials for his account of human knowledge. These also offer a paradigm instance of the constitutive principles of potency and act. It is the desire to understand that characterizes human intelligence. Actual instances of knowing are each accomplishments, but wanting to know marks the human condition itself. Certain persons distinguish themselves by knowing the answer; anyone may pose a question. This openness to whatever can be understood distinguishes the human intellect as such, and invites Aquinas to define the 'scope of our intellectual activity [as] being in general' (1.79.2).

Wanting to know falls short of knowing, yet is ordered to it; and the objects sought after define the range of this desire. Thus Aquinas can state that 'every created intellect, by the mere fact that it is [a power of understanding], ... is to be compared to the gamut of intelligible things · as potency to act' (ibid.). A theory is not being enunciated here. These statements of Aquinas merely assemble some key reminders to establish a basic grammar for the situation of human understanding and development. We would not find anything out without looking for it, and we would not be looking for it if we did not want or need to know about it. Human knowing is tied to personal development and has little to do with haphazard information. We are immediately aware, moreover, when we are being solicited to know more than we want to know.

Aquinas proceeds to mine our native sense that knowing involves more than collecting information. Better, the notion of information itself makes sense only as the answer to a question.[1] He argues that the power to understand must not only want to know, but be able to consummate that desire as well. 'Since nothing can be moved to accomplishment unless by something in act, ... that same power of understanding must possess sufficient force (*aliquam virtutem*),' (1.79.3), in effect, to answer the questions asked. This active component of the power of understanding is called the 'agent intellect.' The desire to know together with its accomplishments, therefore, provide a privileged instance of how potency and act are internally related.

Aquinas demonstrates the need for an active principle from the general phenomenology of the universe offered by Aristotle and contrasted with Plato. According to this picture, most of the things we want to know about could not themselves terminate our quest for understanding because of their material state. So we must be able to take from them what is knowable, and thus accomplish our intent. Were the objects of our inquiry immaterial, Aquinas presumes they could activate our power of under-standing directly. Such objects would terminate an inquiry themselves, as it were, without requiring an active dimension to our power of under-standing: 'since the very fact of immateriality makes something intelligible in act' (ibid.).

He is proceeding in a counter-factual mood here, suggesting what might happen if in fact the 'forms of natural things were to subsist immaterially, as Plato supposed' (ibid.). If such were the case, Aquinas supposes that knowledge would immediately result. Just as opening our eyes normally results in seeing what lies in front of us, so subsisting ideas could (in virtue of their immateriality) inform us willy-nilly. Like roadside signs that impose their message whether we are interested or not, such forms would offer ready answers to questions we had never even thought of.

Put that way, the situation is bizarre, not to say paradoxical. It already warns us how misleading the easy analogy between seeing and knowing can be. In fact, the penchant of Plato to be guided by that analogy offered Aquinas a salient reason for preferring Aristotle's epistemology. Unlike the power of sight, our capacity to understand cannot be merely passive; it must embody both a receptive and an active principle. If Aquinas gives rather technical reasons for this composition stemming from generic considerations of materiality and immateriality, we can suggest some more closely linked to the process of inquiry itself.

Knowledge or information can be assimilated only in the measure we have sought it. This is not to say, of course, that we find only what we're looking for! We may well be surprised. But at least we have to be probing in the area which yields the unexpected knowledge. Inquiry is a heuristic process, and whatever understanding we attain comes as a result of inquiring – even when it upsets our guiding preconceptions. So the intellect, which needs to be receptive to understand at all, must also be actively seeking if what results is indeed understanding. By contrast with seeing, the grammar of understanding calls for an active receptivity. This

121

formal fact appears to be the deeper reason why Aquinas must insist on an active dimension to intellect (*oportet igitur ponere aliquam virtutem ex parte intellectus*).

It also becomes evident why a growing awareness of the structure of inquiry offers a touchstone for the use of both *potency* and *act*. That is exactly how paradigm instances for analogous expressions gain acceptance: sufficiently rich themselves, the situations also provide a way of illuminating other uses of the same expression when we compare those uses with the suggested paradigm. Although each use of *actus* will be a proper one, we find ourselves more at home with that use which helps us to articulate the structure of inquiry. So *actus* itself seems more 'at home' in that particular instance, even though it can be used properly 'away from home.' This peculiar feature of analogous expressions in use shows what makes them analogous. By contrast with ordinary descriptive terms as well as simple metaphors, these can be used properly in utterly diverse contexts. Yet our reliance on paradigm instances when we actually use analogous expressions shows that they never quite cease being metaphors.

Understanding must then be an activity; furthermore, a person is never more active than when he or she is actually understanding. This claim of Aquinas will affect the way he compares contemplative with active forms of life (see chapter 13). It profoundly shapes his theory of action, and in doing so, uncovers yet another dimension of *actus*.

9.2 *Performance and understanding*

Understanding lies at the heart of all activity that is properly called human, as Aquinas anatomizes human performance. Not that so-called 'external actions' are caused by an act of understanding or willing, nor that our performance rests on explicit decisions. Aquinas' model is much more organic than the Cartesian or existentialist alternatives: human action is intention through and through. An act cannot be described without characterizing its object. And it is specifically the office of intellect to identify the object and hence specify an act (2-1.9.1). More concretely, the process whereby we bring ourselves to take up a course of action involves distinct acts of consent (2-1.15) and of counsel (2-1.14). These necessarily must precede any choice of alternatives (2-1.13), if the ensuing action is to be genuinely mine.

It matters more to Aquinas that the action is mine, than that it be effective. There are four factors determining the shape of an act: agent, end, object, and circumstances. Of these, effectiveness hinges on the one factor beyond the agent's grasp: circumstances, i.e. whatever happens to be taking place in the context. That is not to say an agent can control the end or the object, but a person can grasp these in the sense of understanding them. In this precise sense, an action emanates from a person (now an agent). That same person, therefore, can be held responsible – praised or blamed – for it.

This fact remains central to Aquinas as to the medieval perspective and points to the very heart of an act. Effectiveness (or accomplishment in the sense of 'results'), leads one away from the act as described and performed into a multiplicity of concurrent forces. Relevant because they shape the form an act finally assumes, these forces are surely worthy of calculation. None the less, they remain peripheral to action as elucidated by *actus* and grounded in consent and counsel. Such a scheme represents what one could call Aquinas' theory of action. Some details of the process prove illuminating, and show what an intimate role *actus* plays in shaping that theory.

9.21 *Consent to the end*

Willing is for Aquinas a rational appetite (2-1.6.1). Humankind's inclination to its proper end follows upon a person's grasp of that goal. Yet the power of a goal to elicit a response necessitates a complementary capacity in the individual, and that spontaneous tending towards one's perceived good is called willing. It is more like an inclination than a push. This appetite for a goal follows upon perceiving that something is a desirable end, but perceiving alone could not generate the wanting. In this respect, will and intellect remain distinct. As Aquinas sees it, willing is meant to incline towards the goods which reason indicates. The act whereby one tends spontaneously to the end presented he calls 'consent.'

Whatever presents itself as an end is a candidate for consent. Most of them demand deliberation, however, since ends can be ordered as means one to another. The only goal or good which elicits consent with utter spontaneity is the ultimate end (2-1.15.3). For Aquinas that is a logical point: once a goal can be identified as ultimate, we have no choice about wanting it. Yet that fact in no way denigrates our freedom. It simply means that choice is not concerned with the ultimate end, but looks instead to ways of getting there. Something else comes into play when ends are identified, and that is properly called consent.[2]

How can such consent be rational, however, when in this case it is said to be spontaneous? Remember that for Aquinas what distinguishes rational creatures from the rest of animals is their capacity to 'direct themselves to one thing in place of another.' That is what is meant by 'having it in one's power to move oneself' (2-1.15.2). Although rationality bestows distance and hence the capacity for choice, it does not cancel out creatureliness. On Aquinas' analysis, the power which rational creatures have to move themselves does not cease to be originative by the fact that the power must itself be moved. For no mover is itself unmoved, except the first mover. This analysis assures, however, that the motive power moves in one way – by identifying the object and therefore characterizing the act – while it is moved in another. The motive power is itself moved by attraction to what is presented as its proper end. (Technically, these two ways are distinguished as *formal* and *final* causality, respectively.)

Aquinas thus gains a way of characterizing an originative capacity proper to created rational beings. The power to act freely becomes a function of a person's inclination or orientation towards his proper end. Since the person's capacity for apprehending goals ranges over all that is, however, the proper end of rational creatures can be nothing less than their ultimate end. And that ultimate end, of course, is as well the beginning of all things (1.2. Intro). Whenever anyone allows his appetitive power to be spontaneously (and hence conditionally) moved by anything short of the ultimate end, to that extent will the actions be less free.

Freedom, then, admits of degrees without ceasing to be originative and a source of responsibility. By insisting on the transcendence of the ultimate end, furthermore, Aquinas can press his analysis to offer complete freedom to a person, without generating the paradoxes that accompany the notion of freedom as autonomy or absolute indeterminacy. Paradoxes arise when one proffers an ideal of freedom in which reasons appear as constraints. But reasons enter constitutively into our actions, by the mere fact that we cannot help describing what we are doing, quite apart from any need to justify it. Such reasons cannot thus be extrinsic to our actions, as though impeding originativeness.[3]

Nor does Aquinas feel that the ultimate end can be formulated so as to deduce those secondary ends which would then command our consent as means to attaining our proper goal. God's transcendence effectively blocks that route. None the less, Aquinas does insist that the more the ultimate end 'captures' our desire, the freer we are. Inclination to the ultimate end is spontaneous because it is our proper good. And the more we are inclined to what is ultimate, the less will we be moved by less worthy goals. Such goals stunt our growth by restricting our desires and fastening them on something less than all-there-is; they end up determining us unduly. Mankind's natural appetite for the ultimate end, if released and given full play, results in a freedom quite as indeterminate as autonomy might promise. With this signal difference: Aquinas' understanding of freedom emerges as an ideal, following Augustine's 'love God and do what you will.' Indeterminists, on the other hand, presume such freedom at the outset.

We have seen how Aquinas' analysis affords a constitutive place to reasons in human activity, for the power of reason directs our willing (1-2.15.1.1). Yet willing remains a distinct capacity, defined as a natural inclination to one's proper good – specifically, the ultimate end. I have tried to show that the spontaneous act of consent, far from removing one's capacity to be originative, actually empowers it. Such an account offers a way of conceptualizing (if not actually measuring) degrees of freedom. For it is the transcendence of this ultimate end which assures one complete freedom, without the paradoxes attendant upon absolute freedom (or autonomy).

Paradoxes of another sort enter here, of course, as we have noted in treating God's transcendence. One must speak analogously of 'degrees' of freedom, since the logic which maintains transcendence forbids a metric as well. But Aquinas' analysis of freedom complements his treatment of God's transcendence by offering an existential measure. It assumes the form suggested by the Hebrew prophets: any goal short of the ultimate one becomes an idol if we allow ourselves to consent unqualifiedly to it. Where a metric would indicate an objective measure, this test rests with the agent personally. Aquinas' 'degrees' of freedom become an invitation to inner growth.

9.22   *Counsel concerning means*

Aquinas' account neatly avoids what most of us today are persuaded lies at the heart of human action: decision. This divergence becomes even more curious when we reflect how concerned Aquinas was to expose how human action is an originating act. In our time, the activist language of 'decision' offers a paradigm for originative human activity. At the core of any authentically human action is that which makes it an act of the self: a personal decision. Guided by Aristotle's analytic scheme of ends/means, Aquinas reads the situation differently.

Ends are consented to, not chosen, as we have noted. Only means are chosen, and that with a view to their appropriateness in attaining the end. Of course there is much room for discussion about the means. It can continue indefinitely! Indeed, the only way of closing discussion will simply be to act. But the relative weighing of pros/cons, which Aquinas calls 'taking counsel,' hardly qualifies for an existential decision, even if it can only be terminated by a decisive performance. What contemporaries look for in *decision* Aquinas handles more serenely in speaking of consent to ends. We have seen, moreover, that such consent cannot be mindless; it involves assessing which ends merit one's consent. Still, for all that, 'consent' strikes modern ears as too passive for what makes a performance accountable as a personal act.

On reflection, however, consent gains ground phenomenologically as well as systematically. It coheres with Aquinas' insistence that under-standing be receptive, no matter how active that receptivity must be. While consenting is an act of the will since it presupposes inclining towards an end, for Aquinas willing remains an activity of reason, broadly speaking (2-1.15.1). So it is proper that the pattern of receptivity be preserved in the consent which lies at the heart of more manifest voluntary actions like choosing. Furthermore, properly speaking, it seems that ends or goals are rarely chosen or even decided upon. Rather they grow on us. Or is it that we grow into them? Whatever it is, those actions which emerge as fundamental orienting decisions in our lives are rarely *made*. They seem, rather, after the fashion of romance languages and archaic English usage, to be *taken*.

Indeed, it is the recognition of a lacuna here which offers the *prima facie* sanction for invoking *decision*. Since we cannot justify our apparent choice of ends – for choices are justified by recourse to ends – we must simply *decide*. Such decisions, of course, fail to embody the grammar governing deciding, since no reasons can be given. Hence usually we are forced to call them something like 'radical decisions.' Unless, that is, we understood that what looks like choosing an end is really not choosing at all. Then we would not be tempted to speak of decision – something like choice, only stronger – as filling the gap. In fact, if we abandon the language of choice when it comes to ends, there is no gap. It disappears as we learn to speak of a quite different sort of activity: consenting. And if 'consenting' sounds insufficiently active, we need only reflect that 'deciding' conveys a posture too active to be accurate. Perhaps Aquinas is leading us towards a way of reconceiving what is authentically active and accountable. His analysis schools us to think in terms of acts like consenting and understanding, which are themselves as receptive as they are active.

What may appear to be a roundabout introduction of Aquinas' account of choice is offered to explain why he says so little about the matter. For him we simply weigh alternatives, judging those that are conducive to the ends to which we have already consented (2-1.14.3). The ends function like principles (2-1.14.2) guiding the inquiry that we must engage in while taking counsel (2-1.14.1). This process cannot be a deductive one, however, since it moves towards particular actions rather than general conclusions. In fact, as an inquiry in the full sense of that word, it cannot be concluded at all. The process is only a limited kind of inquiry, one leading from an intended goal to a present undertaking (2-1.14.5). What concludes this inquiry called 'taking counsel' is not a proposition but a performance: 'just as the end functions like a principle, so whatever is done for the sake of the end functions like a conclusion' (2-1.14.6).

We take counsel, quite simply about what should be done. This account moves neatly between a hallowed ethical 'ought' and the sheerly in-strumental 'how to get it done.' For with Aquinas, the model of inquiry prevails, even if taking counsel is a special sort of inquiry. The conclusions drawn – the actions to be undertaken – serve to make explicit what we have consented to, since they emerge as consequences following from the end intended. So taking counsel shares in the critical process whereby we assess ends as worthy of our consent. While Aquinas himself does not draw this conclusion, it follows from his insistence that counsel is a kind of inquiry for which ends function as specific principles.

On Aristotle's theory of inquiry, a definition merits its place as the proper principle of a science when it shows that those characteristics judged as essential to a situation follow logically from the definition. If they do not, then we must search for another formula. Neither the definition nor the deductive process, however, identify which characteristics are deemed essential. That judgment reflects the same quality of wit which fastens on likely definitions as well. Aquinas presumes something similar for his analysis of action. Actions which emerge as consequences of consenting to certain ends must be judged appropriate to the situation by an assessment process akin to what elicited consent to the end itself.

There is more than consistency at stake, since deduction forms only one part of the process of inquiry. By drawing consequences, however, we are helping to develop our more basic wit into a critical judgment. By displaying what follows from accepting certain ends we can better grasp the consequences of our original consent. Consent to an end and taking counsel regarding what to do combine to form a sophisticated process. This enables us to become increasingly critical in ascertaining which ends merit our consent, as we grow more adept at canvassing the options they entail. The entire process is then an exercise in what we have come to call 'decision-making.' It should prove useful to compare Aquinas' account with the patterns for rational decision-making developed in management sciences. These have little to do with the 'radical decision' ideology mentioned earlier, even though management theorists presume that one merely chooses ends or has them chosen for him by the goals of the enterprise. Practitioners can see, however, how persons come to re-assess the goals set by an enterprise as the participants perceive certain agenda following from such goals.

9.3   Habitus *or 'first act'*

We have seen how Aquinas' accounts of both understanding and performance demand an active principle. So far discussion has focused on the principle of activity, noting how Aquinas insists that human activity emanates from a source that is receptive as well as active. Yet it is persons, not principles, who are held responsible for actions performed. How can we conceive actions for what they are: the acts of persons?

The contemporary response to this question is immediate: decisions, personal decisions, make my actions mine. But we have remarked how unsatisfactory this answer is, for the action postulated is described in terms that elude our common experience. I have shown how Aquinas offers an alternative analysis of the situation, and how it functions in describing individual choices. Still, how does he account for attributing acts to persons? Not by a decision. Aquinas proposes a much more prosaic process whereby acts accumulate, as it were, into stable principles of action characterizing the individual. These individualized principles are generically called *habitus* (or dispositions), and specifically named virtues.

We have already noted how persons can perform the actions they do perform: by virtue of the active principles belonging to their nature. What we have not yet seen is how these actions themselves contribute to forming the kind of person one is. For most of our actions seem to flow from us with little or no deliberation, though we are no less responsible for them. Aquinas identifies a feedback process whereby actions not only accomplish the deed intended, but also develop a facility in the agent for acting likewise in the future (2-1.51.2). Were not the principle of activity itself receptive and open to many possibilities, an intermediate principle would prove superfluous. Aquinas makes that point in discussing whether dispositions or *habitus* are proper to purely intelligent substances (2-1.50.6). As it is, the human self becomes itself by acting in the ways it does, and these ways come to stamp an individual with his or here particular character.[4] Since that character becomes the proximate source of a person's activity, it is said to be a 'first act' (2-1.49.3.1) or to function like a 'second nature' (2-1.49.2.1).

These descriptive names are revealing. Nature is the primary principle of activity: that by which anything does what it does. The quality which determines a nature initially so indeterminate as a rational one (*capax omnia*) becomes a 'second nature' because it channels the natural powers. But this can be done only because those powers are 'disposed' in certain directions, and brought to a 'stand-by' status whereby they are ready to act. This readiness Aquinas calls 'first act'; the actual performance becomes 'second act.' Hence we assert that we know how to swim without having to perform a stroke to verify the fact. In this way, we become the kind of agents that we are, and which we know ourselves to be.

By showing how we develop those habits of acting which incline us to act in certain characteristic ways (without deliberating to arrive at a decision each time), Aquinas indicates in broad outlines how a self is formed. The radical capacity which each person possesses to be an agent is focused in specific competencies. These sets of skills combine in a particular way to form a responsible self. It did not trouble Aquinas that this intricate complex he terms 'second nature' escapes explanation, yet remains that by which a person acts. For he recognized already that the person-to-be which ultimately characterized each human being also defies description. (And whatever cannot be articulated is a mystery, not a problem.) So what effectively identifies each one of us in a way that can be articulated is that combination of dipositions called one's character.

9.4 *Summary*

Aquinas' analysis of the common-sense conviction that persons are responsible agents thus turns up many latent uses of *actus*. The intellectual activity of understanding demands an active principle: the active intellect. Similarly, the activity of free choice depends upon an act of consenting to ends understood as personal goals. Finally, the repeated performance of actions which make up living demands proximate principles of activity called habits of action (or *habitus*). These must themselves be some sort of act, so they are called 'first act.'

At no time, however, does Aquinas tell us what an act is. Nor do we need to be told, since we perform acts all the time. The aim of his analysis is not to offer a theoretical explanation of performance, so much as to assemble sufficient reminders allowing us to articulate as best we can that in which we are engaged. If we cannot formulate performance in terms other than *actus*, that does not pose a problem for Aquinas. It only corroborates *actus* as a primitive term incapable of being reduced to any other. This fact is underscored as Aquinas proceeds to use it in diverse yet related contexts. For *actus* belongs to that set of primitives which must function analogously to do the job they are called upon to do.[5]

We come to understand what Aquinas means by *actus* as we grasp the different roles he asks it to play. In the measure that his analysis offers us a hold on our own performance, we will begin ourselves to use *actus* in analogous ways. It is at this point that one appreciates how a philosophical analysis works, especially in dissolving pseudo-problems. I have remarked how Aquinas' analysis of action appears truncated. For it seems that the development of *habitus* as a proximate principle of activity demands one more step: to articulate what it is who acts. Such a step would carry us to the 'transcendental ego.' But Aquinas neatly avoids that problem by recognizing there is no step at all. The one who acts, as Aquinas views the matter, is articulated in the remote and proximate principles of action. Nothing more need be said because nothing more can be said: the self we know is known by those characteristics which mark it.

Aquinas can assert that what remains is a mystery. He does that here just as he asserts that to-be is an act, and that God's creative activity is expressed in the to-be of each creature. But what remains is not a remainder, *something* left over for philosophy to analyze. Logic shows two points: there is that which remains, and what remains escapes articulation. This cannot, therefore, emerge as a 'problem,' though it must be respected as an unknown. The positive term Aquinas bestows on such unknowns is 'mystery.' It is not an idle term, for one can display (as in the case of *actus*) how certain expressions gesture towards what cannot be expressed.

Such terms do this by the way they function – analogously. As we notice them recurring in diverse but related contexts, we can grasp the meaning of the expression by observing how the roles relate to one another. We may try to formulate that relationship. In the case of inherently analogous terms like *actus,* we find that whatever formulation we adopt itself contains analogous expressions. So we must settle for identifying a paradigm instance, and relating the other uses to that.[6] *Actus* is a privileged example, since the paradigm instance turns out to be one's own self as a human agent.

10

Natural Process: *Actus* and Causality

Aquinas certainly wishes to recommend human intentional activity and performance as the working paradigm for a term so analogous as *actus*. He must, however, gradually wean our attention from the physical processes which first attract it. Action is manifested most clearly in power, specifically in the power to change. Whether it builds up or tears down, such power impresses us by what has been done. Generation and corruption perhaps offer the most conspicuous mode of activity, and in each case we want to know what made it happen. The *actus*, or principle of activity in question is called a cause. We begin a search for causes in order to understand what fascinates us. To explain a happening is to identify its cause.

In the context of physical process, then, the relevant sense of *actus* is captured by 'cause.' Aquinas' investigation into the way a cause operates will help us grasp the use of *actus* by showing how it functions in this context. Physical process itself is, furthermore, a plausible candidate for a paradigm use of *actus*. If we accept 'cause' as the primary analogate among the other (admittedly analogous) uses of *actus,* then we have to relate intentional activity explicitly to physical process in our effort to understand it. That is, of course, the customary movement today. Aquinas attempted the reverse.

By examining the way he proceeds we should be able to locate relevant differences from contemporary styles of explanation. In particular, how he uses *actus* to offer a stringent philosophical critique of some ordinary conceptions of causal operation can be noted. Aquinas manages to clear away certain endemic yet misleading ways of conceiving causal process by refusing to accept 'cause' as the primary meaning of *actus*. With such clarifications he closes the discussion; nothing presses him to develop a theory of causality. Yet the grammatical observations Aquinas does make remind us forcibly how analogous terms can clarify matters when used by one who knows how to employ them.

Perhaps the most facile way to think of a cause acting to effect change is to imagine something passing from mover to moved. The activity of sperm fluid in the process of natural generation would be a characteristic image. It was easy enough for Hume to make his point against causal activity by noting that whenever A strikes B, one observes nothing more than B's moving following upon that of *A*. There are only two moving things; no motion can be detected passing from one to another. A crude conception when spelled out that way, no doubt, yet it manages to lay bare the force of Hume's critique.

But how are we to conceive what has come to be called the 'causal connection'? There must be more sophisticated ways of thinking about A's causing B to move. When the general way of describing what happens settled so easily on the expression 'connection,' however, what alternative language can we adopt? Must we conjure up an unobservable power passing from cause to effect, or is there another way entirely of grasping this process?

10.1 *From* actus *to* relatio

Aquinas is concerned to safeguard the fact that the mover be able to move without itself changing. With Aristotle, he wants to develop a notion of agent which embraces an unmoved mover as well as moved movers. But unlike Aristotle, Aquinas seeks to conceive the unmoved mover acting in a more direct way than merely 'as being desired.'[1] This particular systematic motivation leads him to ask whether it is ever necessary to regard an agent's role as involving change in the agent itself. While the ordinary conception of something passing from cause to effect would force us to say Yes, Aquinas' analysis leads him to say No. The difference lies in the way he puts the notion of *actus* to use.

Let me first put it paradoxically: the act of making something happen (causation) is not itself an action. As Aquinas analyzes it, causing an effect is properly a relation. The fact that A causes something to happen to B requires acts, of course, but it itself is not an action distinct from these. What is required above all is that A be *in act;* it may also be necessary that B be moved into proximity with A. (A fire-storm will succeed in drawing a range of combustibles into its vortex as well as igniting them; a simple flame will burn only what comes close to it.) Once something susceptible to being changed in the way A can change it comes within A's scope, that thing will be so altered: combustibles burn when brought in contact with a flame.

But what actually happens in such a situation? When we ask a question of this sort, we are looking for an answer which only a physical theory can provide. In the case suggested that answer is given in terms taken from the chemical reaction of oxidation – terms quite appropriate to the expectations built into the question. But since Aquinas was operating on the level of grammar rather than physical theory, let us examine what he did say rather than fault him for what he did not say nor could have anticipated. Negatively he discouraged us from looking for 'an accident in transit from one subject to another' (*de Pot* 3.7). Positively, Aquinas asserted that one and the same act actuates both potencies (*In* 3 *Phys* 4 (9)), and that this act is the motion produced in the object moved (*In* 3 *Phys* 4(7)).[2]

When A causes something to happen to B, then, the act of the thing moved (B) is identical with that of the mover (A). In short, what happens is what we see happening to B (or in B). We say that A is causing this to happen, not because we ascertain that something is going on *between* them (whether by seeing or positing it), but simply because we understand that B depends on A to this extent. A burning flame need only burn in order to ignite a piece of paper thrust into it. Nothing is altered but the relationship – in this case the relative location – between flame and paper. Whatever is itself *in act* in the relevant respect need not do anything further to be a cause. Something else may have to happen, but that consists in altering the relative order, not the agent itself. Thus causing does not have to be explained as a further act by the agent. It is, in fact more accurately structured as a relation of dependence. This relation is initiated so that the agent thereby becomes cause as well, as its act activates the effect.

10.2   *Role* actus *plays*

Yet what Aquinas offers as an analysis of the causal situation may be no more than a verbal sleight of hand, and the example I have selected could be too simple to capture richer cases of causality. What about the instance where one speaks and another hears? It seems that something must pass between them. And does not this *medium* explain how it is that the other can hear? Of course. But the history of attempts to explain just what is going on between speaker and hearer confirms rather than challenges Aquinas' analysis. For an elastic medium is demanded precisely so that the action of speaking can affect anything within earshot capable of hearing. Besides speaking, we need do nothing further so that a person in the vicinity might hear. To speak within earshot is to be heard.

We might move one step further to ask whether we can cause anyone to understand what is heard. Then our response must hark back to Aquinas' treatment of understanding as active receptivity: though indeed we can make ourselves heard, we cannot thereby expect to make others understand. That is what Aquinas means when he asserts that no one can properly be said to teach another, except by ministering in an extrinsic manner to that person's innate power of understanding, much as a doctor assists the body in the healing process (1.117.1.1). While a speaker may cause another to hear, then, that same speaker cannot cause someone to understand what is being said. The difference lies in locating the active principle. In hearing, it is the speaker who actively activates the hearer; in understanding, the active principle lies within the one addressed.

When Aquinas insists that the act whereby the agent is agent becomes the act of the thing moved, he effectively shifts the stage of the discussion from *actus* to *relatio*. Causality itself becomes 'simply the relation of dependence in the effect with respect to the cause.'[3] By so directing the grammar of this discussion, he succeeds in sidestepping our initial expectation to find something passed on from cause to effect. Such a move, in fact, opened the way to those functional explanations which were to emerge as mathematics developed. Stopping short of a theory himself, Aquinas carried out the requisite preliminary therapy by removing causality from its *prima facie* location as an accident (or accidental action), to locate it in the formal category of relation.[4]

We might understand better how the act of the mover can become the act of the thing moved without being passed on, if we reflect on the grammar of ordinary usage. For we can say with equal propriety: A causes B to Y, or A effects Y in B. To cause something to happen is to effect it. An effect of the match's burning is the paper's burning; my speaking is effective when it makes another hear. What causes also effects. Such usage offers grammatical evidence for Aquinas' analytic assertion that causality occurs when the activity of the object changed can be described in terms identical with those describing the active power of the agent. The fact of causality is adequately explained by the activity of the agent itself, together with the relative order of mover and moved. No further activity is required. *Actus* conveys a sense of agency sufficient to display a connection of mover with moved, without needing to posit any qualitative transfer between them.

10.3 *Conclusion*

By shifting attention to the act which empowers an agent and to that agent's relationship with other things susceptible of being changed, Aquinas succeeds in discouraging our initial search for something transferred. Causation does not require a supplementary act on the agent's part. At most, the relation between mover and moved needs to be altered. And that activity, too, will be similarly explained by Aquinas. While not positing a theory of causation, his grammatical analysis nevertheless clears the way for the kind of consideration we call 'theoretical.' It encourages us to explain causality by a set of relationships rather than to look for something passed on. If we can countenance the inverse-square law as an explanation, it is because Aquinas has taught us to look for relations of dependence in accounting for causation.

11

Divine Activity: Creative and Immanent

Since Aquinas has freed himself from a merely descriptive use of *actus*, he is free to use it in ascribing things to divinity. For he can assure us that no description is intended. From the useful yet tautological identification of God as *actus purus,* Aquinas goes on to speak of two activities proper to God: the primary production of all things, and the intercourse proper to divinity as revealed in Christian tradition. We name the first 'creation' and the second 'Trinity.' In this chapter, we can see how the grammar proper to *actus* allows that expression to cover these transcendent activities.

11.1 *Creation*

That God is creator is an article of faith for Aquinas, of course, yet it is never enough merely to affirm the fact. Indeed, 'facts' of this sort can mislead us if we proceed to assert them just like any other. Creation is an organizing or formal fact; it is not a statement about a situation. Rather creation states something about any situation: whatever is is thereby related to one originating principle. That statement assuredly cannot be tested just as the relation cannot be discerned, for it is nothing other than the creature itself (1.45.3.2).

As a real yet non-empirical fact about everything, then, creation must be a formal fact. And the concomitant relation – ' "creation" taken passively' – is an internal one. Yet stating that something is a creature certainly involves more than remarking that anything we consider is thereby one. *Unity* offers a working paradigm for formal facts; *created* functions similarly, but adds an existential note. The assertion that something is created enters, after all, as an article of faith, and not as the term of a logical analysis of discourse with its presuppositions. It elicits from us something besides a nod of recognition, for such a statement offers

135

more than a reminder about the grammar we have always employed.

To acknowledge God to be creator becomes a turning point in one's life, as Augustine testified.[1] Josef Pieper identifies this affirmation as the central though often hidden element in Aquinas' philosophical discourse.[2] Creation thus functions like a formal fact in organizing an entire field of discourse. Unlike a notion such as *unity*, however, creation – or the fact that something is created – requires on our part an affirmation quite beyond what analysis of presuppositions might warrant. This affirmation, furthermore, must be self-involving if it is to be truthfully made.[3] For that is the logic of the matter.

11.11 *Logic of creation*

Aquinas telegraphs his awareness of these logical matters while commenting on Aristotle's arguments for an unmoved mover in the *Physics*: 'the universal production of being by God should not be taken as motion or as change, but rather like a simple emanation. Hence "to become" and "to make" are used equivocally [when employed to span the] universal production of things as well as other productions' (*In* 8 *Phys* 2 (2002)). We have to resort to such expressions, of course, just as Aquinas used 'production' in making his grammatical point. That reliance is a human exigency, for our manner of signifying follows the way we understand things (1.13). And it goes without saying that the universal production of being is not a fact of our experience, while other productions are (1.45.2.2).

By calling our attention to the equivocation that will ensue, however, Aquinas reminds us that any talk about creation will be inherently analogous. His explicit allusion to question 13 (on our manner of understanding and of signifying) is a warning not to be misled by solemn phrases such as 'the universal production of being' or by metaphors like 'simple emanation.' We must use them, but they cannot be deemed descriptive. Aquinas offers them rather to display how unfamiliar this territory is, and to alert us regarding how special an activity is involved in 'the emanation of all being from the universal cause, which is God' (1.45.1).

Aquinas appreciated how something so central as creation could simply escape one's consideration (*de Pot* 3.5). He also showed that it was impossible to decide the more specific issue whether the created world had a beginning or had always existed (1.46.1). That he could leave such a matter as this in the air already indicates the direction Aquinas' conceptual analysis of creation will take. Properly speaking, neither a motion nor change, the act of creation will be located not in the category of action or passion, but in that of relation (*de Pot* 3.3). A relation of dependence would be compatible with either temporal arrangement: creator and creature coextensive, or creature beginning with time.

In the face of a formally undecidable situation, revelation may demand adherence to one alternative without doing violence to reason. The traditional reading of Genesis takes creation to imply a beginning of the universe, and Aquinas expresses this as the stance of Christian belief (1.46.2). In the wake of Augustine, he goes on to show that such a beginning cannot be located *in* time, but rather brings time along with it (1.46.3.3).[4]

11.12. *Arguments for a picture*

For most of us the temporal paradox is less problematic than the very notion of creation as *ex nihilo facere*. Aquinas, however, finds creation itself to be philosophically compelling, as well as an article of faith. So besides showing us how to read the *ex* in *ex nihilo* (parallel to the *in* in *in time*), he argues that it makes no sense to assert anything to be which is not created by God (*de Pot* 3.5). More positively, Aquinas' thesis will be that it is necessarily true that whatever is be created by God (1.44.1). As we examine his arguments, however, we are struck by their indirect character.

One cannot demonstrate creation from what little we can say of the nature of God, since creation has been understood traditionally as a free act of God (1.45.6). Alternatively, to argue from creatures to a creator would proffer one more *quia* demonstration of God's existence – at best out of place here. Aquinas' arguments seem designed rather to persuade us to regard the universe as a created one. Having begun with what can be said of that which we know not (to be God is to be), the author of the *Summa* frames a complementary assertion to fit everything else: whatever is not God *has* being (*participents esse*). From there it is but a small step to suggest that anything which has its being must receive it from the 'one first being' whose nature it is to be (1.44.1). Aquinas facilitates that step by noting how fitting it is to root in one principle the diversity exhibited by the ways things participate in being.

It should be clear that Aquinas is not fashioning a demonstration so much as arguing for a picture. He cannot, as we have seen, proceed demonstratively, either *propter quid* or *quia*. Furthermore, since God must be a transcendent cause, that relation whereby a creature is cannot be an identifiable feature of the object in question (1.4.3). In fact, that relation is nothing more than the creature itself, considered as having its being from God (*de Pot* 3.3.2). Yet there is no way of locating the being of an object independent of the object itself. We saw that when Aquinas asked whether anything created resembled God (1.4.3). What we are asked to do here, then, is to conceive created to-be as itself a relation of dependence from the one whose nature is simply to be.

That feat is urged upon us by Aquinas' using the Platonic language of participation, and by his brief history of philosophical opinion on the matter (1.44.2). This sketch moves progressively to 'Plato, Aristotle and their followers, who arrived at a consideration of universal being itself (*ipsius esse universalis*), and therefore alone posited a universal cause of things by which all other things came into being. . . . Such an opinion is congruent with the catholic faith' (*de Pot* 3.5). Beyond collating assertions congruent with the claims of faith, however, Aquinas does not produce a proper argument in the more extended *de Potentia* treatment either. He offers what he takes to be the arguments of Plato and Aristotle; from Avicenna he supplies one which moves from participated to unparticipated being. In responding to an objection, though, Aquinas remarks that 'God, as first cause, does not enter into the essence of created things. Nevertheless, the to-be which is in created things cannot be understood except as derived from the divine to-be, just as no proper effect can be understood unless it can be derived from its proper cause' (*de Pot* 3.5.1).

11.13 *Sense of the picture*

We have seen how Aquinas' later considerations deprive such overtly metaphysical assertions of any possible use. While affirming to-be as the proper effect of God, the *Summa* reminds us that both to-be's remain ineffable (1.3.4.2, 1.4.3). If so, then the invitation to conceive created to-be as derived from uncreated amounts to replacing an already mysterious affirmation by one explicitly transcending our grasp. It seems as though the affirmation of creation, which Josef Pieper identifies as the organizing element in Aquinas' philosophy, is itself a mystification. Can we manage to recoup Aquinas' account at all? Recall the elements: creation is not a change or motion (1.45.2.2); it purports to speak 'not of something's becoming this or that, but of making anything to be at all' (1.44.2); hence nothing is presupposed (1.45.1), and temporal conditions are concomitant with coming into being (1.45.2.3). All these are features of an activity solemnly described as 'the emanation of all being from the universal cause which is God' (1.45.1). The proper effect of this emanation is 'that which is presupposed to everything else, namely the simple fact that something exists (*esse absolute*)' (1.45.5). Created to-be is thus causally related to God's creative activity, so that the creature itself *is* a relation (1.45.3.2).

So run the assertions. 'Emanation' offers little direct help in understanding the activity involved. Aquinas adopts the metaphor, no doubt, to remind us that we are not speaking of any ordinary production. Nothing is presupposed, and the proper effect is the sheer fact that something exists. Yet we have seen that to-be is not a mere given for Aquinas. He proposes that we understand something's being on the model of what it might do. Recall that he suggests a way of offering some intelligibility to the fact of existence by thinking of it as an act. Analogously, to be sure, since I cannot exercise my existence. But that something exists, we have noted, is directly analogous to affirming a proposition hitherto only entertained. This analogy especially recommends Aquinas' maneuver.

The assertions which constitute his scheme for affirming the radical dependence of each created to-be also reinforce the proposal to consider *esse* as *actus*. Seen from this angle, the statement which sounded at first like further mystification plays a more positive role. To assert that something's to-be is derived from the one whose nature it is to be, offers that much more incentive to think of existing as an act. We cannot conceive how such a derivation might occur. Nor do we need to. The mere assertion of dependence provides greater warrant for including to-be within the analogy of act. That God's nature, otherwise utterly unknown, must be affirmed simply to be, gives a warrant of sorts for taking to-be as an act. For the source and goal of all things must itself be act. Tautologies these are, and they remain so. Yet Aquinas could put tautologies to work, showing us how to go on in regions where we have no other guidance.

11.14 *Creation as a self-involving affirmation*

I have spoken of affirming creation as though it were tantamount to accepting a certain picture of things – or all things. 'Picture' is doubtless a faulty expression. But I use it to convey the force which a series of affirmations has on us, even when we cannot formulate their connection into a working theory. Not all affirmations coalesce into such a picture; they must have something to do with the shape of the world or of our lives.

In the case of creation, both are at stake: the world and ourselves. Without discriminating any feature of the universe, we are asked to think of it and of each thing and situation in it as dependent for existence on a first existent: God the creator. We are invited to think of things also as relations – as terminating a relation of radical dependence, and hence as creatures. We have no language available for doing this, of course. Hence I have spoken of a picture. If creation cannot make a difference in the way we discourse about things, however, what can it mean to regard them so?

The difference will come primarily in our comportment towards the world. By accepting the invitation to regard the world as itself related to God, our relation to the world is affected. That relation is changed by way of compensation and congruence. Since we are unable to shift our grammar, we can only alter our manner of speaking and acting.[5] We have expressions which try to convey in language new ways of using language: words like 'reverence'. To utter them, nonetheless, is to recognize how inadequate they are. For such expressions mean to convey a form of life, a whole way of speaking and acting. And these realities cannot be contained within a language since they refer to the manner in which an entire language is used. Believers express their new relatedness in ritual, and ritual in turn offers us explicit postures to assume. In deliberately assuming them, we come to appreciate the import of the relatedness we have affirmed. This happens by imitating that relatedness in our comportment towards the world and its creator.

The affirmation of creation thus holds out to us a new way of relating to the world, even if it cannot‚ supply a new language in which to comprehend it. For the act of creation itself, as well as the relation of dependence it engenders, exceeds our grasp. The most we can affirm is that each thing's being what it is can be considered on the model of act, since it is derived from the one whose nature is simply to be. The only way available for us to express that transcendent relatedness lies in our comportment: how we actively engage the world. One should be able to note a qualitative difference there. If it cannot be spelled out, it can nonetheless be recognized. Such is the logic of expressions like 'reverence' and of the attitudes and postures they seek to express.

Since comportment and the character it engenders are usually communicated by stories, belief in creation finds its expression in these and not in theories. If human activity is the subject of stories, however, those which embody a revelation nevertheless tell of something more. Such stories are designed to show how certain forms of life exhibit a way of relating to the world as dependent. And that, indeed, provides an indirect image of creaturely relatedness. Moreover, the difference that regarding the world as created makes in our comportment expresses something about the world, not merely about us. What it expresses is a formal fact about the world: its actual relatedness to the one whose nature is to-be. Because this formal fact (unlike such transcendental notions as *unity*) is an existential fact as well, it must be reflected in activity. The activity appropriate to reflect it is, of course, human activity, since humankind enjoys intentional relatedness as part of its own formal structure. Augustine marked the intellectual turning point in his journey by an attunement to the things about him, hearing them say 'we did not make ourselves.'[6] And his way of incorporating that realization into the record of a personal journey gives us a model for grasping the central fact of relatedness which is creation.

11.2   *Activity immanent to God: persons as relations*

At first glance it appeared that to account for causality (and the connection between cause and effect), a specific action on the part of the agent was required. On closer scrutiny, however, this common-sense approach turned up an infinite regress: what could explain the particular action of causing except another of the same kind? We saw how Aquinas avoided this paradoxical route by calling attention to the act proper to the agent as such and focusing on the relation between agent and patient. When the requisite ordering between the two is attained, what results is the activity known as causality.

The process of causation, then, is best analyzed as a relating between two factors, one of which is already *in act* with respect to the other. No distinct activity is involved over and above the act appropriate to the factor which becomes agent. The merit of Aquinas' analysis is to exorcise the demand that a specific action be identified as 'the causal process.' He succeeds, moreover, in locating 'the causal nexus' squarely in the category of relation. Causality can thus be explained as an ordering relation, given the capacities to act and to be acted upon inherent in the factors so related. Ironically, it is this analysis which prepared the way for later scientific explanation in the mathematical mode characteristic of the seventeenth and eighteenth centuries. But Aquinas' specific intent was to account for divine creative activity without needing to postulate any change on God's part.

On the part of what comes into being, however, there is certainly a great deal of change! In fact, changes or shifts in scene are what we observe above all. So considerable intellectual therapy is always required to render plausible a formal or relational account of causality. Aquinas was well aware of that – and of how much is demanded in asking us to conceive of an activity utterly devoid of change. Undoubtedly for many the very notion will be incoherent.[7] Yet it is precisely such a notion which Aquinas needs to find an analogy for activity proper to divinity. And he finds instances of such activity in those intellectual activities of understanding and of intending with which we are familiar.

Aristotle had already called attention to the linguistic peculiarities characteristic of describing intellectual activities: to see is to have seen, to recognize is to have recognized, to decide is to have decided.[8] The language itself is devoid of process; the terms employed announce an attainment. They belong to a category of expressions called more recently 'achievement-terms.' For example, words like 'win' may presuppose a process (viz. running), but do not themselves denote one. To win a race is to have won it. Similarly, expressions describing intellectual activity are used in conjunction with process-terms such as 'looking,' 'deliberating,' 'thinking,' yet the activities themselves are never described in process language.

11.21 *A logic germane to revelation*

Aquinas developed Aristotle's observations into a theory of intellectual activity grounded on the very act of misunderstanding. And this theoretical development, in turn, offered him an analogy for an activity interior to divinity itself: the classical Christian doctrine of the Trinity.[9] Unlike creation, mankind could have no inkling of this divine life had God himself not revealed it. What was revealed was not what the Christian tradition has called the doctrine of the Trinity, of course, but rather a set of relationships implying an interior activity belonging to God alone.

The Trinity, then, is really a shorthand term for expressing the heart of the Christian revelation of God in Christ: 'God was in Christ reconciling all things to himself.'[10] The formula – Father, Son, and Holy Spirit – by which one is baptized a Christian, encapsulated an invitation to enter into fellowship with the divinity by sharing in God's own personal activity.

Against the background of Aquinas' properly agnostic philosophical theology, we can appreciate how startling he regarded such a revelation to be. For even should we recognize ourselves to be God's creatures, that recognition provides no hope of discerning what God is like. If we may speak in a generic sense of belief in a creator, then believers and unbelievers would share the same ignorance of that creator's nature. To believe that God reveals himself in Jesus, however, already offers some privileged access to the nature of divinity. As that revelation has been classically understood, Jesus is not regarded as a simple mouthpiece, but is himself taken to be the revelation of God.

The canonical books of the New Testament express this fact in various ways. And the early councils of Nicea (523) and Chalcedon (451) pressed certain philosophical and common terms into special service trying to articulate Jesus' unique relationship to God. One thing was clear to the community: in addressing God as his father, Jesus initiated a new era by exhibiting a singular relationship to the divinity. Nicea spelled out that faith by insisting that 'Jesus Christ, the only-begotten Son of God, ... [is] begotten, not made, of one substance with the Father.' As Nicea grasped the problem, the only way to assure Jesus' divinity was to assert him to be uncreated. God alone is uncreated, and God is one, hence Jesus must be 'of one substance with the Father.'

But if God be one, how can God be both Father and Son? The series of affirmations which Christians found themselves compelled to make led directly to this question. For the Jew, and later the Muslim, that question alone gave reason enough to reject the claims of Christianity. To watch it arise was like observing Christianity generate its own *reductio ad absurdum*.

Christian thinkers, however, regarded the problem as a challenge. They sought ways to dissolve the apparent contradiction by transforming it into a question for speculative theology. How could one conceive a divinity whose unity is beyond question as being both Father and Son? The earliest systematic response followed closely the grammar of 'father' and 'son', noting how the terms function relatively to one another.[11] While common usage presumes father and son to be different individuals, the expressions themselves do not state that fact. Taken directly and precisely (*absolute*, the medievals would put it; *neat*, we might say), the terms state only a relationship whereby father generates son while son is generated by father. A relationship between two individuals, we want to insist! But that observation stems from the general presuppositions governing our discourse, rather than anything stated by the terms themselves.

What if 'father' and 'son,' when used within divinity, were to refer simply to a relationship? Not a relationship between two individuals, but neatly to one relationship begetting, which calls forth its complement, begotten. Since the generative relationship is not reflexive, begettor must be distinguished from begotten (and vice versa), even when nothing can set them apart as distinct individuals. That is simply the grammar of the situation – no matter that we cannot conceive it. In fact, we cannot conceive a relation subsisting, as it were, with substantial termini. None the less, this is precisely what the Cappadocians ask us to affirm in the divinity revealed by and in Jesus.[12]

To be sure, they are not requiring us to subscribe to an authority; there is nothing contradictory in the assertion. It is simply that such an affirmation goes beyond the normal presuppositions for our use of '*x* is related to *y*', even though it adheres to the rules which govern that use. Father and Son, one divinity, differ solely in that father generates son, and son is generated by father. Beyond that, there is no difference. Of course, we cannot conceive of such a case, since it belies the ontology presupposed to our discourse, where relations terminate in different subjects (or substances).

The logic of the situation as it obtains in divinity might be summarized by saying that father and son are conceived not as distinct substances but as subsistent relations. But this phrase offers no more than a misleading shorthand for the grammatical observations already made. Recall that we have no way of conceiving how relations might subsist. Yet it should not surprise us that we cannot conceive how father and son, while distinct, subsist as one God. Could we anticipate being able to describe those relations interior to divinity itself? It suffices to have found a category – relation – which can be extended so far beyond its accustomed use.

If our manner of extending it brings little illumination, that category has none the less served its purpose. By the strictest interpretation of the logic of relations, Aquinas manages to show that the New Testament language of Father and Son, when said of God, need not militate against the unity which divinity must exhibit. Furthermore, the fact that we cannot properly conceive Father and Son counts in favor of using the category rather than against it; divinity continues to outreach our understanding, especially in the life proper to it. Yet we have attained by reflection, as it were, some intimation of that life proper to God as such. In a manner beyond our ken, God's own life must be thought of as a kind of relating.

11.22   *Relating as activity*

In his *de Trinitate*, Augustine carried the issue beyond the spare logic of relations to the region of intentional activity.[13] This domain is rich in analogies, and any activity which qualifies as intentional is *ipso facto* a relating as well. What Aquinas added to Augustine's triad of *memoria*, *intelligentia* and *amor*, was a cognitional analysis which showed how *verbum* and *amor* each represent activities within divinity. More exactly: how the activity generating an interior word goes on to elicit a loving assent. In this ordered activity of intellectual generation Aquinas comes up with his most refined use of *actus*.

The analysis was no doubt encouraged by his desire to find an analogue for that activity of relating which the Christian tradition had come to associate with the inner life of God. The analysis itself, however, adheres explicitly to that form of philosophical reflection which tries to delineate the structure of human understanding. Whether we call this mode of reflection epistemology, cognitional theory, philosophical anthropology, or metaphysics of knowledge, it represents the aim of every philosopher whose thought merits the title 'critical.' Aquinas' way of proceeding will itself indicate how one should classify his effort.

The number of divergent Thomistic epistemologies suffices to remind us that Aquinas never worked out a theory of knowledge as such.[14] Nowhere does he devote a single treatise to the subject, although portions of the *Questiones Disputatae de Veritate* as well as the *Summa Contra Gentiles* and *Summa Theologiae* deal directly with epistemological issues.[15] That these issues are usually taken up in another context, however, accounts for our sense that Aquinas lacked an elaborated theory of knowledge. Furthermore, his manner of reflecting on human knowing follows a pattern quite foreign to contemporary epistemologists, while later Thomists were inclined to find it insufficiently metaphysical.

Thanks to the painstaking exegetical work of Bernard J. F. Lonergan, collected in his *Verbum: Word and Idea in Aquinas*, we can identify the theory of knowledge which Aquinas generally employed, and used to elaborate an analogy for the trinitarian activity in divinity. By a careful analysis of the statements Aquinas does make, positioning them in context both topically and chronologically, Lonergan has pieced together the theory of knowledge which Aquinas failed to elaborate. Lonergan leaves it to each reader of *Verbum* to assess the accuracy of his interpretation, by the 'measure of exactitude, extent and light' which it offers in elucidating the various statements Aquinas makes about human understanding (181).

Satisfied with Lonergan's accuracy, I shall attempt a summary of Aquinas' theory in a more common philosophical idiom. Then we must ask how to position this inquiry of Aquinas into human understanding: what manner of statements go to make up his theory of knowledge?

Finally, the analogy which the acts of understanding and loving offer to the trinitarian life of God will emerge as a quite natural result of the inquiry. Such was certainly Aquinas' intention, and so it turns out.

12

The Act of Understanding:
A Theory and an Analogy

Aquinas' reflections on understanding begin by noting the conviction of Aristotle that knowing demands identity. The duality of subject and object follows from a more basic requisite for knowing: identity in act.[1] Unless the act of understanding is able to reproduce the act of the thing it seeks to understand, how can understanding occur? Moreover, when the act of understanding does reproduce that of the thing sought after, this identity alone suffices to effect understanding. Nothing more is required. Since the identity is not a passive congruence but an intentional identification, furthermore, knowing is a conscious act. Bringing an act of understanding to explicit consciousness requires a special effort of attention. But this consciousness is not an additional act of knowing, for we are concomitantly conscious of understanding whenever we understand anything at all.[2]

Statements which lead off so boldly as these, and make such straightforward claims about understanding, knowing, intentionality and consciousness, certainly require some warrant. How can Aquinas simply assert them, where in fact he does? Or how can Lonergan offer these as a reconstruction of Aquinas' working theory of knowledge? What sort of claims are these, and what evidence do they require?

The question poses itself somewhat differently for us than it might for Aquinas. He was proceeding, after all, along lines established by Aristotle, whose theory in the main he appears to have accepted. We must ask the prior question: on what grounds did he find Aristotle's treatment of knowledge generally acceptable? The grounds seem to be no different in make-up from those adduced for epistemological claims today: a judicious combination of grammatical reminders with pointed appeals to each person's own experience of knowing or understanding something.

Thus, Aristotle asserts that knowing does not itself involve a coming-

146

to-be, or a change properly so-called. He defends this position by recalling how *know* and cognate expressions display definite atemporal characteristics: to know is to have known; to see, to have seen; to decide, to have decided.[3] Contemporary epistemologists argue similarly when they insist that whatever we can be said to know must be able to be formulated in a proposition. That is so because the proper object of the verb *to know* is a that-clause.

Grammatical observations about recurring that-clauses lead inevitably to talk about propositions as a class of entities. In like fashion Aquinas took Aristotle's distinction between actions entailing change and those which do not to demarcate a set of actions called *intentional,* and to characterize a domain called *spiritual.* This region is set off from that of material substances by the simple fact that a spiritual power does not need to be changed to be activated. And since *matter* names the substratum present in every alteration, properly so-called, the domain of activities which do not involve change is fittingly called *immaterial* or *spiritual.*

It may seem rash to introduce an ontological domain on the strength of a grammatical peculiarity, until we recall that we have no more trustworthy indicators than these. What we must monitor carefully is the manner in which the philosopher goes on to describe that domain. Should he exceed the evidence adduced by the grammar – in this case, that of intentional activity – he may be accused of perpetrating metaphysics, in the nefarious sense. If not, he is simply reminding us of structures or patterns to which our very discourse already commits us.

Hence the mixed appeal: to grammar and to our experiences of knowing. An appeal to experience, in cases like these, is never that far removed from the grammatical. We are offered a description of an act of understanding, and asked whether that is what it is like to know something. In other words, we are asked whether it makes sense to us to describe it that way. Descriptions make sense to us, however, only when they succeed in rendering an experience coherent with our larger grasp of the situation, that is, with our understanding of its context. But how best elicit our understanding of the larger context? By making explicit the patterns displayed by those descriptions which have proved successful in this domain.

In short, it is only by bringing to light the grammatical structure of successful descriptions that we can develop norms for judging those which do not recommend themselves directly. Descriptions one may offer of the act of understanding would necessarily be of this sort, since we can only advert to what it is we are doing by a reflexive turn. Hence descriptions of the act of understanding stand a better chance of being judged successful, the more they themselves succeed in helping us to recall recurrent patterns in describing things, patterns which offer the implicit grammar for the domain of knowing itself. Such descriptions appeal to experience precisely by making us that much more conscious of its structure. They would seem to be successful in the measure that even these indirect descriptions also serve as grammatical reminders.

The appeal, then, is not so mixed as it first appeared. Descriptions of the act of understanding, like claims about knowing, will render a coherent account of our experience in proportion as they make us more aware of the grammar (and hence the logical structure) of those statements we feel entitled to make about anything at all we know. It follows that we would be foolish to demand a warrant for every such description. For we come to an awareness of structure only gradually, and statements designed to evoke that awareness should be allowed to accumulate. We may test any set of these descriptions, however, when we feel it strategic to do so.

12.1 *Aquinas' theory of knowledge*

Since knowing is not an observable activity – not a piece of behavior, if you will – a theory of knowledge will not be susceptible of verification in the manner by which we are accustomed to test scientific theories. So if one prefers to retain scientific theories as paradigm instances of theoretical proposals, a theory of knowledge will not fit that pattern. The expression is proposed here, however, to signify a set of descriptions of the act of understanding which display a certain coherence, enough to be consistent among themselves and to be distinguished from other ways of formulating this activity.

Following Aristotle, Aquinas calls attention to those features of the act of knowing which are manifested in the grammar of cognitional expressions. These point to an activity which is immanent, rather than transitive.[4] Although knowing that something is the case may result in altering a person's behavior, the fact that a person now knows something he did not know before need not be displayed in any discernible manner. None the less, the person is a different person for the knowledge he possesses: the knower is really related to the thing known, through knowing it.[5]

Aquinas expresses this fact by stating that whatever is known is in the one knowing it, albeit in an intentional manner.[6] In that sense the knower is the known, just as someone who knows how to swim can be called a swimmer.[7] Knowing how to swim makes one a swimmer; the capacity is now part of that person and belongs among his or her descriptions. Furthermore, the modification is a relational one: knowing something relates a person to the object known.

It is this fact which led Aquinas to distinguish the activity of knowing from any determinate behavioral alteration. Relation is too comprehensive a category to be constrained by material considerations. The distance or temporal gap between knower and known, for example, would be

148

irrelevant to the manner in which knowing the object might affect the knower. On the other hand, precisely because knowing represents a relational modification of the subject, it should affect the way a person deals with what he has come to understand. When we know something, we are related to it differently; therefore, we should relate differently to it. In fact, our comportment is a better test of our understanding than our power of verbal repetition, and normally serves to discriminate under-standing from mere memorizing.

We must use *should* rather than *will* in describing how comportment follows upon knowing, however, because of the strategies of dissimulation that characterize intentional capacities. We can know perfectly well that something is the case, and yet fail to advert to that knowledge in relevant circumstances. Simple inadvertence can be classed as forgetfulness, but a recurrent failure to bring our knowledge to bear on our behavior reflects the *prima facie* contradictory situation of self-deception. Although that situation is indeed recognizable to any one of us, it proves notably resistant to straightforward description. In a careful analysis, Herbert Fingarette identifies self-deception with a disingenuous avoiding to 'spell out' the consequences of our actual engagements.[8] His use of the metaphor 'spelling out' calls attention to a critical step in Aquinas' reconstruction of the activity of human understanding.

12.11   *Knowing as producing a word*

The act of understanding something makes over the one knowing by really relating him to what he knows. If the new relation is to last, however, and have a chance to alter his comportment, he must be able to express this new understanding. In the act of expressing or making explicit what it is we understand, we come into possession of our understanding, and it has an opportunity to take possession of us. Since understanding, as an intentional activity, is *ipso facto* conscious, to express what we know is to express it to oneself, even if that be not the purpose of the expression. Everyone learns something more about a subject in the act of writing about it.

The language here is inevitably metaphorical and indirect, for our awareness of the activity of knowing is a concomitant one: the intellect knows itself in knowing something else (1.87.1). Aquinas is reluctant to identify an act of understanding with a specific expression, for the simple reason that we recognize more than one expression can mean the same thing. Translation would be impossible if understanding were tied uniquely to a fixed expression. On the other hand, we do not feel that we really understand something until we can articulate it in some way. For this activity allows us to connect what we have just come to understand with things we already understand, and also to ascertain some of the consequences of our new-found understanding.

A simple enough affair at the outset, an act of understanding becomes a syntactical fact almost before we know it, as the flash of discovery seeks expression of its own accord. There is seldom any discernible gap between insight and articulation, since one completes the other. The order laid down is often reversed, in fact, as the effort itself to articulate a complex situation leads to fresh understandings. These in turn find expression, and the account takes on a verisimilitude as it begins to mirror the complexity of the situation, yet also manages to illuminate it by showing how the parts connect with one another.

What I have referred to as expressing, articulating, making explicit, or 'spelling out,' Aquinas calls producing an inner word.[9] His language for describing such a singular activity is borrowed from language itself, which offers the controlling metaphors for describing this phase of understanding. The syntactical structure of language seems designed, as it were, for making explicit what would otherwise remain implicit. Aristotle had already noted the parallels between implication and predication; in fact, one can regard his *Prior Analytics* as an attempt to display the unique relation of universal predication by showing how it could be elaborated into an entire system of consequences.[10] As the sentence makes explicit the implications of the subject term, so any sentences which can be deduced from the original serve to make explicit the meaning of that sentence. To ask what an expression means is to call for a variant or to demand what one could infer from a statement employing the expression. Both procedures converge, since we would check a suggested variant by seeing whether statements employing it implied the same things as the original expression did.

If expressing our understanding amounts to 'spelling it out,' it is but a small step in the same direction to begin spelling out its consequences as well. Articulation, whether linguistic or not, is already a systemic activity. And because language offers a nearly transparent metaphor for understanding, Aquinas describes this activity as the immanent production, or emanation, of an inner word. The term 'production' will appear too crude when Aquinas wants to utilize this theory as an analogy for the begetting of the Word in God; indeed it seems already misplaced in an epistemic description.[11] For if the act of understanding itself does not involve change in an ordinary sense, neither should the further act of expressing what it is we understand. While that expression can take many forms, each of which involves producing things (sounds, ciphers, gestures), the inner word which guides these productions cannot itself be one of them. Hence Aquinas gradually shifted to the vaguer term *emanation*.[12]

Described as the act of an act (*actus actus*), this intellectual emanation is said to complete an act of understanding by expressing it. The metaphor is taken from language, and the analogy runs strictly parallel to language itself. The need to complete an act of understanding by expressing it represents a peculiarly human concern, where any single act of understanding is bound to be partial and needs to be developed by connecting it with others. It is the expression which allows us both to notice and to establish these connections, for the expression introduces the act of understanding into a systemic field of force.

The inner word, as a word, must be a syntactic entity. That is the specific role it plays for Aquinas, and so it becomes the instrument whereby what is latent can become overt. Furthermore, as symbol or ikon, that word can itself occasion yet further insight. Human understanding could not develop without this capacity for expression (language); moreover, it is the partiality of any single act of understanding which demands that such an expression be produced to complete it. Hence the capacity to generate an appropriate expression is at once characteristic of the singular activity called understanding, yet it remains a distinctive feature of that understanding termed human.

12.12 *Towards an analogical use*

By distinguishing the act of understanding from its expression, Aquinas not only accounts for translation and alternate expressions. He also designates understanding as an activity so analogous that it allows him to speak of God's knowing as an act of understanding. Understanding in God will not be a distinct act from the act whereby to be God is to be, of course, since everything said of God must be reducible to that defining formula. Furthermore, in that single act by which God is, God also understands all that is, each according to its mode of being. And where God understands something to be, it is. For all that our syntactic utterances manage (not) to say, one thing is clear: expression would be redundant to God. God's act of understanding needs no completion. In it, by it, and through it, everything which can be understood is understood.[13]

Thus the analogy Aquinas will want to make between human understanding and the generation of the Word as a distinct 'person' in divinity remains a remote analogy. The divine act of understanding requires no such expression. Rather than a defect, however, this feature turns out to meet a demand of Christian doctrine: that the inner life of God be so hidden that we could not conclude to it from our natural (and inevitably negative) knowledge of divinity. Aquinas' description of distinctively human understanding as requiring an intelligible emanation to complete each act (by expressing and opening it to discursive development), offers a way of approaching that expression of divinity in a 'word' without asserting its necessity. In fact, a closer look at this analogy will help to clarify some imprecisions in Aquinas' theory of knowledge and in my rendition of it.

12.2 *Language and 'Word' in God*

When Aquinas speaks of the act of understanding as expressing an 'inner word' or 'species,' the first analogy borrows from language, the second from vision. The analogy from language will prove more helpful. If we think of language as a system which one knows how to employ to make a point, Aquinas' 'inner word' comprises the myriad ways we have of attaining a systemic grasp of anything – including the system itself. His vague use of 'inner word' should not be interpreted woodenly, as though Aquinas envisaged a set of 'interior' elements matching the words which make up our language. *Verbum* is closer to *ratio* (or *logos*) than to *nomen*; it is better presented by a formula than a term. And the formula can convey a rule of inference or a definition, an hypothesis or simply an intelligent question. What is required is that the 'inner word' complete the act of understanding by introducing it into a framework or system.

The system need not be a conventional language, of course. All it must offer is a set of elements susceptible of diverse orderings, so that the patterns emerging can convey 'information.'[14] Dance, art, or music constitute alternative forms of expression to the verbal, but because they provide a pattern of responses designed to communicate, we often call them languages. In fact, it is generally helpful to speak of any systemic expression as linguistic, provided we do not limit that description to conventional languages.

It seems quite impossible to conceive of the roles Aquinas assigns to the 'interior word' without thinking of it as embodied in a particular expressive medium. The language he uses to show this word's necessity is modeled so closely on the role language itself plays in understanding that the analogy fast becomes an identity. How better characterize the primitive function of predication than by the metaphor of expressing: making explicit what the subject term implicitly conveys? By means of predication and its extended analogue, implication, we are able to draw out what we purport to know, and thus complete our understanding. Such metaphors as these, then, govern Aquinas' arguments for the necessity of an inner word to complete a hiterto inchoate act of understanding.

Since the major reason for differentiating act from expression in understanding is to account for our capacity to recognize equivalent terms and thus move with some ease among variants, it would seem superfluous to qualify the word as 'inner,' unless Aquinas wants to call attention to the fact that any expression we employ is already more than syntactical. To complete an act of understanding, we have seen, an expression must introduce it into a framework. So it is a necessary condition for any word that it function syntactically. But because the person who understands can also use the expression to evoke that same understanding in another, we must think of a word in use as more that syntactical.

Of course, we could take this 'more' to be the word's very use, which is contributed by the act of understanding – the source of the expression. Then Aquinas' predilection for 'inner word' would serve primarily to remind us that no expression can stand alone as a syntactic object. In that case, 'inner' is not contrasted with 'outer,' since every expression requires a medium. Rather 'inner' betokens that a merely objective consideration of linguistic expressions is misleadingly abstract. Equally and oppositely abstract would be an expression without a medium. We can indeed characterize a language as an ordered set of elements prescinding from the nature of those elements, but such a characterization is a deliberate abstraction. Calling the word 'inner' would offer a way of acknowledging the demands of intentionality as well as of logic. At least such an interpretation of Aquinas' qualification would be compatible with his descriptions of the act of understanding and the word expressed, if due allowance were given to the vagueness of his account.

12.21   Interpreting Aquinas' terminology

Aquinas uses the more inclusive term *verbum*, doubtless for its biblical allusions, but also for its power to convey an entire linguistic scheme rather than a mere element of language. The other metaphor he resorts to, *species*, is a less felicitous one; it stems not from language but vision. Yet Aquinas' very manner of employing this visual metaphor is frankly linguistic. He speaks of the angels as knowing through *species*, not expressed by them but given to them by God (1.55.1). These *species* are connatural to the angels as intellectual substances, and through them as by a 'universal medium, [they] can know each of the things which are properly contained in it' (1.55.3.2). Similarly, 'angels know singulars by universal forms, which nevertheless are the images of things both as to their universal, and as to their individuating principles' (1.57.2.3).[15]

Whatever the origin of the metaphorical term *species*, and however Aquinas may refer to it as an image, his conception of an intelligible species comes directly from a general term or principle. He understood a principle as that in which one can grasp many things precisely because one knows how to draw them out as implications. Aquinas' use of the vague *verbum* and *species* should not then obscure the inherently linguistic conception he has of any expression generated by an act of understanding. Nor should we overlook his highly syntactical grasp of language.

There is simply no evidence, however, that Aquinas conceived of these *verba* and *species* as themselves constituting an 'inner language' parallel to or patterning the language we actually use. Although later medievals (notably Ockham) spoke in this fashion, Aquinas never did. Hence my conclusion that he deliberately carried out his epistemological descriptions at a level of vagueness appropriate to the enterprise in which he was engaged. I have suggested one way of making his notion of 'expressing an inner word' more precise. My interpretation cannot be offered as Aquinas' own, yet I would defend it as more compatible with his account than one which attempts to oppose *inner* and *outer* expressions, as some later medievals did. Aquinas generally avoided multiplying entities, orders or modes. And most importantly, he opted for embodiment more often than outright dualism.

12.22   *An analogy for 'Word of God'*

But what then of the trinitarian application? Orthodox Christians want to say that the Father expresses the fullness of divinity in a Word which is God, but is nonetheless distinct from God the Father because expressed by the Father. They would not want to say, however, that this expression demands a medium, for the very notion of a *medium* is repugnant to divinity.[16] Yet, on my interpretation, to speak of an expression without a medium leaves out one of the features integral to human understanding. But it was only human understanding, we should recall, which demanded that the act of understanding be expressed to be completed.

This difficulty is only an apparent one, since the notion of an inner word was never conceived by Aquinas as more than an analogy for the generation of the Word in God. Some theologians would doubtless prefer that the expression he conceived as an immaterial emanation; the analogy with divine emanation would then be more plausible, at least on the face of it. I shall attempt to show that the greater plausibility of such a view is merely *prima facie*. While the application to divinity would certainly be more direct, we actually end up with less of an analogy to work with. An immaterial emanation offers us little upon which to ruminate. On the other hand, the notion of a syntactical expression-in-use offers a richer analogy, although its application to divinity is more remote. We must first determine, however, whether it is too remote to be able to offer us any help in understanding what church theologians have identified as processions within divinity.

Given the systematic notion of expression (or inner word) elaborated here, what would it mean for the Father to express the fullness of divinity in a Word? (We need not worry that our categorization is abstract at this point, since we are deliberately employing it as an analogy.) The Father's Word must not, first of all, be so construed as to improve or complete God's self-understanding. No expression is needed to serve that purpose in

God, who in one act (equivalent to the act whereby to be God is to be) knows himself. So God's expression will be an utterly gratuitous one, adding nothing at all to his self-understanding. What does it add, then? Or if it adds nothing, why call it an expression? To what end the analogy with human understanding?

To express is, most generally, to articulate. That God does not gain greater insight into himself by articulating his self-understanding tells us something about God's mode of understanding. What we would call an intuitive grasp suffices for God to see at a glance all that (we would say) it entails. Without attempting to characterize such an act of understanding, we can nevertheless affirm it to be true of God. Should that act of understanding be expressed, however, it would by that fact be articulated. Failing that, the metaphor of expressing would seem to offer no help at all.

Could it mean that the act of understanding itself is simply replicated? This approach appears even less felicitous since orthodox Christianity insists on one act of understanding in God: Father, Son and Holy Spirit. These cannot be three gods, but one. So we are left with trying to conceive of the Father as articulating the divine self-understanding. in a Word, where the Word is otherwise indistinguishable from that very act. To do this would require a concept of articulation as a sheer ordering – an ordering which presupposes no elements to order.

While we cannot conceive of such an ordering (any more than we can of an immaterial emanation), we should none the less be able to affirm it in God. How? By reflecting on the fact that each articulation or order we do know presupposes elements to be ordered, yet can be characterized as the set of relations holding between those elements. In other words, a particular set of ordering relationships (like before, after, greater than, smaller than) can be characterized independently of the elements they presuppose. Such a characterization will be irremediably abstract; it will be done in terms of the formal properties of relations themselves. But it remains possible. (This degree of abstractness warrants my initial observation that we cannot conceive of such an ordering – in the sense of imagining or reproducing it.) Yet as characterizing an order, it offers a firm if slim analogy for articulation *in divinis*.[17]

Aquinas did not have to go to such lengths. The language he used allowed him to speak directly of a conception proceeding from the very act of understanding, called 'the word of the heart' (1.27.1). It is this 'intention understood,' a 'certain likeness of the thing understood conceived in the intellect, ... which the exterior words signify' (*CG* 4.11.6). What is essential to the trinitarian analogy is that the procession remain within the one understanding as the immanent intellectual term of the operation (*CG* 4.11.13). In fact, since the 'exterior vocal sound is called a word from the fact that it signifies the interior concept of the mind, ...

it follows that, first and chiefly, the interior concept of the mind is called a word' (1.34.1).

Even though the expression 'word' derives from our use of language and its structure, nevertheless the primary sense of that term shifts under the pressure of the kind of semantics Aquinas articulates here. If the words we speak are called that because they signify interior words, then however metaphorical the origins of our use of *word,* the interior word enjoys the primacy. Aquinas cites Augustine for support here: 'whoever can understand the word, not only before it is sounded, but also before thought has clothed it with imaginary sound, can already see some likeness of that Word of whom it is said: "in the beginning was the Word" ' (1.34.1).

Certainly it is difficult but not impossible to understand (the notion of) a word before it is sounded, either actually or in one's imagination. That is, in fact, what we accomplish by formal or syntactical characterization. But it is incoherent to try to understand a word that does not express a thought. A word which fails to complete an act of understanding by introducing it into a matrix of systemic connections is simply impossible to grasp. If an examination is to be an intelligible one it must partake of that systemic character, since the necessary condition for an expression to express something is that it assume a syntactical role. In short, the kind of intelligibility that expression brings is at least syntactical. That is what 'intelligibility' means for Aquinas, as his original arguments for 'intelligible emanation' show.[18]

It is even possible to characterize the ordering structure which affords intelligibility without referring to any specific medium of expression. I have argued that any such characterization remains abstract; it prescinds from an element integral to the notion of expression as we use it. But such abstract characterizations remain useful. They clearly would suffice as a base for the analogous way Aquinas wants to use the notion of intelligible emanation. What is essential is that 'in the act of understanding, the intellect conceives and forms the intention or the essence understood' (*CG* 4.11.13), and that the act remain within the intellect.

Such a conception – the act of an act – assures the act of understanding both (a) its intelligibility and (b) its interiority. Now, intelligibility conceived (or essence understood) implies articulation, by contrast with the simplicity of the act of understanding 'prior' to expression. Thus interiority cannot cancel out this feature essential to expression. Rather than attend to those material elements forming a medium of expression, interiority must be used to underscore that aspect of articulation which assures the very intelligibility of articulation. At this point, it might be helpful to invoke the semantic scheme which Aquinas recalls from Aristotle's *de Interpretatione,* whereby the words we speak gain their intelligibility by signifying interior words. Or one could have recourse to a semantics in which the lingusitic schemes we employ in speaking are interior to the expressed intention itself. Aquinas' key notion of 'intelligible emanation,' however, is neutral to the semantics one adopts. And the notion serves as an analogy of the Word in divinity in the measure that it conveys a sufficiently full-blooded sense of expressing what it is one understands.

Aquinas makes it clear that the use of this notion of inner word as an analogy for the Word in God in no way contradicts his previous strictures against knowing what divinity is like. As Lonergan summarizes it:

> though our *intelligere* is always a *dicere,* this cannot be demonstrated of God's (*de Ver* 4.2.5). Though we can demonstrate that God understands, for understanding is pure perfection, still we can no more than conjecture the mode of divine understanding and so cannot prove that there is a divine Word (*de Pot* 8.1.12). Psychological trinitarian theory is not a conclusion that can be demonstrated but an hypothesis that squares with divine revelation without excluding the possibility of alternative hypotheses (1.32.1.2). Finally, Aquinas regularly writes as a theologian and not as a philosopher; hence regularly he simply states what simply is true, that in all intellects there is a procession of inner word (*Verbum,* 196).

Lonergan's final observation explains why Aquinas could content himself with mentioning a semantics which I have found it necessary to amend. Yet Aquinas uses the analogy of the interior word in some detail to clarify specific contested points in trinitarian doctrine. It is as if he himself wished to corroborate that the notion of intellectual emanation is quite independent of the semantics one adopts.[19]

12.3 *Love as the tendency completing expression*

Loving is an activity as immanent as understanding, for Aquinas, although the manner of presence differs. Whatever is understood 'is in the intellect by reason of the likeness of its species;' while the thing loved 'is in the will of the lover as the term of a movement' (*CG* 4.19.4). But these are also related, of course, since whatever is in the lover as loved 'would not be loved unless it were somehow known' (*CG* 4.19.8). Hence whatever is loved is at once in the intellect by a likeness and in the will as an inclination towards the object loved. Present in this way, as an inclination, 'love is said to transform the one loving into the object loved, in the measure that the one loving is moved by love to the very thing loved' (*CG* 4.19.7).

How are these diverse immanent activities linked one to another? Aquinas' answer is clear: 'every inclination of the will arises from this: by an intelligible form a thing is apprehended as suitable or affective' (*CG* 4.19.3). Lonergan's commentary spells out this connection in terms of the faculties involved: 'as complete understanding not only grasps essence and in essence all properties but also affirms existence and value, so also from understanding's self-expression in judgment of value there is an intelligible procession of love in the will' (*Verbum,* 201). While knowing the good does not of itself suffice for doing the good, it follows that recognizing a good as the good for me suffices to incline me towards it.

What Lonergan calls a judgment of value represents a step beyond mere understanding to a reflexive grasp of this particular good as my own good (or inversely, of my own good as congruent with this good). It is akin to the judgment that a certain proposition in fact obtains, or that a situation hitherto only entertained really exists. A judgment of this sort does suffice to incline me towards that good, for 'the will is related to intellectual things as natural inclination to natural things' (*CG* 4.19.3). While the faculties differ and the mode of immanence varies from similitude to inclination, nevertheless love adds to knowing only a further consequentiality. This is the consistency Socrates demanded, asking not just that one's thoughts hang together, but that a person's action also match his thought.

An ideal, no doubt, for the discrepancy in faculties offers critical space for the failure we call sin. Yet it remains a constitutive ideal. For it is precisely this 'necessity of intelligible procession from intellect to will,' Longergan reminds us, that drives a sinner 'either to seek true peace of soul in repentance or else to obtain a simulated peace in the rationalization that corrupts reason by making the false appear true that wrong may appear right' (*Verbum,* 202). In other words, failure to align our performance with what we judged to be right and good is understandable enough. But it must be acknowledged as a failure. An attempt to offer any other kind of explanation lands us squarely in self-deception. This inescapable fact forces us to regard the inclination of love arising out of a judgment of value as a further 'spelling out' of what we understand to be the case, albeit in a different way: in actions rather than words.

To render this description of will as an intellectual appetite (and love as an intellectual inclination) more plausible, consider how we protect ourselves from situations we sense we are 'unable to deal with.' Characteristically, we refrain from spelling them out in detail, and content ourselves with vague descriptions. By glossing over those things which, if spelled out, would create conflict, we manage a tenuous peace. Our premonition of conflict stems directly from the fact that consistency requires us to avoid a situation whose description is manifestly inhumane.[20] So we do our best to mask the situation in such a way that we will not be placed at odds with ourselves.

The language here is borrowed from intellectual consistency precisely because actions should follow statements with the same consequentiality that links propositions into a cogent argument. Nor is this 'should' a special moral 'should' for Aquinas; it is simply constitutive of an intellectual nature: 'from an intelligible form there must follow in one who understands an inclination to his proper operations and his proper end.' And 'this inclination in an intellectual nature is the will' (*CG* 4.19.2). So the will represents for Aquinas not an independent faculty alien to understanding, but simply the inclination natural to an intellectual nature. Of course willing differs from the understanding, as inclination differs from likeness; as an activity, however, willing cannot be understood independently of understanding.

It would take us too far afield to trace the permutations in the descriptions of these complementary faculties of intellect and will, especially under the subsequent influence of Kant and later of romantic philosophers like Nietzsche.[21] Nonetheless, it is worth noting that thinkers of a pragmaticist bent, such as Peirce and James, tended to reach back to a conception more akin to Aquinas.

12.31 *The analogy of love in divinity*

As an analogy offering intelligibility to the revelation of God as Father, Son and Holy Spirit, Aquinas' description of the emanation of love is peculiarly fruitful. Since 'the beloved is not in the lover by a likeness of species,' but by way of inclination, Aquinas can neatly distinguish the procession of Spirit from the generation of Son (*CG* 4.19.9). Furthermore, while the inclination 'proceeds from a word' (*CG* 4.24.12), still it tends towards the thing itself understood in the word. Thus Aquinas can affirm that 'the love by which God is in the divine will as a beloved in a lover proceeds both from the Word of God and from the God whose Word he is' (*CG* 4.19.8).

That love proceeding from God speaking and spoken is identified as the Holy Spirit, who in the formulation of the Council of Nicea accepted by Aquinas is said 'to proceed from the Father and the Son.' The tradition always associated this same Spirit with love. (1.37.1). Even more specifically, the Spirit has been identified with the love uniting Father and Son, although Aquinas cautions that this locution may be misleading (1.37.2). In explaining how Father and Son may properly be said to 'love each other and us, by the Holy Spirit as by love proceeding,' Aquinas presses the analogy for maximal clarity (1.37.2).

For me to press further along these lines would be to enter into that mode of understanding sought by faith, which the Christian tradition calls theology. So far, although I have made constant reference to the trinitarian relations in God, it has only been to mention them as terms for testing the analogical reaches of Aquinas' epistemological descriptions. I have spelled out those analogical applications in some detail only to demonstrate the range over which Aquinas can extend his notion of *actus*. Lest this exercise in analogical understanding appear as little more than a *tour de force*, however, a brief theological observation seems in order.

12.32 *Role of Trinity in theology*

What is the point of pursuing so intently a trinitarian formulation? The need to understand is natural enough, of course, so the question really asks about the precise role that the assertion of distinct 'persons' in God plays within Christian tradition itself. Aquinas' response is direct and illuminating:

> The knowledge of the divine persons was necessary [for us] for two reasons. The first was to give us the right idea of creation. To assert that God made all things through his Word is to reject the error according to which God produced things by natural need; and to place in him the possession of love is to show that if God has produced creatures, this is not because he needed them for himself nor for any other cause extrinsic to him; but rather through love of his goodness (1.32.1.3).[22]

This first reason contrasts dramatically with the position taken later by the group of religious thinkers known as 'process theologians.' I have already suggested how their conclusions follow as a matter of course, once we contrast the initial positions of these theologians with an orthodox trinitarian doctrine. In formulating the role that doctrine might play in organizing Christianity's understanding of itself, Aquinas has articulated key points of opposition between 'process theology' and its particular characterization of 'traditional theism.' Aquinas sees clearly how the revelation of God as trinitarian offers an explicit corroboration and defense of that utter transcendence which reason had to affirm of divinity, but which remains a scandal to humankind.

In offering his second 'reason' for the trinitarian revelation, Aquinas shows how a proper grasp of the role of 'persons' in divinity can attenuate the scandal of transcendence. But that happens only by raising yet further scandals and follies:

> The second reason and the principal one was to give us a true notion of the salvation of the human race, salvation which is accomplished by the incarnation of the Son and by the gift of the Holy Spirit (1.32.1.3).

12.4 *Concluding reflections*

Since the act of understanding represents Aquinas' paradigm for the notion of *actus,* it merits – and has received – extended treatment. Following Lonergan, moreover, I have sought to delineate the main lines of Aquinas'

160

theory of knowledge in a relatively short compass. Along the way we noted how *actus* provides Aquinas with a working analogy for explicating orthodox trinitarian assertions. What demanded closest attention is the particular manner in which he develops the act of understanding to serve this special purpose.

If doctrine is understood as a set of assertions winnowed by tradition to guide the faithful in their grasp of revelation, one can appreciate how this process has already incorporated much effort at clarification. We had noticed the role played by the logic of relations in reconciling assertions regarding three 'persons' with those about one God. In formulating their grammatical statements, the church councils deliberately eschewed requiring Christians to adopt one or another theological explication. The work of the Cappadocians on relations and of Augustine on an epistemological analogy thus remains extrinsic to what an orthodox Christian is asked to believe. If believers desire to make what sense they can of the conciliar statements, however, these routes are open to them.

The extent to which one's faith entails a theology depends largely on how inquisitive a person is. If the doctrinal assertions raise questions, then one is pressed to more precise understanding than the assertions themselves can offer. Here is where a theologian such as Aquinas can bring to bear conceptual tools like the logic of relations or a developed theory of knowledge. In the measure that these analogies bring greater understanding, they also enhance an inquirer's faith. Theological interpretation is in that way woven into the fabric of skills which constitutes the intellectual dimension of a working faith.

Often enough, the conceptual tools themselves become sharpened in the process. We observed how this happened as Aquinas put his grasp of the act of understanding to a theological use. Not only was the immanent character of the act itself required, but also its expression as the act of an act was needed. Beyond that, there was the spontaneous tendency of the expression to issue in an inclination of the will towards whatever was judged to be good. The relations among these intellectual activities were themselves clarified as the act with its emanations was used as an analogy for the activity interior to divinity.

This entire process illustrates once again how Aquinas worked out the dynamics of faith employing reason to seek understanding. In those places where his philosophical skills remained underdeveloped, I have extended Aquinas beyond what he actually said. In doing this, however, my hope has been to be faithful to the spirit of Aquinas in displaying the same relation between philosophy and theology which he constantly employed. That specific interface exhibits his expertise better than any other – and stands as a challenge to us.

13

Paradoxes of Action:
Some Structural Parallels

We have sampled the range of uses to which Aquinas turns *actus*. Interesting as the survey might be, it serves a higher purpose: to discover why this term alone is used of God in arguments showing how no expression could properly be predicated of divinity. The founding arguments in question 3 all turn on God's being 'pure act' (*actus purus*).

The phrase can slip by because we are prone to value action implicitly, assuming its contrast to be inaction. But we have seen how 'action' is susceptible of many paradigm uses. Some of these generate contrast terms which we might prefer to the mode of action expressed. So Aristotle deemed a contemplative life superior in itself to an active, political one; and just war arguments presume a moral preference for defensive reaction over aggression, even if field commanders naturally would rather seize the initiative. And so on.

This fact of usage makes 'action' (*actus*) a likely candidate for use *in divinis*. It strikes us normally as a favorable expression, yet gives way in some contexts to its opposite. Ambivalence of that sort allows a term to express transcendence, provided the shifts are sufficiently monitored. We must examine some of these contexts to see whether the reversal of roles is more apparent than real. Such considerations could turn up more effective paradigm uses for *actus*. I have selected two of these contexts for closer scrutiny: Aquinas' treatment of martyrdom (2-2.124), and his mini-treatise comparing the active and contemplative lives (2-2.179-82).

These cases will move us towards genuine paradoxes, however, as we come to appreciate how Aquinas relies upon his paradigm use of *actus*: intentional activity. The paradoxes arise notably in a western mind-set, which links action neatly with accomplishment. When we praise someone for his or her actions, we implicitly acknowledge the work done as that person's accomplishment. The one praised will usually demur, allowing that several hands, including fortune, conspired to bring the work to completion. But demurals of this sort remain a formality. A person will consider it equally normal to accept the praise, as he was invited to do, though it would have been poor form not to gesture towards renouncing it.

I shall show how Aquinas' paradigm for *actus* – intentional activity – in no way countenances any inherent connection between action and accomplishment. Furthermore, it is precisely this conceptual independence from accomplishment which opens *actus* to the range of uses it enjoys, as well as making it appropriate for transcendent use. Observing certain parallels in eastern religious and philosphical discourse can show us how to detach action from accomplishment more plausibly. The western mind has linked them so closely that anything to the contrary looks perverse, if not contradictory.

If entire traditions, however, view that connection as the quintessence of *hubris,* and hence an inexhaustible source of illusion, something has to give way.[1] On a careful analysis of descriptions and the role they play in framing actions, we will be able to understand how commonsensical are many Buddhist observations about illusion. Once the seemingly paradoxical can be accepted as quite matter of fact, we will have gained some critical purchase on the presumed link between action and accomplishment. Conscious of our own cultural bias, we should then be able to recover something of the finesse with which Aquinas employs the notion of *actus*.

13.1 *Some contrasting uses of* actus

Christian tradition placed a premium on suffering as well as contemplation – two practices at least *prima facie* opposed to action. Given the privileged role which *actus* plays in his thought, it should be illuminating to watch Aquinas deal with these two issues. Since *actus* is not a categorial, but an analogous term, we should be prepared to find him resolving the *prima facie* difficulty by a yet more exalted or interior mode of activity. Whether these moves are merely formal, or whether they genuinely advance the effective range of *actus* can be judged only as Aquinas develops the case. I have chosen his article on martyrdom (2-2.124) to illustrate one treatment of suffering. The comparison of active with contemplative states of life (2-2.179-82) offers his mature statement on contemplation.

13.11 *Martyrdom as an act of fortitude*

The Christian church valued witnessing to the faith with one's life above any other act, on the grounds that nothing short of an overpowering love of God could master the animal tenacity with which we hold on to our lives. For that very reason, tradition set certain guidelines for discriminating authentic witnesses from imposters. Persons who turned themselves over to hostile authorities, for example, were normally distrusted. Since courage classically represents a judicious mean between cowardice and bravado, who would presume to endure the ordeal? Human endurance most certainly would not suffice, and neither ought one test the Lord's help.

The tradition was thus wary of possible aberrations, yet retained an extraordinary place for the suffering and death of martyrs: witnesses to the truth of Christian faith. Aquinas asks whether enduring pain in this way unto death is an act of fortitude (2-2.124.2). He is not simply inquiring whether suffering demands courage (which it obviously does), but asking whether suffering is itself a courageous act. His answer recapitulates a prior analysis of fortitude: 'the chief act of fortitude is endurance: to this and not to its secondary act, which is aggression, martyrdom belongs' (2-2.124.2.3).[2]

Aquinas here leans as usual on Aristotle: 'fortitude is more concerned to allay fear than to moderate daring' (*Ethics* 3.9). But the argument proceeds by appealing to a psychological economy: the act of standing fast faces fear directly, and thus displays more fortitude than does lashing out (2-2.123.6). He takes on the obvious objection that enduring is not an action but a passion, by distinguishing: 'endurance denotes indeed a passion of the body, but an action of the soul cleaving most resolutely to good, the result being that it does not yield to the threatening passion of the body' (2-2.123.6.2). Whereas standing fast is not itself an action, some powerful activity is required to stem the body's own autonomic reactions to violence. Aquinas' reference to soul, then, echoes Socrates' retort to Cebes: '. . . by Dog! I fancy that these sinews and bones would have been in the neighborhood of Megara or Boeotia long ago (impeled by a conviction of what is best!) if I did not think it was more right and honorable to submit to whatever penalty my country orders.'[3]

Aquinas backs up his position with a curious observation: 'He that endures fears not, though he is confronted with the cause of fear, whereas this cause is not present to the aggressor' (2-2.123.6.3). It is as though the one who stands fast contends with fear directly, while the one who takes action against the hostile power can avoid confronting his own fear. Occupying himself with taking the offensive, 'the aggressor looks upon danger as something to come' (2-2.123.6.1). The cause of fear is not present to the aggressor because the activity of aggression sets up its own static, and thereby manages to create the illusion that the danger is yet to come. Aggression responds more nearly to that 'narcissism [which] keeps men marching into point-blank fire in wars: at heart one doesn't feel that *he* will die, he only feels sorry for the man next to him.'[4]

Standing fast, however, must draw on something interior, precisely in the measure that one 'is confronted with the cause of fear.' Hence Aquinas judges endurance 'the principal act of fortitude' (2-2.123.6), thereby opting for a sense of *actus* more interior than behavioral. But he is not content simply to call such an act an 'action of the soul.' Aquinas goes on to explain why that ontological status is required: to overcome the instinctual reactions which would drive us to seek safety, and which also animate an offensive reaction to danger.

13.12   *Active or contemplative life?*

In Robert Bolt's play *A Man for All Seasons,* Cardinal Wolsey, closeted with Thomas More, complains:

WOLSEY: Then the King needs a son; I repeat, what are you
           going to do about it?
MORE: I pray for it daily.
WOLSEY: God's death, he means it . . . . You'd like that,
           wouldn't you?
           To govern the country by prayers?
MORE: Yes, I should.[5]

Many have found in More someone who embodied the political virtues of a man of action, yet retained a contemplative spirit. We shall see how such a combination would merit Aquinas' highest commendation (2-2.182.1.3).

In a perfectly classical manner, Aquinas distinguishes active from contemplative modes of life by attending to the prevailing orientation of one's intentional activity, affective as well as intellectual: 'the life of every man would seem to be that wherein he delights most, and on which he is most intent . . . .' Accordingly since certain men are especially intent on the contemplation of truth, while others are especially 'intent on external actions, it follows that man's life is fittingly divided into active and contemplative' (2-2.179.1). This division adequately describes the primary orientations of 'human life as derived from the intellect, [since] the intellect is divided into active and contemplative' (2-2.179.2).

Nothing unusual here. To speak of a 'life' in this fashion is simply to suggest an habitual, though not exclusive inclination. A person who failed to exercise the complementary capacity of his intellect would be a truncated human being. But skills require focus and practice to become habitual, and so most individuals are content that one orientation prevail. Teachers, however, will always be torn between the two tendencies (2-2.181.3).

Aquinas deals with the issue of the active or contemplative life rather summarily, without a hint of the conflict Aristotle feels in the *Ethics* (10.7-8). The Greek philosopher obviously prizes the *homo politicus,* deeming it to realize one's humanity most fully. Aristotle's anthropology forces him to acknowledge the intrinsic superiority of contemplation, but only by virtue of something divine in man: *nous* or intellect. Leadership and direction of human affairs galvanize most of the virtues we link with human excellence.

Aquinas, however, leaves aside most of these anthropoligical considerations, allowing himself to be guided by scriptural traditions exclusively. He quotes Gregory more than Aristotle, and glosses *Luke* 10:42: 'Mary has chosen the better part; it is not to be taken from her,' as his central text. He does not even cite Paul's dilemma: 'I want to be gone and be with Christ, which would be much the better, but for me to stay alive in this body is a more urgent need for your sake' (Phil. 1:23-4). But Aquinas does recognize the call of human need: 'in a restricted sense and in a particular case one should prefer the active life on account of the needs of the presenᵗ life' (2-2.182.1).

In arguing for the intrinsic superiority of the contemplative life, of course, Aquinas can rely on the reasons Aristotle offers, reinforcing them from the scriptures and fathers of the church (2-2.182.1). His principal criterion for preferring the contemplative life is found in the article where he asks whether the active life is of greater merit than the contemplative. Aquinas' response is systemic: 'the root of merit is charity, and . . . the love of God is by itself more meritorious than the love of our neighbor' (2-2.182.2). If someone argues that spending oneself for the good of mankind can be a telling expression of one's love for God, he answers: 'a much more expressive sign therof is shown when a man, renouncing whatsoever pertains to this life, delights to occupy himself entirely with divine contemplation' (2-2.182.2.1).

If anything, Aquinas sounds more Greek and less Christian than Aristotle, as he neatly resolves what Paul and countless other Christians have experienced as an acute dilemma: 'life to me, of course, is Christ, but then death would bring me something more; but then again, if living in this body means doing work which is having good results – I do not know what I should choose' (*Phil.* 1:21-2). A life of contemplation as Aquinas envisages it could be tantamount to death, from the viewpoint of accomplishment, especially should one 'renounce whatsoever pertains to this life.' The most Aquinas will countenance is that 'through excess of divine love a man may now and then suffer separation from the sweetness of divine contemplation for the time being, that God's will may be done and for his glory's sake' (2-2.182.2).

The frequency with which 'delight' appears could lead some to conclude that Aquinas is forced to this position, since he follows Aristotle in ranking happiness higher than duty among human goods. But the article on merit suggests a more specific response, when he acknowledges that 'an excess of divine love' would allow a person to 'suffer separation from the sweetness of divine contemplation.' This divine love is not the person's love for God, but rather God's love for the individual, indwelling (1.43.3) and directing a person's intentional responses with 'quickness and joy' (1-2.109.3.1). What is clear is that Aquinas values the activity of sanctification wrought by God within the person over any action – however good – that the person may accomplish.

For Aquinas, actions are valued precisely in the measure that they dispose us to be attuned to this divine activity within us (2-2.182.3). Allowing God's sanctifying action to take one over is, in fact, to fulfill one's wildest aspiration, 'because contemplation of the divine truth . . . is the end of the whole human life' (2-2.180.4). So Aquinas is calmly yet relentlessly taking this opportunity to remind us that nothing is to be preferred to the love of Christ. It is not our satisfaction, or even our delight, that is at issue, but rather a mode of life which attunes one to the saving and sanctifying action of God at work in the world. And since contemplation is the action which best attunes to this transforming action of God, the life when contemplative activity prevails is simply and neatly to be preferred – unless that same divine agent asks something else of a person.

Aquinas offers no description of the 'external works' associated with an active life, except to consider them as giving witness to a Christian's love of neighbor. So we should consider all of the traditional activities for 'temporal welfare' to be included. Aquinas seems to be unaware of a social and political context which could give such work the cohesion we link with 'human development.' Perhaps this explains his failure to capture Aristotle's urgency or to feel Paul's dilemma. For Aristotle spoke out of a lively concern for the *polis,* which Paul was actively engaged in initiating Christian communities. Nevertheless, one might still translate Aquinas' clear notion of the 'end of the whole human life' into a socio-political context. Then the measure of development – the test of its humanness – would be a society's capacity to prepare human beings for the delights of contemplation. A fantastic notion, certainly, yet no more or less off-base, certainly, than Thomas More's retort. A closer look at action should help us judge whether such criteria are as eccentric as they appear. They could show the way to a more fixed center for activity.

13.2 *Action and accomplishment*

The most trenchant contemporary objector to linking action with accomplishment is certainly Wittgenstein. The fiercely uncompromising way in which he severs intention from effectiveness cannot fail to take us aback. Most commentators waffle the issue by offering genetic observations about Schopenhauer, or by consigning the entire ensemble of pointed remarks to Wittgenstein's mystical tendency.[6] The scholarly dodge via genetic accounts is demeaning to Wittgenstein, of course, who should be presumed to have reasons for adopting an idiom as his own. The other way of avoiding the issue really betrays one's own biases, and only works when they are presumed to be shared.

Without entering into the tangle of Wittgenstein interpretation, however, a simple collation of key statements from the *Tractatus* will show how squarely he challenges the presumed conceptual link between action and accomplishment:

The world is independent of my will (6.373).

Even if all that we wish for were to happen, still this would only
be a favor granted by fate, so to speak: for there is no *logical*
connection between the will and the world, which would guarantee
it, and the supposed physical connection itself is surely not something
that we would will (6.374).

If good or bad acts of will do alter the world, it can only be the
limits of the world that they alter, not the facts, not what can be
expressed by means of language.
In short, their effect must be that it becomes an altogether
different world. It must, so to speak, wax and wane as a whole.
The world of the happy man is a different one from that of the
unhappy man (6.43).

Minimally, Wittgenstein's insistence that our wanting to change the course of the world has little effect on the world or its course warns us not to rely upon a causal model for spelling out the reaches of intentional activity. In this respect, his initially paradoxical assertions have a shock-effect, forcing us to articulate the paradigm that in fact governs our discussions. They can also have the positive therapeutic effect of suggesting a new paradigm. As we will be using his remarks – to illuminate how Aquinas actually proceeds – they serve both purposes: to ferret out tacit presuppositions about *actus,* and to insinuate a clearer paradigm for extended use.

There is no doubt that we normally think of our actions as changing the course of events. If not, why bother? Furthermore, we think of them so in both a weak and strong sense: (1) we simply presume they have some effect, and (2) our description of them includes that presumed effect. So the model we quite naturally adopt is a straightforwardly casual one, where the description of both cause and effect is so constructed as to include the other implicitly, as the two senses of 'deed' suggest. In the absence of some *a priori* connection, the link between action performed and accomplished would be a merely contingent one. Since a contingent connection would be no connection at all for the Wittengenstein who was writing the *Notebooks* and the *Tractatus,* I have suggested that his radical statements stand as warnings against our presuming a causal connection between human activity and whatever is accomplished.

A causal model misleads us, moreover, when we inquire into the source of action. That road leads one to adopt the language of *will*. We have already noted how elusive a notion *will* is, in exploring Aquinas' psychological analogy for the Trinity. His account of the procession of love has been consistently misconstrued, primarily because we presume the will to be a cause and to function quite independently from understanding. Actions, however, require justifications rather than explanations – precisely in the measure that they are actions and not movements. Whoever understands actions to be the sort of thing for which the agent takes responsibility appreciates the import of this distinction. Hence Aquinas insisted that the will is an intellectual appetite, thus consciously adopting an intentional rather than a causal model in accounting for action.

So despite our native tendency to adopt it, a causal model seems less than helpful the more carefully we regard either the origin or the consequences of human activity. This preliminary analysis displays a certain symmetry, moreover, since the pattern of ethical argument known as 'consequentialism' regards results precisely as justifications: reasons we can offer in support of the line of action we have taken. Others want to argue that foreseen consequences may be relevant but cannot be central to the ensemble of reasons that suffice to justify an action. Wittgenstein's uncompromising assertions help to clarify this difference. His observations about the inevitable slippage between intending something to happen and what actually happens remind one of the doctrine of the *Gita*: whoever wishes to act authentically must renounce the fruits of their actions.[7] This teaching, translated effectively into our century by Gandhi, echoes the teaching of the *Ramayana* that any accomplishment is a miracle.[8]

13.21 *Actions and movements*

These statements can be made not only plausible but also commonsensical if we reflect on the way we describe actions by their goals, freighting the movements with our intent. We can succeed in washing a car in the measure that we bring ourselves to make enough of the movements which combine to achieve that result. And if nothing else happens (an interestingly compulsive condition!) it will remain clean for a short while. Results can be achieved – 'look how clean the car is!' – so long as they are described in terms sufficiently close-hauled to the very movements which we can make.

But there are other things we set out to do of quite a different sort: to make a go of a marriage, to achieve a modicum of collaboration among the faculty, to teach freshman to apply criteria of cogency to arguments, to bring peace to the Middle East. All these actions display Wittgenstein's point immediately. And those things which we tell ourselves we ought to do, *actions* which come under ethical scrutiny, are closer to this paradigm once we begin to describe them as actions and not movements.

Teaching offers a useful example, and one which works symmetrically for its complement, learning. Teaching is an activity, the central activity of many persons' lives. But we come to realize before long that it is not the sort of thing we can *do*! That is, we translate the activity of teaching into motions we habitually make, and which we think have some connection with students' learning. Yet the frustration with this state of affairs manifests itself in multiple ways, the most common being to slip into a straightforward causal model for teaching and to proceed to bully. All this happens even when we know how inappropriate and demeaning is the image of a teacher pouring something into a student's head. The frustration should tell us something about this activity and the way it relates to the motions we might make.

Aquinas translated this state of affairs admirably. Using 'cause' in the analogous way in which medievals were wont, he observed that a teacher can at best be no more than an inadequate secondary cause of anyone's learning anything. Secondary because that person's own power of understanding would be primary; and inadequate, I take it, because one never quite knows which motions will help and which hinder the process.[9]

I have distinguished between motions and actions, but the term 'action' is analogous enough to cover both. By distinguishing between them, I intend to call attention to different classes of descriptions: reserving 'action' for the more far-reaching (which include the results in the description), while limiting 'motion' or 'movement' to those (descriptions of) actions whose results are co-terminal (or nearly so) with performing them. The activity of murdering someone requires certain motions, one of which might be pulling a trigger. The latter too is an action, of course. The point of discriminating among descriptions in this way is to remind us that paradigm instances of actions tend to involve the intent in such a way that Wittgenstein's dicta and the doctrine of the *Gita* and *Ramayana* sound less paradoxical and more commonsensical.

To think that we have ever achieved or accomplished something like teaching another how to reason properly appears as the grossest illusion. No more argument is needed. We get the point. Perhaps we ordinarily miss this point because we really act so rarely. What we call actions are usually set responses called for by our social roles, and so more properly termed reactions. It is only when we try to step out of the routine reserved for us that we sense ourselves launched on a path of action. And this path frightens us precisely because we cannot tell where it will lead. When we step out of a predictable pattern, the *fact* that we cannot secure the results of our actions (or intentions) is driven home to us. Conversely, so long as we remain within that pattern, where movement and results appear linked in a predictable way, we sense that we are not acting so much as functioning within a system. (Think of a department chairman signing a requisition: he is not *doing* anything; he is simply making a movement. The system does the rest.) Establishments assure that things get done. But were the persons involved to think themselves to be acting in a full-blooded sense, they would be deceived in that pervasive way that creates illusion.

Observations like these about systems give rise to anti-establishment sentiments and radical critiques precisely because we sense such a collective illusion to be entropic. And of course it is, and so offers an apt illustration of the Judaeo-Christian symbol of original sin: a state of self-deception projected and hence objectified, originating in and sustained by avoidance routines designed to forfeit my responsibility for what otherwise might be my actions.

But what alternatives remain? What does authentic action look like? If it cannot achieve anything, why engage in it? How can we know what to do, if we have nothing but the negative guidance: renounce the fruits of your actions? Is it simply that in renouncing them, in releasing oneself from the illusion created by thinking that we could accomplish what we set out to do, that we can then truly act? Something like this is at stake for Wittgenstein, I feel, close as it is to his convictions about philosophic activity as therapeutic or maeiutic: released from a deceptive or misleading picture, one simply will understand. The activity of renouncing, however, is no easier to articulate or to carry out than is the skill of philosophical therapy. Yet like all other activities whose very description defies our accomplishing them, certain movements appear to be more or less conducive to releasing one from the illusions of acting. These could free a person to do what he or she can do, and hence to act truly.

Such movements are embodied in traditional spiritual disciplines, and gestured at by terms like 'prayer' and 'meditation,' terms which carry a great deal of promise. Yet these very terms also entail certain practices and movements. From the Christian scriptures, the Gospel of Mark offers an illustrative narration. After having been sent on a tour of the villages with 'authority over unclean spirits,' 'the apostles rejoined Jesus and told him all they had done and taught. Then he said to them, "You must come away to some lonely place all by yourselves and rest for a while"' (6:8, 30). They do so, but are followed by a multitude. Out there in that lonely place, the apostles manage to feed that multitude by distributing what they had with them. The headiness that ensued from their turn at working wonders demanded some time apart to put things in perspective, to remind themselves by what power they had in fact accomplished those things. The object lesson was of a humbler sort though in the very same vein: they managed to feed everyone by doing what was in them to do. Mark's version of the Kingdom and its power exploits the gap between action and result to find space for the power of God. In similar fashion, Matthew will show how the Kingdom puts us in touch with a new power and releases us to act, by contrasting it with the inertial religious establishment.

171

Coming away to a lonely place represents a movement conducive to renouncing any credit we might be tempted to take for whatever we may have accomplished, whenever the things we did happened to accomplish something. Taking credit for accomplishing those things is natural enough, for it appears that we did *do* them. It becomes a temptation, however, precisely because any connection between the movement we carried out and the results which ensued remains fortuitous. And we know it. The temptation, more precisely, consists in taking credit not for the movements we may in fact have made, but for the action which we are prone to describe in terms far more inclusive than the mere movements. That is what we set out to do by making the movements we made; so what the *Gita* calls 'fruits' fall quite naturally within the scope of our actions as we intend them. Hence a deliberate effort must be made to 'renounce the fruits of our actions.'

What would it be like, then, to act without illusion? To act truly? One is reminded of Socrates' announcement in his *Apology:* 'The truth of the matter is this, gentlemen,. Where a man has once taken up his stand, either because it seems best to him, or in obedience to orders, there I believe he is bound to remain.' (29a). Whatever his grounds, he must undertake what he sees to be right: that is, he must perform those actions which he assesses to be conducive to the state of affairs which he deems it his duty to promote. That some calculation may be required in the manner in which one acts is the well-coded message of the *Crito*. But beyond that, a man can only do what is in him to do: he can only make the movements which he judges to be conducive to the intended results. Whatever more eventuates is beyond him; he can neither take credit for it nor assume blame for its failure.

Prudence is a necessary step, but the justification (and hence the proper cause) lies elsewhere for the movements undertaken in the name of action of a certain sort. Gandhi called it 'truth-force' and the New Testament speaks of the Spirit and the power of God. Both insist that right action is action emanating from that dimension of power. The respective traditions stemming from Gandhi and Jesus offer movements designed to put one in touch with those levels of oneself where contact with such power can be obtained.

Such language is indirect to the point of oddness, yet the nature of those very disciplines wards off any hint of magic formulae. For we cannot purchase assurance of success even at the level of contact with the Spirit or with truth-force. In fact, that very 'contact' seems to be so linked with the renouncement we have spoken of as to make success redundant. Even more, what counts as success is transformed by our being led beyond the initial framework in which we were prone to describe our undertaking. Thus anyone who acts from that spiritual power will achieve something. In more classical terms familiar to us from Plato and Aristotle, the just man acts without hope of reward, since virtue carries its own. But such thoughts become mere sentiments when the keystone virtue, prudence, diminishes to a form of calculation, or if this entire process is supported by a naive theory of action producing results. So the parallels from other traditions recall what must have been tacit presuppositions for Aristole.

13.22 Actus *as primarily intentional*

A meditation of this sort, designed to mine some of the deeper veins in our grammar of action, returns us to Aquinas' comparison of active and contemplative lives. It also reminds us of his treatment of will as an intellectual appetite, whose specific activity of loving represents that appetite's spontaneous inclination towards what one's intellect judges to be a person's good. In short, to act rightly and to be attuned with 'the end of the whole human life' is to act without illusion. This formula does not pretend to be sufficient to guide specific choices. It understands perfectly well the role prudence plays, and that a disdain for concrete conditions can account for the failure of an action to achieve its goal. The claim is rather that prudence, like Socrates' *daimon,* may modify, postpone, or call off an action, but can never account for undertaking it.

Something else must be satisfied, for the heart of an action remains this side of its intended effects. And to act *from* that heart is to act authentically. At such a point, we are far from the 'external actions' which Aquinas took to be characteristic of an active life, and much closer to that activity he called contemplation. Perhaps his sense of this dialectic made him so secure in ordering activity to contemplation. For contemplation is more clearly the goal of action when we also see it at the heart of the activity we find most conducive to human intercourse and to personal development. It was the eastern religious and philosophical traditions, however, which supplied the clues to allow us to spell out this reversal.

These reflections confirm my initial claim that intentional activity offered the paradigm for *actus* in Aquinas. They confirm that claim by showing how even the paradoxes inherent in action find some resolution if we can manage to detach ourselves from the causal model that spontaneously suggests itself to us. The alternative is an intentional one, and by using it therapeutically we can attain some grasp of this paradigm use without being asked for a theory of intentionality. Such a theory cannot be found in Aquinas. Intentional activity cannot be explained precisely because it functions as the paradigm for every other use of *actus*. Fortunately, however, we all know what it is to understand, in the connatural sense that we know the thrill of getting the point. And that thrill, Aquinas contends, is the best clue we have to our humanity and to its sources.

13.3 Actus *as the transcendent expression*

One of the ways we could miss the direction of Aquinas' analogical use of *actus* would be to understand the paradigm, intentional activity, as something *mental*. That notion, which carries its geneology from Descartes through British philosophy, fails to capture the initiating and even generative character of intentional activity, as the medievals understood it. Nor ought we to confuse such activity with a process of becoming. The distinction among actions which Aristotle noted remains in force: most involve change, but certain kinds do not. The metaphor of 'energies' conveys much of what medieval Christian writers used 'spiritual' to evoke. Yet the term 'spiritual' lost its metaphorical moorings as it came to adorn scholastic disputations. From suggesting something vital, filled with life, or even energized, 'spiritual' came to demarcate an ontological realm beyond our experience, thus covering for one's ignorance. If we lose sight of the metaphor alive in 'energies,' the expression could reach a similar end.

Intentional activity seems able to reconcile opposites. Hence contemplation, for those moments we enjoy it, marks the most 'energized' of human states. A contemplative moment not only can free us from space and time; it can also resolve impasses by allowing hitherto incompatible horizons to merge. Such an activity itself requires no effort, though disposing oneself for it normally demands a rigorous discipline. The activity itself bears no resemblance to our attempts to sort things out, yet many confusions come unraveled in its wake.

The loving act of understanding which I am describing is more like a pregnant silence than a complex formula. In Aquinas' terms, it is fitting that the act of contemplating what lies beyond our capacity to articulate makes contact, in its simplicity, with the initial act of understanding which must precede any articulation: the spontaneous 'I see.' This process of articulation between the two comprises the better part of a lifetime, and makes demands of consistency in word and in deed that go to fill the ensuing silence.[10]

It is this notion of *actus* which Aquinas feels justified in using of God, when he states without hesitation that God is pure act. As an analogous notion, whoever employs it responsibly recognizes how far from the paradigm his present application lies. In the case of *actus,* furthermore, the paradigm use also denotes an experience. It is one which resolves confusions but is also nourished by wonder, and even generates wonder at its own performance. If anything is able to characterize the first principle of all, *actus* seems the best candidate.

If we let the intentional activity which illuminates and resolves guide our use of *actus,* that very activity will allow us to comprehend the dictum of Aquinas: 'the extreme point of the human knowledge of God consists in knowing that God is unknown to us in the sense that his proper being passes beyond all we can understand of it' (*de Pot* 7.5.14).[11] Understanding Aquinas' use of *actus* may even enable us to utter such a statement ourselves with insight and responsibility.

Notes

Preface

1 Two notable exceptions to which I owe a great deal are Ralph McInerny, *The Logic of Analogy* (The Hague, 1961); and Herbert McCabe, 'Categories,' originally published in *Dominican Studies* 7 (1954), 147-79, reprinted in Anthony Kenny, ed., *Aquinas: A Collection of Critical Essays* (New York, 1969).

2 Cf. M.-D. Chenu, *La Théologie au douzième siècle* (Paris, 1957).

3 For a fuller treatment of analogy, not as a theory but as a disciplined way of utilizing the resources latent in one's language, see my *Analogy and Philosophical Language* (New Haven and London, 1973).

1 Background: Philosophical Grammar

1 M.-D. Chenu, *La Théologie au douzième siècle* (Paris, 1957), ch. 4, 'Grammaire et theologie.' Norman Kretzmann presents a summary of medieval speculative grammar in Paul Edwards, ed., *Encyclopedia of Philosophy* (New York, 1967), vol. 7, 374-5. G. L. Bursill-Hall offers a modern linguist's critical viewpoint in *Speculative Grammars of the Middle Ages* (The Hague, 1971).

2 It is in his 'metaphysical' reflections as well as his observations on the symbolic role played by notation itself that C. S. Peirce exposes the presupposition of isomorphism: Charles Hartshorne and Paul Weiss, eds, *The Collected Papers of C. S. Peirce* (Cambridge, Mass., 1931-58).

3 Aquinas' remark can be found in *In 4 Metaphysica*, 4, 574 (Rome, 1950): 'Philosophus [differt] a dialectico secundum potestatem. . . . Philosophus enim . . . procedit demonstrative.' I am indebted to James C. Doig's study, *Aquinas on Metaphysics* (The Hague, 1972), for this lead.

4 While utterly uninformative, tautologies need not prove useless, especially when we can put them to use in reminding ourselves of the contours of a logical space. At any rate, this is what I take from Wittgenstein's observations on tautologies in the *Tractatus Logico-Philosophicus*, trans. by D. F. Pears and B. F. McGuinness (New York, 1961), 4.4611, 6.12, 6.124, 6.22.

5 The medievals were not in possession of a notion of *referring* distinct from that of signifying – if, in fact, there be any such. My contention is an extrapolation in contemporary terms of Aquinas' observation that predicate is to subject as form is to matter (*In* 1 *peri Hermeneias* 8, 98). That is, they have diverse but related roles to play; and it is in virtue of this internal relatedness of predicate to subject that the proposition manages to say one thing. One implication of this grammatical observation is that if we are to use the notion of *refer* at all, it is the proposition which most plausibly can be said to refer (cf. my 'Substance: A Performatory Account,' *Philosophical Studies* (Maynooth) 21 (1973), 137-60). I am indebted to Wilfrid Sellars for focusing my concern on these issues – cf. particularly, 'Naming and Saying' in *Science, Perception, and Reality* (New York, 1963).

6 In this matter I am in substantial agreement with Victor Preller in *Divine Science and the Science of God* (Princeton, 1967), and this position nicely contrasts with that offered by M. J. Charlesworth in *Philosophy of Religion* (London, 1972).

2   The Unknown

1 On this quite polemical point Richard Rorty's response to Mortimer Adler is instructive: 'Do Analysts and Metaphysicians Agree?', *Proceedings of the American Catholic Philosophical Association,* 41 (1967), 39-53.

2 I have argued this in summary fashion in *Exercises in Religious Understanding* (Notre Dame, Indiana, 1974), ch. 3, 'Aquinas: Articulating Transcendence.' For a clearly contrasting position, see M. J. Charlesworth, *Philosophy of Religion* (London, 1972).

3 'Classical theism' becomes a position when concocted as a foil for Charles Hartshorne and William Reese in *Philosophers Speak of God* (Chicago, 1953), Schubert Ogden in *The Reality of God* (New York, 1966), and others to develop an alternative set of metaphysical categories to handle certain issues in natural theology. The attitudes embodied are familiar enough, of course, and William Blake exposes them for what they are in *The Marriage of Heaven and Hell.*

4 The expression 'formal feature' does appear in Wittgenstein's *Tractatus,* but I am indebted to Eddy Zemach's essay, 'Wittgenstein's Philosophy of the Mystical,' *Review of Metaphysics* 18 (1964), 38-57 (reprinted in I. M. Copi and R. W. Beard, eds, *Essays on Wittgenstein's Tractatus* (New York, 1966)), for so precise a characterization of formal features.

5 For one contemporary reading of Aristotle's stipulations, see my 'Substance: A Performatory Account,' *Philosophical Studies* (Maynooth) 21 (1973), 137-60.

6 The contrast between what we can say with our language and what we can *show* through it finds contemporary expression in the form of Wittgenstein's *Tractatus* and explicit mention at 4.1212. The strategy, however, stems from Aristotle's way of dealing with *aporiae* in the *Metaphysics,* where continual recourse to grammatical structure recalls us to positions too basic to argue.

7 For a treatment of such isomorphisms quite continuous with medieval 'speculative grammar,' see Wilfrid Sellars, 'Naming and Saying,' in *Science, Perception and Reality* (London and New York, 1963).

8 Aristotle, *Physics* I, 7.

9 Aquinas, *ST* 1.85.1; cf. Herbert McCabe, ed., *Knowing and Naming God; Summa Theologiae*, vol. 3. (New York, 1964), Appendix 1: Knowledge. And Karl Rahner, *Spirit in the World*, trans. by William Dych (New York, 1968).

10 'The word "God" is applied to him because of the operation peculiar to him which we constantly experience . . . .' *ST* 1.13.9.3.

11 Aristotle, *Posterior Analytics* I, 9-11.

12 Cf. Ludwig Wittgenstein, *Philosophical Investigations,* trans. by G. E. M. Anscombe (New York, 1953): '*Essence* is expressed by grammar' (371); 'Grammar tells us what kind of object anything is' (373).

13 Plato, *Phaedo* 105b.

14 The explicit thesis of P. F. Strawson, *Individuals* (London, 1959).

15 See the critical edition of Joseph Bobik, *Aquinas on Being and Essence* (Notre Dame, Indiana, 1965).

16 Wilfrid Sellars, 'Empiricism and Philosophy of Mind,' in *Science, Perception and Reality* (London and New York, 1963). Sellars' attack on the 'myth of the given' takes its cues from C. S. Peirce's sustained criticism of 'foundationalism.' Among medievals, Aquinas would line up with Sellars and Peirce, while Scotus displays the foundational urge and embodies the drive to philosophy as theory. Cf. my *Analogy and Philosophical Language* (New Haven and London, 1973), ch. 5, 'John Duns Scotus: The Univocity of Analogous Terms.'

17 In speaking of a Judaeo-Christian picture of God, I am referring to what a philosopher might call the ordinary conception of God consonant with Judaeo-Christian religious practices. It is a college of attitudes, aphorisms and generalizations which coalesces into something best described as a picture of God. Theology neither reinforces nor supplants this picture. Its role is rather to exercise critical watch over it, now unraveling confusions and inconsistencies that arise from it, now checking it with *praxis* to offset its stereotypical drift, now challenging it as a lazy simplification. So a grammatical inquiry makes its impact on religious life indirectly, by an ongoing critique of the conceptions which mediate life to us, thereby guiding our attitudes towards it as well as our participation in it.

18 Cf. Frederick Crowe, SJ, 'Complacency and Concern in the Thought of St Thomas Aquinas,' *Theological Studies* 20 (1959), 1-39, 193-230, 343-81.

19 For C. G. Jung's treatment of the symbolic form of the mandala, cf. *Collected Works of C. G. Jung,* vol. 9.1 (New Jersey, 1953).

20 This is the point at which Jung speaks of 'archetypes,' Kant of 'ideals of reason,' and C. S. Peirce of 'leading principles.' So long as one does not treat these constitutive patterns as axioms serving as the basis for an argument, recourse to them seems natural enough and innocent of any 'foundational' aspirations.

21 Cf. my 'Substance: A Performatory Account.'

22 For some characteristic references see note 3 above.

23 *ST* 1.13.7; cf. Merold Westphal, 'Temporality and Finitism in Hartshorne's Theism,' *Review of Metaphysics* 19 (1966), 550-64.

24 This is Schubert Ogden's characteristic form of argument in *The Reality of God* (New York, 1966), 156-67, 174-5.

3 *Showing a way* : Esse

1 I often abbreviate this formula when I use it for a shorthand summary of Aquinas' position: hence, to be God is (simply) to-be. It does not seem to be misleading to express it that way, and it is certainly more euphonic. But for purposes of analysis the complete formula is a must. I hyphenate the final 'to-be' to distinguish it from its indexical neighbor and to indicate that the infinitive form is being put to a substantival use here, as a predicate nominative.

2 Aquinas clarifies his position again in *ST* 1.3.4.2: 'The verb "to be" is used in two ways: to signify the act of existing, and to signify the mental uniting of predicate to subject which constitutes a proposition. Now we cannot clearly know the being of God in the first sense any more than we can clearly know his essence.'

3 Cf. Joseph de Finance, *Etre et Agir* (Rome, 1960); and Etienne Gilson, *Being and Some Philosophers* (Toronto, 1952).

4 P. F. Strawson clarifies the way Aristotle had of presupposing the fact of existence, in *Introduction to Logical Theory* (New York, 1952).

5 See Joseph Bobik's edition, *Aquinas on Being and Essence* (Notre Dame, Indiana, 1965); G. E. Moore's essay can be found in his *Philosophical Papers* (London, 1959).

6 Bernard J. F. Lonergan suggests the working analogy: essence:existence:: understanding:assenting, in *Verbum: Word and Idea in Aquinas* (Notre Dame, Indiana, 1967), and develops it in *Insight* (London, 1958). One finds remarkable affinities with J. L. Austin's discovery of a performative dimension to language in *How to Do Things with Words* (Cambridge, Mass., 1962).

7 Cf. my 'Method and Sensibility: Novak's Debt to Lonergan,' *Journal of the American Academy of Religion* 40 (1972), 349-67.

8 Gerald Phelan's *St Thomas and Analogy* (Milwaukee, 1941) offers a clear example of this tendency, which finds its source in the considerable work of Jacques Maritain.

9 *In 4 Metaphysica* 4, 574 (Rome, 1950); cf. James C. Doig, *Aquinas on Metaphysics* (The Hague, 1972).

10 See Stephen Toulmin, 'Ludwig Wittgenstein,' *Encounter* 32 (1969), 58-71.

11 *ST*: 'Effects can give comprehensive knowledge of their cause only when commensurate with it' (1.2.2.3), 'Now nothing is commensurate with God; though he is called the measure of all things, inasmuch as the nearer things come to God, the more fully they exist' (1.3.5.2).

12 For an introduction of the 'bare particular' topic, see I. M. Copi, 'Objects, Properties, and Relations in the *Tractatus*,' in I. M. Copi and R. W. Beard, eds, *Essays on Wittgenstein's Tractatus* (New York, 1966). For a discussion of Aristotle see my 'Substance: A Performatory Account,' *Philosophical Studies* (Maynooth) 21 (1973).

13 Kierkegaard defines a human person by the activity of 'relating oneself to oneself,' in *Sickness unto Death* (Princeton, 1941). I have associated this constitutive activity with the experience of critical reflection in 'Beyond a Theory of Analogy,' *Proceedings of the American Catholic Philosophical Association* 46 (1972), 114-22.

14 *Expositio super librum Boethii de Trinitate* (Leiden, 1959): 'Since our understanding finds itself knowing God most perfectly when it knows that the
divine nature lies beyond whatever it can apprehend in our present state, we
can be said to know God as unknown, once we sum up what knowledge we
have of him' (1.2.1).

4 Analogical predication

1 The theoretical formulation represents a much later work of Cajetan (Tomasso
de Vio), *The Analogy of Names,* trans. by E. A. Bushinski (Pittsburgh, 1953).
For a contemporary discussion, compare Ralph McInerny, *The Logic of Analogy*
(The Hague, 1961) with my *Analogy and Philosophical Language* (New Haven,
1973).
2 *Categoriae,* 1.
3 Cf. Ralph McInerny's discussion: ' "Analogy" is analogous,' in *Studies in
Analogy* (The Hague, 1968).
4 Cf. Emil Fackenheim, *The Religious Dimension in Hegel's Thought* (Blooming-
ton, Indiana, 1969).
5 Aquinas insists that analogous expressions can be 'used literally of God'
(proprie competunt Deo) without thereby demanding that a literal (or proper)
use be univocal (ST 1.13.3). Paul Tillich, on the other hand, follows the
contours of common sense to insist that symbolic use must be tethered down
by a univocal sense: cf. *Courage to Be* (New Haven, 1952), especially ch. 6,
'Courage and Transcendence.' He is not the first, nor the only person, of
course, to be misled by the multiple senses of 'literal': cf. Owen Barfield,
Saving the Appearances; A Study in Idolatry (New York, 1965) 74-5, 87. In fact,
his conclusion represents a quite spontaneous conclusion: cf. Schubert Ogden,
The Reality of God (New York, 1966), 59.
6 The argument of Bernard J. F. Lonergan's *Insight* (London, 1957) is designed
to show that argument itself is grounded finally not in premises but in
performance. Such a strategy is quite compatible with C. S. Peirce's sustained
arguments against 'foundationalism.'
7 Alistair McKinnon, *Falsification and Belief* (The Hague, 1970, pp.80, 89).
8 James McClendon and James M. Smith, *Analyzing Religious Convictions* (Notre
Dame, Indiana, 1975).
9 Gottlob Frege, 'Uber Sinn und Bedeutung,' *Zeitschrift für Philosophie und
philosophische Kritik* 100 (1892), trans. as 'On Sense and Reference,' in Peter
Geach and Max Black, eds, *Translations from the Philosophical Writings of Gottlob
Frege* (Oxford, 1960).
10 C. S. Peirce remarks how one can be brought to an understanding of the
signifying relation as 'thirdness' by coming to realize that 'it is inexpressible
by means of dyadic relations alone' (*Collected Papers of C. S. Pierce,* ed. by
Charles Hartshorne and Paul Weiss (Cambridge, Mass., 1931-58, 1.345)).
11 I have shown how this characteristic helps to define analogous expressions in
Analogy and Philosophical Language (New Haven and London, 1973).
12 Alistair McKinnon is helpful here in showing how any particular conception
can (and must) be overturned when applied to God: *Falsification and Belief,* 50,
58-61, 76-8.

5 Truth in matters religious

1 On, 'Protestant principles' see Paul Tillich, *A History of Christian Thought,* Carl E. Braaten, ed., (New York, 1967), 280-3.

2 This less polemical subtitle of the *Summa Contra Gentiles* has been adopted for the English translation, Anton C. Pegis, ed., (Garden City, New York, 1955-7).

3 Ludwig Wittgenstein, *Philosophical Investigations,* trans. by G. E. M. Anscombe (New York, 1953): 'If language is to be a means of communication there must be agreement not only in definitions but also (queer as this may sound) in judgments' (242). 'That is not agreement in opinions but in form of life' (241).

4 Cf. Thomas Merton's Introduction to *Gandhi on Non-Violence* (New York, 1965).

5 Carlos Castaneda, *The Teachings of Don Juan* (Berkeley, Calif., 1968); *A Separate Reality* (New York, 1971); *Journey to Ixtlan* (New York, 1974); *Tales of Power* (New York, 1974).

6 J. King and M. Oakes, eds, *Where the Two Came to Their Father: A Navaho War Ceremonial* (New Jersey, 1969), 24.

7 Cf. Ludwig Wittgenstein, *Philosophical Investigations* (New York, 1953); 'Essence is expressed by grammar' (371); 'Grammar tells us what kind of object anything is' (373).

8 In an early work, *The Myth of Sisyphus,* trans. by Justin O'Brien (New York, 1955), Camus scored Soren Kierkegaard for introducing a 'leap of faith' at the critical juncture of reason with revelation. Camus mistook the use Kierkegaard was making of the leap-image, as many have shown. Moreover, Camus' own use of 'the absurd' represents a logical leap beyond the evidence of incongruities which he adduces.

9 Cf C. S. Peirce, 'A Neglected Argument for the Reality of God,' in *Collected Papers of C. S. Peirce* ed. by Charles Hartshorne and Paul Weiss (Cambridge, Mass., 1931-58), 6.452-93. It is significant that so logical a wit as Peirce perceived this opening and took this route.

6 A Philosophical Objection: Process Theology

1 The clearest summary statement of Hartshorne's position is to be found in the *Review of Metaphysics* 21 (1967), 273-89: 'The Dipolar Conception of Deity.' More extensive treatment can be found in *Philosophers Speak of God,* co-authored with William Reese (Chicago, 1953), and in *The Divine Relativity.* (New Haven, 1948). Schubert Ogden displays how deeply influenced he has been by Hartshorne's critique in *The Reality of God* (New York, 1966), especially pages 44-74. All are indebted to A. N. Whitehead, notably to his *Process and Reality* (New York, 1929), *Religion in the Making* (New York, 1926), *Adventures of Ideas* (New York, 1933), and *Modes of Thought* (New York, 1938). Each of these books differs in approach. Whitehead, quite proleptic in expression, is consciously reaching out beyond his ken to make what remarks he does about God; yet those remarks remain the inspiration of the movement. Hartshorne freely elaborates these and his own seminal insights

into a position, animating scholastic thoroughness with passionate wit. Ogden promotes the neo-classical thought-posture as the most fitting conceptuality for handling existential theological issues of the sort raised by Heidegger and Camus, as well as by Bultmann and Bonhoeffer.

2 Cf. Ogden, *Reality of God,* 94.

3 I have worked this out for five thinkers, from classical to modern, in *Exercises in Religious Understanding* (Notre Dame, Indiana, 1974).

4 Ogden, *Reality of God,* 19; cf. review by Langdon Gilkey in *Interpretation* 21 (1967), 447-59.

5 The expression is Richard Rorty's, and his judgment that Whitehead went as far as one could without incorporating that critical turn has helped me to define my own posture towards the entire 'process' orientation: 'The Subjectivist Principle and the Linguistic Turn,' George Kline, ed., *Alfred North Whitehead: Essays on His Philosophy* (Englewood Cliffs, N.J., 1963), 134-57.

6 'Dipolar Conception of Deity,' 282. See *Philosophers Speak of God,* 119-33. Aquinas is the exemplar – 'we are not aware of any important advance upon his treatment ... in the seven centuries since he wrote' (120) – of the thoroughly unacceptable position labeled 'Classical theism.' 'Is this really the best that theism can do? If so, how strong indeed would be the position of positivism, holding that the idea of God is a mere confusion or absurdity!' (133). Here we can trace the roots of both Hartshorne's and Ogden's passion.

7 *Philosophers Speak of God,* 81, 111.

8 For a masterful example of this sort of interpretation, see Leo Strauss's structuralist introduction to the Bollingen edition of Moses Maimonides' *The Guide of the Perplexed* (Chicago, 1963).

9 'The Dipolar Conception of Deity,' 274, 279.

10 Ibid., 279.

11 *ST* 1.13.11. Cf. *CG* I, 22 (10), where Aquinas adopts the passage from Exodus 3:13 to indicate how 'our Lord himself showed that his own proper name is *He who is.*'

12 Thus he introduces question 8: 'An unlimited thing [question 7] ought, it seems, to exist everywhere in everything; we must therefore consider whether this is so of God.' And in the context of this consideration he will allow himself to assert: 'now to-exist is more intimately and profoundly interior to things than anything else.' (*ST* 1. 8.1).

13 Thus, 'being good does not really differ from existing, though the word "good" expresses a notion of desirability not expressed by the words "existent"' (*ST* 1. 5.1).

14 Among others, cf. James W. Felt, SJ, 'Invitation to a Philosophic Revolution,' *New Scholasticism* 45 (1971), 87-109.

15 Cf. Bernard J. F. Lonergan, *de Deo Trino* (Rome, 1961), 215-22; for a list of patristic sources, 195, n.4.

16 *ST* 1.14.8: 1.19.4, 1.44-5. Cf. Walter Stokes, SJ, 'Is God Really Related to this World?' *Proceedings of the American Catholic Philosophical Association* 39 (1965), 145-51, for a careful sketch of creation as a personal activity of God.

17 Hence, while discussing the logical and physical improprieties in speaking of creation *from* nothing, Aquinas observes: 'It follows that the production of all things from God involves neither motion nor change, but is more like a

simple emanation. Thus "to become" and "to make" are used equivocally here'
(*In* 8 *Phys* 2 (974)).

18 To see what can happen when someone fails to discriminate among levels of
discourse, cf. Felt, op. cit. He protects himself while blurring our focus by
aiming at 'traditional Thomism,' which he insists 'cannot philosophically
allow that God loves us' (106), and neither 'God's knowledge nor his love
could be admitted to relate Him to creatures with a "real" relation [roughly,
a relation which makes a difference to God]' (103). Most of the interpretative
blunders of the 'process theology' movement are employed or mentioned
herein. In all honesty, I do think this chapter, however critical, contributes to
Felt's final and more conciliatory invitation: 'Let us develop a wider viewpoint
under which the fruitful conceptualizations of both Thomas and Whitehead
may be found complementary rather than antithetical' (109). I feel that less
reliance on slogans, coupled with a keener use of logic as well as a sharper eye
for philosophical grammar, can help us attain such a viewpoint. An exemplary
study in this regard, and one which gave me the courage to undertake this
extensive critique, is that of Merold Westphal: 'Temporality and Finitism in
Hartshorne's Theism,' *Review of Metaphysics* 19 (1966), 550-64.

19 Hartshorne, 'The Dipolar Conception of Deity,' 274; *The Divine Relativity*,
passim.

20 Ogden, *Reality of God,* 175, especially note 22.

21 For an account of analogous expressions and an analysis of accounts thereof
which offer an alternative to Ogden, while concurring in his skepticism
regarding the claims of analogy to 'work' in algorithmic sense, see my *Analogy
and Philosophical Language* (New Haven and London, 1973).

22 *Analogy and Philosophical Language,* 237-41: semantic structure of perfection-
language must be analogous.

23 Daniel Taylor, *Explanation and Meaning* (Cambridge, 1970), ch. 5.

24 For a grammatical analysis of this commonly shared situation, see Herbert
Fingarette, *Self-Deception* (London, 1969).

7 *A Psychological Objection: Jung and* Privatio Boni

1 *Questiones Disputatae de Malo* (Rome, 1953) 1.1: 'ipsum malum ... est ipsa
privatio alicuius particularis boni.'

2 *Collected Works of C. G. Jung* (New Jersey, 1953) 9.2, 54'. These volumes will
be cited in the text by volume number followed by page. Volume 9 is
published in two parts, hence 9.1 or 9.2.

3 *QD de Malo* 1.1.2: 'illa proprie dicuntur contraria quorum utrumque est
aliquid secundum naturam, sicut calidum et frigidum, album et nigrum; sed
alia quorum unum est secundum naturam et aliud recessus a natura, non
opponuntur proprie ut contraria.'

4 Plato, *Meno* 77e.

5 As Aquinas' overweening scheme of natural capacity or inclination puts it: 'the
will naturally and necessarily wills happiness; no one is able to will misery.'
(*QD de Malo* 3.3).

6 Jung cites his experience with a patient misled by the formula: 'I should never

have dreamt that I would come up against such an apparently out-of-the-way problem as that of the *privatio boni* in my practical work. Fate would have it, however, that I was called upon to treat a patient, a scholarly man with an academic training, who had been involved in all manner of dubious and morally reprehensible practices. He turned out to be a fervent adherent of the *privatio boni,* because it fitted in admirably with his scheme; evil in itself is nothing, a mere shadow, a trifling and fleeing diminution of good, like a cloud passing over the sun.... It was this case that originally convinced me to come to grips with the *privatio boni* in its psychological aspect' (11, 304).

7 A revealing summary statement from an essay of Jung's on conscience reads: 'There is scarcely any other psychic phenomenon that shows the polarity of the psyche in a clearer light than conscience. Its undoubted dynamism, in order to be understood at all, can only be explained in terms of energy, that is, as a potential based on opposites. ... It would be a great mistake to suppose that one could ever get rid of this polarity, for it is an essential element in the psychic structure' (10, 447).

8 *QD de Malo* 1.1 It is not the case, however, that *privation* cancels out contrariety, as Jung thinks (11, 168).

9 Note the mystification which excessively abstract language produces. No classical philosophical grammar ever proposed a substantial status for 'good'; *capacity* was reserved for it. Similarly, evil was never considered non-being simply, but rather a specific privation.

10 C. S. Peirce, *Collected Works* (Cambridge, Mass., 1931-58), 2.199.

11 *Confessions*, book 2.

12 Cf. Bernard J. F. Lonergan's careful tracing of Aquinas' arguments to this conclusion in *Nature and Grace* (New York, 1972), an exercise to which I am greatly indebted. For quite independent testimony, cf. Herbert Fingarette, *Self-Deception* (London, 1969). It has been argued that self-deception is at the root of all evil activity (Sartre's 'inauthenticity'), and Fingarette traces the paradox of self-deception to a *failure* to spell out one's involvements.

13 Lonergan, *Nature and Grace,* 80-4.

14 *ST* 1.63.3. Aquinas' treatise on the angels (1.50-64) reads like an exercise in constructive epistemology: to anatomize the workings of a pure intelligence not confined to the step-wise procedures of reason.

15 What I have presented will be recognized as a faithful summary of Jung's therapeutic practice, but it also finds explicit voice. In the *Answer to Job* he notes how 'in Christ's sayings there are already indications of ideas which go beyond the traditionally "Christian" morality ..., sayings in which the moral criterion is consciousness, and not law or convention' (11, 434). Elsewhere he states: 'One of the toughest roots of all evil is unconsciousness, and I could wish that the saying of Jesus, "Man, if thou knowest what thou doest, thou art blessed, but if thou knowest not, thou art accursed, and a transgressor of the law" [Luke 6:4, see Jerusalem Bible note], were still in the gospels, even though it has only one authentic source. It might well be the motto for a new morality' (11, 197). Jung is fond of citing that particular logion, which epitomizes for him 'what I would call a *differential moral equation.* For instance, it is good if evil is sensibly covered up, but to act unconsciously is evil' (11, 434).

16 Cf. Ludwig Wittgenstein, *Philosophical Investigations,* trans. by G. E. M. Anscombe, (New York, 1953), 179.

17 Cf. 11, 305 and 11, 169, where Jung assumes *privatio boni* to be a name for evil and for Satan.

18 Jung appears to take *privatio boni* here as a *name* which the Christian theological tradition has given to the devil; a clear example of how one can be misled by failing to recognize a grammatical statement for what it is; or (in other terms) by confusing abstract with substantive discourse.

19 Cf. my extended discussion of this point in ch. 5 of *Exercises in Religious Understanding* (Notre Dame, Indiana, 1974).

20 Reference is to P. F. Strawson's *Individuals* (London, 1959), yet it is not anachronistic, since Aquinas holds that the object proper to human understanding is an embodied nature (*ST* 1.84.9). Cf. Karl Rahner's *Spirit in the World,* trans. by William Dych, (New York, 1968) for an extended commentary on this dictum so central to Aquinas' epistemology.

21 Here we can see that Jung's references to the ambivalence of *prima facie* good and evil and to the intrinsically antinomial cast of the unconscious miss the mark. They do not succeed in confronting the classical anatomy of good and evil, even if he thought they did. What Jung's discoveries do show is the plethora of material ingredient in any ethical assessment, and the numerous pitfalls we must negotiate to make an authentic one. Once we have deflected his polemic against *privatio boni* and neutralized his predilection for gnostic solutions, we can better appreciate Jung's own sketch of the grammar of ethical decision-making; cf. *Memories, Dreams, Reflections* (New York, 1961), 330.

22 Albert Speer's memoirs, *Inside the Third Reich* (New York, 1970), offer literary and biographical confirmation of this collusion: without Speer's genius for planning, Hitler's power could have been dissipated in mad ravings; yet without Hitler's inspiration, Speer's career would have been a quite ordinary one.

23 Cf. my discussion of Kierkegaard in *Exercises in Religious Understanding* (ch. 4). To *be* human or Christian is to be smitten with an inescapable imperative to *become* human and Christian.

24 Jung, *Memories, Dreams, Reflections,* 331. See ch. 5 in my *Exercises in Religious Understanding,* for a careful analysis of Jung's language here.

25 'From the beginning I had a sense of destiny, as though my life was assigned to me by fate and had to be fulfilled. . . . I did not have this certainty, *it* had me. Nobody could rob me of the conviction that it was enjoined upon me to do what God wanted and not what I wanted. That gave me the strength to go my own way. Often I had the feeling that in all decisive matters I was no longer among men, but was alone with God' (*Memories, Dreams, Reflections,* 48).

8   Actus: *an Inherently Analogous Notion*

1 Joel Feinberg, 'Action and Responsibility,' in Alan R. White, ed., *The Philosophy of Action* (Oxford, 1968), 119.

185

2 Bernard J. F. Lonergan offers careful analysis of Aquinas' idea of causation in ch. 4: 'St Thomas' Theory of Operation,' *Grace and Freedom* (New York, 1971), 64-9.

3 See Dorothy Sayers' introduction and notes on the controling notion of retribution, in her translation, *The Comedy of Dante Alighieri the Florentine* (Harmondsworth, Middlesex, 1949). e.g., Cantica I, Hell: 'Neither in the *story* nor in the *allegory* is Hell a place of punishment to which anybody is arbitrarily *sent*: it is the condition to which the soul reduces itself by a stubborn determination to evil, and in which it suffers the torment of its own perversions' (68). Helen Luke develops this theme at length in *Dark Wood to White Rose* (Pecos, N.M., 1975), 19-24, 31-4.

4 Bernard J. F. Lonergan, *Verbum: Word and Idea in Aquinas* (Notre Dame, Indiana, 1967).

5 Bernard J. F. Lonergan, *Insight* (London, 1958); for a defense of this way of reading *Insight*, cf. my 'Method and Sensibility: Novak's Debt to Lonergan,' *Journal of the American Academy of Religion* 40 (1972), 349-67.

9 *Intentional Activity and Performance: Paradigm for* Actus

1 For a discussion of *information* as the answer to question, see K. M. Sayre's treatment of choice and degree of uncertainty, in 'Choice, Decision and Origin of Information,' F. J. Crosson and K. M. Sayre, eds, *Philosophy and Cybernetics* (New York, 1968), especially 74-5.

2 Cf. Frederick Crowe's exhaustive study: 'Complacency and Concern in the Thought of St Thomas Aquinas,' *Theological Studies* 20 (1959), 1-39, 198-230, 343-95. I prefer to use 'consent' to translate both *consensus* and *complacentia*, as they occur.

3 Stanley Hauerwas: *Character and the Christian Life: A Study in Theological Ethics* (San Antonio, 1975), 18-34. Hauerwas shows how ethical preoccupation with decision and with justifying our decisions reflects a notion of freedom as sheer indeterminacy, and obscures the fact that reasons inform a human action prior to any explicit demand to justify what we have done. The contrast can be overdrawn, since in adopting the descriptions we do, we tacitly prepare a justification. None the less, the logical priority is to be respected, if the ensuing justification is to accomplish its intent, and not be caricatured as a merely extrinsic and *post-factum* 'justification.' Such is the logic of the matter.

4 Hauerwas shows how this feedback characteristic originates in Aristotle and is developed by Aquinas: *Character and the Christian Life,* 35-82.

5 The very notion of a 'primitive term' has been unfortunately tied to a phenomenalist analysis of language and the world. Hence the paradigm candidates for 'primitives' become the quality words naming those 'sense-data' out of which we are supposed to have constructed our world. Yet the logical notion of a primitive term is separable from that particular picture of language and the world. For Aquinas, primitives are more apt to be analogous terms, grasped by an ordered set of examples. Cf. *ST* 1.13.5.1: 'all univocal predications are based on one non-univocal, analogical predicate, that of "being"'; and my *Analogy and Philosophical Language* (New Haven and London, 1973), 81, where the reference is to Aristotle.

6 Simple as it sounds, this tactic requires judicious practice. In *Analogy and Philosophical Language,* I have shown how such a practice translates Greek and medieval preoccupation with analogous usage better than any hope for a theory of analogy. My indebtedness to G. E. L. Owen should be clear, notably his 'Logic and Metaphysics in Some Earlier Works of Aristotle,' in I. During and G. E. L. Owen, eds, *Aristotle and Plato in Mid-Fourth Century* (New York, 1960).

10 *Natural Process:* Actus *and Causality*

1 Cf. Bernard J. F. Lonergan, *Grace and Freedom* (New York, 1971), 63-91, especially 84.
2 Ibid., 65.
3 Ibid., 65.
4 What theoretical explanation seeks to lay bare is the 'intelligibility immanent in the immediate data of sense,' but as 'it resides in the relations of things, not to our senses, but to one another' (Bernard J. F. Lonergan, *Insight* (London, 1958), 78). This account squares nicely with that of Wilfrid Sellars, 'The Language of Theories,' in *Science, Perception and Reality* (London and New York, 1963), 106-26.

11 *Divine Activity: Creative and Immanent*

1 *Confessions of Saint Augustine,* trans. by R. S. Pine-Coffin (Baltimore, 1961): 'I considered all things that are of a lower order than yourself, and I say that they have not absolute being in themselves, nor are they entirely without being. They are real in so far as they have their being from you.' (VII, 11 (147)). Cf. also VII, 20 (154), and X, 6 (212). There is also the Hasidic tale cited by Heinrich Ott: 'As Levi Yitzhak returned home from his first trip to Rabbi Shmelke of Nikolsburg, which he had undertaken against the will of his father-in-law, the latter jumped on him: "Now, what did you learn from him?" "I learned," answered Levi Yitzhak, "that there is a Creator of the world." The old man called a servant and asked him: "Are you aware that there is a Creator of the world?" "Yes," said the servant. "Of course," cried Levi Yitzhak, "they all say so, but do they also learn it?"' ('What is Systematic Theology?' in J. M. Robinson and J. B. Cobb, eds, *The Later Heidegger and Theology* (New York, 1963), 110-11).
2 Josef Pieper, *The Silence of Saint Thomas,* trans. by J. Murray and D. O'Connor (New York, 1957), 47-50.
3 Donald Evans, *The Logic of Self-Involvement* (London, 1963).
4 Cf. *Confessions of Saint Augustine,* XI.
5 In *Time and Myth* (New York, 1973), John S. Dunne shows how relatedness has always been the mark of spirit, so that assuming a new relation to the world especially characterizes inward activity.
6 *Confession,* IX, 10 (198).
7 This is one of the arguments which process theologians employ to build an antecedent case for accepting their shift to a new basis for conceiving divinity.
8 Aristotle, *de Anima* II, 5; III, 4-5.

9 Beginning with *Verbum: Word and Idea in Aquinas* (Notre Dame, Indiana, 1967) the work of Bernard J. F. Lonergan has been devoted to tracing this connection between cognitional theory and theological effort. Lonergan's subsequent major works, *Insight* (London, 1957) and *Method in Theology* (New York, 1971) extend these conceptual connections into regions quite beyond those suggested by Aquinas.

10 For a classical treatment, see D. M. Baillie, *God Was in Christ* (rev. ed. New York, 1955).

11 See I. Chevalier, *Saint Augustin et les pères grecs; Etudes des relations trinitaires* (Fribourg, 1939); J. N. D. Kelly, *Early Christian Doctrines* (New York, 1960), 109-137, 252-79.

12 Cf. R. Arnou, *de Deo Trino,* Part I (Rome, 1933), 130-40.

13 Books X and XV argue for the triad of memory, understanding, and will or love as the best human image of Father, Son, and Holy Spirit respectively: see *de Trinitate* X, xi.17-18; XV, xxii.39-xxiii.43 (in *Library of Christian Classics,* vol. VIII (London, 1955); or in *Corpus Christianorum,* Series Latina, vol. 50 (Libri I-XII) and 50A (Libri XIII-XV), W. J. Mountain, ed., (Turnhout: Typographi Brepols Editores Pontificii, 1968).

14 Standard divergences can be found by comparing Jacques Maritain, *The Degrees of Knowledge* (New York, 1955), with Charles de Koninck (bibliography in *Mélanges à la Mémoire de Charles de Koninck* (Quebec, 1968), 7-22) and with Fernand van Steenberghen, *Epistemology,* trans. by L. Moonan (Louvain and New York, 1970).

15 *Summa Contra Gentiles* (= *On the Truth of the Catholic Faith* (New York, 1956)), vol. 2, chs 46-101; *ST* 1.79-89.

12   *The Act of Understanding: A Theory and an Analogy*

1 Aristotle, *de Anima* III, 4, 430a3ff; *Metaphysics* XII, 9, 1075a3ff.

2 See Bernard J. Lonergan, *Verbum: Word and Idea in Aquinas* (Notre Dame, Indiana, 1967) 184-5, especially for the way Aquinas contrasts with Platonist alternatives.

3 Aristotle, *de Anima* II, 5; III, 4-5.

4 For a clarification of grammar as it leads (or misleads) us regarding formal features of actions, see *ST* 1.37.1.2. For a discussion of the immanent/transitive distinction, see Lonergan, *Verbum,* 119-24.

5 *ST* 1.13.7; also 1.34.3.2, 1.28.1.2, 1.19.3.3, 1.19.4.

6 *ST* 1.85.2.1; also *de Ver* 10.8.

7 This point is more easily grasped if we adopt Herbert Fingarette's suggestion to view consciousness as a set of skills (in Aquinas' language, *habitus*): *Self-Deception* (London, 1969).

8 Fingarette, *Self-Deception,* 39-51.

9 Lonergan, *Verbum,* 33-45, 98-106; Aquinas, *de Ver* 4.2.

10 Cf. my 'Entailment: "E" and Aristotle,' *Logique et Analyse* 7 (1964), 111-29.

11 Lonergan, *Verbum,* 197.

12 *ST* 1.27.1; Lonergan, *Verbum,* 33-45.

13 Evil, as an 'absolute objective falsity' - a surd - remains opaque even to God,

who must understand it as a lacuna; Bernard J. F. Lonergan, *Grace and Freedom* (New York, 1971), 112-16.

14 The classic source is Claude Shannon and Warren Weaver, *The Mathematical Theory of Communication* (Urbana, Ill., 1949). Representative texts include Norman Abramson, *Information Theory and Coding* (New York, 1963); and Robert Fano, *Transmission of Information* (Cambridge, Mass. 1963).

15 Aquinas' entire treatise on the angels – *Summa* 1.50-64 (Eyre and Spottis-woode/McGraw-Hill, vol. 9) – represents an exercise in intellectual play utterly characteristic of twelfth- and thirteenth-century inquiry.

16 Hence Hegel's notion of a God who must express himself – on penalty of otherwise remaining *an sich* (or 'abstract,' in Hegel's sense) – as well as his identifying the medium of that expression to be world history, makes him doubly suspect to Christian theologians. Medievals would be quick to point out that he modeled the act of understanding too closely on the *process* of human understanding.

17 I am indebted to the work of K. M. Sayre, *Consciousness*; *A Philosophical Study of Minds and Machines* (New York, 1969) for assistance in showing how such formal characterizations may be used.

18 The necessity for articulation is tied to those processes of human under-standing which language displays. Victor Preller's *Divine Science and Science of God* (New Jersey, 1967) shows how syntactical a matter intelligibility is for Aquinas.

19 In *CG* 4.13 and 14, Aquinas uses the understanding gained by the analogy from intelligible emanation to resolve *aporiae* raised by the assertions of trinitarian doctrine, to wit: that there is but one Son in divinity (4.13); that generation *in divinis* implies no potency whatsoever but 'is like the origin of act from act, as is brilliance from light and an understanding understood from an understanding in act,' and that the Son is 'necessarily co-eternal with God whose Word He is, for an intellect in act is never without its word' (4.14.3); that 'the substance given to the Son does not cease to be in the Father, for ... the word of our intellect owes it to the very thing understood that it contains intelligibly that very same nature' (4.14.4); nor 'need there be in the Son of God something which receives and something else which is the nature received, ... for it is not thus that a word arises within an intellect: ... in its entirety the word has its origin from the intellect' (4.14.5).

20 A perfect example is provided in Albert Speer's memoirs, where he recalls a Nazi functionary warning him not to inquire into the workings of certain camps in Poland marked for Jewish deportees. Speer observes, from Spandau prison, '... from fear of discovering something which might have made me turn from my course, I had closed my eyes': *Inside the Third Reich* (New York, 1970), 481.

21 For a treatment at once classical and contemporary, cf. Martin D'Arcy, *Mind and Heart of Love* (New York, 1956).

22 Mary T. Clark, whose translation I have used here, glosses the apparently redundant phrase 'through love of his goodness' with 'the desire to share' (*An Aquinas Reader* (Garden City, N.Y., 1972), 429). Others speak of an overflowing or a superabundance; the point is clear: divinity needs nothing more to fulfill itself.

13 *Paradoxes of Action: Some Structural Parallels*

1 In his study of eastern religious thought, *Mysticism and Morality: Oriental Thought and Moral Philosophy* (New York, 1972), Arthur Danto simply assumed action to be linked with accomplishment, without suspecting that link might represent an ethnocentric view. The result is a seriously flawed treatment, and that from an insightful theorist of action (*Analytical Philosophy of Action* (Cambridge, 1973)) and an articulate expositor of other positions (*Nietzsche as Philosopher* (New York, 1965)).

2 For a sensitive contemporary treatment, see Josef Pieper, *Fortitude and Temperance* (New York, 1954), ch. 4: 'Endurance and Attack.'

3 Plato, *Phaedo* 99A, *Last Days of Socrates* (Baltimore, Md, 1954), 157.

4 Ernest Becker, *The Denial of Death* (New York, 1973), 2.

5 Robert Bolt, *A Man for All Seasons* (New York, 1960), 12-13.

6 Thus P. M. S. Hacker, *Insight and Illusion* (Oxford, 1972), 66; and G. E. M. Anscombe, *An Introduction to Wittgenstein's Tractatus* (London, 1959), 171-2. The revelant remarks can be found in the *Tractatus Logico-Philosophicus* (London, 1961) and in an earlier version in *Notebooks 1914-1916* (Oxford, 1961) at 5.7.16. I am indebted to John Robinson for some helpful leads here, in his unpublished doctoral dissertation: 'Seeing the World Aright: A Study of Wittgenstein's Pretractarian *Notebooks*' (Unpublished PhD thesis, University of Notre Dame, Indiana, 1975).

7 *The Bhagavad Gita; A New Verse Translation,* by Ann Stanford (New York, 1970), e.g., 5.12, 18.5., 18.23, 18.26.

8 The precise phrase comes from a contemporary dramatic version of the Ramayana; its sense may be found throughout a standard poetic collation, such as *The Ramayan of Valmiki,* trans. by Ralph T. H. Griffith, re-issued in the Chowkhamba Sanskrit Studies, vol. 29 (Varanasi-1, India, 1963).

9 Although the precise formulation is not Aquinas', 'inadequate secondary cause' offers an accurate summary of his treatment in *ST* 1.117.1, and *de Ver* 11.1

10 Bernard J. F. Lonergan, *Method in Theology* (New York, 1972) for the role conversion plays in allowing one to go on, that is to understand, in these regions.

11 For a treatment of the knowledge of divinity which corroborates mine, see Henri Bouillard's careful comparison of Karl Barth with Anselm and Aquinas: *Knowledge of God* (New York, 1969).

Index

abstract and concrete: Aquinas contrasts, 4-7, 9, 22; Hartshorne's distinction, 81
'achievement terms', 141
active or contemplative life? Aquinas' view, 165-7
actuality, 28, 37; *purim actum,* 37
actus
    actions and movements, 169-73; action and accomplishment, 167-9; active/contemplative life, 165-7, 173; as active receptivity, 120; and causality, 131-4; characteristic uses, 116-17; consent, 123-5, 126, 127; degrees of freedom, 124-5; ends and means, 125-7; *habitus,* or 'first act', 127-8, 129; act of martyrdom, 163-5; as master metaphor, 116; paradigm use, 118, 131, 162-3, 173-5; performance and, 122-3; as primarily intentional, 173, 174; as transcendent expression, 174-5; willing, 123, 124, 125; *see also* understanding, act of
aims of Aquinas, 69
Ambrose, St, 71
analogical predication, 55-67; Aquinas' treatment, 62-3; grammatical observations, 60-2; literal usage, 63-5; naming God, 58; no theory of analogy, 55, 56-8; 'perfection-words', 65-6; preoccupation of Aquinas' followers with proportionality, 56; ways of speaking, 59-60; *see also* analogous expressions
analogous expressions 55, 57-8; and act of understanding, 151-2; analogy of love, 159-60; art of using, 69-71; and creation, 138-9; inherently analogous expressions:

actus, 116-19, 129-30; paradigm uses, 118, 122, 130; and teaching, 170; for 'Word of God', 154-7; *see also* analogical predication; metaphorical expressions
angels, 102, 103, 107, 110, 153
Apology (Socrates), 172
archetypal factors, in consideration of good and evil, 100, 102, 104, 105
Aristotle, 12, 20, 21, 37, 49, 84, 121, 174; active *v.* contemplative life, 165-6, 167; being not genus, 24; categories, 52-3, 91; causality, 117, 132, 136; creation, 138; distinguished from Aquinas, 44; expressions and their senses, 55; 'first philosophy', 78-9; account of 'good', 30, 31; potency/act, 14-15, 45, 46, 50; predication and identity, 5; principles of logic, 17; and 'process theology', 87; scheme of ends/means, 125; 'substance', 78; system of consequences, 150; theory of inquiry, 127; treatment of knowledge, 146, 147, 148; *see also individual works*
Augustine, St, 20, 37, 124; and creation, 136, 137, 140; divine transcendence, 71; the eternal, 39; motives and influences for evil, 100, 102; preoccupation with *ordo,* 84; the Trinity, 144, 161; word of God, 156
Avicenna, 138

Basil, St, 99
Bible, the: *Genesis,* 28, 137; Gospel of Mark, 171; New Testament, 142, 172; use of language in, 3-4